Forgotten Crisis

Forgotten Crisis

The Fin-de-Siècle Crisis of Democracy in France

Robert Elliot Kaplan

BERG PUBLISHERS
Oxford • Washington, D.C.

First published in 1995 by
Berg Publishers Ltd
Editorial offices:
150 Cowley Road, Oxford, OX4 1JJ, UK
13590 Park Center Road, Herndon, VA 22071, USA

Library of Congress Cataloging-in-Publication Data

A catalogue record for this book is available from the Library of Congress.

British Library Cataloguing-in-Publication Data

A catalogue record for this book is available from the British Library.

ISBN 1 85973 032 9

Front cover: left — Godefroy Cavaignac; right — René
Waldeck-Rousseau.

Printed in the United Kingdom by WBC Book Manufacturers,
Mid Glamorgan.

For Shoshana

Contents

Acknowledgements

It is fitting here to restate the obvious: no historical research can be accomplished without libraries and archives and the people who make them work. For this study I have relied primarily on the Bibliothèque Nationale, the New York Public Library, the Cornell University Library and the Israel National Library in Jerusalem. May they and all other such institutions prosper!

This study has benefitted from the reading and comments of Kim Munholland, Frederick Seager, Joel Blatt, Michael Smith, Joel Colton, Mordechai Nisan, Harvey Chisick, Marjorie Farrar, Donald Wileman and the anonymous referees of *French Historical Studies* and Berg Publishers. By forcing me to clarify my writing (and thinking) they all contributed to this work. I thank them all with heartfelt gratitude.

Though it is not reflected by a plethora of footnotes, the conceptual framework of this study is based on my teacher Edward W. Fox's brilliant *History in Geographic Perspective: The Other France.* Anyone familiar with the work of Professor Fox should recognize his influence on my own.

Without the support and encouragement of my wife Shoshana this work would never have seen the light of day. I thank her deeply. I can only hope that my children Eliah, Moshe Matanel, Chayut Miriam and Uziah Leah, will some day understand in some positive way the investment made by their *abba* in this study.

General Auguste Mercier

General Deloye
Director of French Artillery

Commandant Walzin-Esterhazy

120mm Short, Model 1890

Captain Alfred Dreyfus

Commandant Rimailho

General Sainte-Claire Deville

Commandant Ducros

Lieutenant-Colonel Deport

Ducros's accelerated-fire field cannon
modified version of 80mm de Bange

Introduction

The period between the Panama scandal and the Dreyfus Affair – between early 1893 and late 1897 – is generally considered to have been a period of calm in France.[1] Yet even a casual perusal of the press reveals that for France's haute bourgeoisie – the wealthiest 1 per cent of the population, which owned more than 30 per cent of the national wealth – far from being a time of calm, 1893 to late 1897 was a time of intense nervousness. The historian Pierre Sorlin was not mistaken when he observed that 'between the municipal elections of 1892 and the general elections of 1898, fear of socialism was the dominant characteristic of French political life.'[2] While historians have discerned no significant *attempt* at revolution in the 1890s, the *fear* of revolution among the wealthy is impossible to miss. Senator Emile de Marcère warned in 1894 that 'socialism is extending itself and preparing a revolutionary era in which France could perish'; the bourgeois publicist Anatole Leroy-Beaulieu spoke in 1896 of 'the dangers [of social revolution] which increasingly menace the country and society'; and Georges Picot, leader of the bourgeois political organization the *Union Libérale*, wrote of the need for an organization to defend against 'revolutionary socialism'.[3]

This study was begun as an attempt to understand the haute bourgeoisie's fear of revolution between 1893 and 1898. On what was that fear based? Was it the result of labor unrest, which was particularly intense in the 1890s? Was it inspired by anarchist bombs, which caused those years to be known as the 'Terror'? Was it the result of the heavy rioting by students and workers in the streets of Paris in the summer of

---

1. Gordon Wright, *France in Modern Times* (Chicago: Rand McNally, 1960), p. 321; Paul Boujou and Henri Dubois, *La Troisième République*, 5th edition (Paris: Presses Universitaires de France, 1965), p. 56; Pierre Sorlin, *Waldeck-Rousseau* (Paris: Armand Colin, 1966), p. 358; Guy Chapman, *The Third Republic of France – The First Phase, 1871–1894* (London: MacMillan & Co., 1962), p. 368; Jacques Chastenet, *Histoire de la Troisième République*, vol. III, *Le Republique Triomphante, 1893–1906* (Paris: Hachette, 1955), p. 51.
2. Sorlin, *Waldeck-Rousseau*, p. 358.
3. Emile de Macère, 'Chronique Politique', *Nouvelle Revue*, LXXXVIII (May 1, 1894), p. 21; Georges Picot, 'La lutte contre le socialisme revolutionnaire', *RDM*, CXXXII (Dec. 1, 1895), pp. 591–625; *Economiste Français*, April 18, 1896, pp. 491–492.

– 1 –

1893? Was it due to Socialist electoral successes, which resulted in more socialist deputies than ever before? Conceivably each of these or a combination of several could have been what inspired fear of revolution among the haute bourgeoisie. Surprisingly, bourgeois leaders expressed no fear that any of these threats to the status quo had any chance of success. In fact, what really frightened the haute bourgeoisie was that the Chamber of Deputies might enact an income tax graduated from 2 to 5 per cent – an *impôt sur le revenu* – on incomes over 10,000 francs. This was the menace which terrified the haute bourgeoisie. Léon Say warned that to create such a tax 'would follow the star of collectivism'. Paul Leroy-Beaulieu denounced the *impôt* as 'an instrument of oppression and torture for the rich and well-to-do classes . . . a true fiscal Terror.'[4]

The French hauts bourgeois believed that an impôt sur le revenu could destroy them and feared that they had no adequate means to prevent one from being enacted. In a broader sense the issue was democracy itself. The haute bourgeoisie feared that the non-wealthy 'many' of universal suffrage was on the verge of taking control of government and, with the power of taxation, confiscating their wealth and destroying civilization as they knew it.

Daniel Halévy, in *Le fin des notables*, described the haute bourgeoisie's apprehension of universal suffrage in the early decades of the Third Republic. Universal suffrage, he wrote, was viewed as 'that formidable phenomenon, the enormous craving for power which threatened to destroy those states that did not learn how to curb it . . . If it were suddenly to dominate France, where the revolutionary tradition was so strong and the State so apparently crippled, what form would the upheaval take? "It is possible," wrote a fine essayist, Dupont-White, "to predict the impact of a pressure group [referring to the many of universal suffrage] still unconscious of its power, one that is destined to play such a great role and that is still harboring such formidable memories and grudges." It was safe to expect a catastrophe.'[5]

Few historians have recognized that the impôt sur le revenu was the chief political issue between 1893 and 1898. Even a meager description of this issue is absent from most general histories of France.[6]

4. France, *Journal officiel de la République française: Débats parlementaires, Chambre des Députés* (1896), pp. 729–732; Paul Leroy-Beaulieu, *Economiste Français*, March 28, 1896, p. 285.
5. Daniel Halévy, *The End of the Notables* (Middletown, Ct.: Wesleyan University Press, 1974 [Paris: 1930]), pp. 54–55.
6. Two of the few historians who gave sufficient recognition to the issue of the impôt sur le revenu were the archivist Charles Braibant and Marcel Marion, the historian of French finances. Braibant wrote that between 1893 and 1898 the issue of the impôt sur le revenu was the touchstone of French politics. Marion wrote that 'from about 1894 to

Introduction

The present study aims to correct this failing and to establish the importance of the issue of the impôt. To the politicians who advocated it, the impôt sur le revenu was a democratic reform, a means to counteract the regressiveness of the French fiscal system which relied heavily on consumption taxes. But to the haute bourgeoisie, the impôt was the very essence of socialistic revolution.

Although France is the subject of this study, it should be borne in mind that in the 1890s the fear of socialist revolution was not unique to that country. In 1895 the Frenchman Edmond Villey observed: 'The wind of socialism blows like a storm over the world . . . Never has there been posed a problem more pressing.'[7] It should also be borne in mind that in that period the issue of income tax was important throughout the Western world. As the American authority on taxation Edwin Seligman wrote, 'with the beginning of the nineties we enter upon a new and modern epoch of the income tax'.[8] In Italy an income tax was approved in the 1890s although its implementation was far from effective. In England the same period saw the first serious consideration of a progressive tax on total income although the country had long had a tax on 'sources' of income. It was in Prussia, the dominant state of the German *Reich*, that the progressive income tax was enacted most successfully in the 1890s. Seligman wrote that 'the great Prussian tax reforms of the nineties' put that country far in the lead in acquiring a modern fiscal system. One of the most important of these reforms was the 1891 graduated tax on family incomes over 900 marks.[9]

In the United States, Congress approved an income tax for the first time in 1894. The proposed tax rate was 2 per cent and exempted the 98 per cent of Americans with annual incomes under $4,000. Wealthy Americans reacted to the income tax quite as hysterically as wealthy Frenchmen did to the impôt sur le revenu. Senator John Sherman described it as an insidious venture in 'socialism, communism, devilism'. Congressman Dun challenged it as 'class legislation which would create such a financial revolution in this country as would shake the government

---

1898 the question of the impôt global et progressif sur le revenu completely dominated our political life.' Charles Braibant, *Félix Faure à l'Elysée, Souvenirs de Louis le Gall* (Paris: Hachette, 1963) p. 37; Marcel Marion, *Histoire financière de la France depuis 1775* (Paris: Rousseau & Cie, 1931), pp. vii–ix. To date the only monographic study of the issue of the impôt sur le revenu is Arthur Minnich's essay 'The Third Force, 1870–1896' in Edward Mead Earle (ed.), *Modern France* (Princeton: Princeton University Press, 1951).

7. Edmond Villey, 'Les causes morale et sociales du socialisme contemporaine', *Revue Politique et Parlementaire*, V (July 10, 1895), pp. 1–3.

8. Edwin Seligman, *The Income Tax* (New York: Macmillan Company, 1911), pp. 179–180.

9. Seligman, *The Income Tax*, p. 251.

to its very foundations.' Joseph Choate, the legal luminary, stated that the tax of 2 per cent was 'communistic in its purposes and tendencies' and was 'defended on principles as communistic, socialistic – what shall I call them – populistic as ever have been addressed to any political assembly in the world.' In his plea to the United States Supreme Court to declare the 2 per cent income tax unconstitutional, Choate warned: 'If you approve this law, with its exemption of $4,000, and this communistic march goes on and five years hence a statute comes to you with an exemption of $20,000 and a tax of 20 per cent upon all having incomes in excess of that amount, how can you meet it in view of the decision which my opponents ask you to render? . . . for once it is settled that the many can tax the few, it will be impossible to take any backward step.'[10]

The American upper class was saved from the 2 per cent income tax by the Supreme Court's decision in the Pollack case and the victory by the opponents of the tax in the bitterly fought 1896 presidential election. In France the haute bourgeoisie was saved from the impôt sur le revenu by the Senate's 1896 defeat of the Radical ministry which sought it and the restructuring of French politics by René Waldeck-Rousseau in 1899.

The Radical ministry, whose primary goal was the impôt sur le revenu, held office from November 1895 to April 1896. But even if this ministry had not come to office, the significance of the issue would not have been materially different. Bourgeois leaders realized, from the 1893 general election onward, that such a ministry was increasingly a real possibility. They also realized that the general elections of 1898 returned a clear majority of deputies willing to support a government seeking the impôt. With this in their minds, bourgeois leaders vigorously opposed what they considered to be a profound threat to their class and civilization itself. As means of social defense, bourgeois leaders in the 1890s considered electoral reform, constitutional reform, administrative decentralization and paternalistic enterprises to benefit society's less wealthy members.

In fact it was Waldeck-Rousseau's 1899 restructuring of the majority coalition in the Chamber, which I call the 'dreyfusian revolution', which finally overcame the threat of 'revolution' by taxation. This restructuring divided the coalition which had maintained Léon Bourgeois's Radical ministry in office. Provincial Radicals (who took anti-clericalism as their main issue) supported Waldeck-Rousseau. Parisians (who emphasized nationalism) opposed him. More important, perhaps, Radical politicians came to feed at the trough of political patronage and, for the first time, received campaign funds from haut bourgeois-financed campaign committees.

10. Louis Eisenstein, *The Ideology of Taxation* (New York: Ronald Press, 1961), pp. 18–19.

An accurate understanding of how French politics was restructured by Waldeck-Rousseau was purposely obscured by those who organized and benefitted from it. The representatives of the haute bourgeoisie who organized Waldeck-Rousseau's 1899 majority described it as a 'coalition of Republican defense'. It would have been contrary to their purposes to describe it as 'coalition to bury the impôt sur le revenu', but that is nonetheless what the coalition was. For obvious reasons, Radical politicians who supported the Waldeck-Rousseau ministry and thereby exchanged pursuit of a graduated income tax for plums of political patronage could not announce publicly that this was what they were doing.

The purpose of the 'center' coalition of 'Republican defense' organized by Waldeck-Rousseau was, presumably, to defend the Republic against anti-Dreyfusards who sought to overthrow it. Those 'threats to the Republic' will be seen to have been insubstantial indeed. The organizers of the Waldeck-Rousseau coalition stated clearly months before it came to office that a 'center' coalition was needed to avoid an impôt sur le revenu, and that to be durable it should be presented in 'positive' terms as a coalition to defend the Republic rather than in 'negative' terms as a coalition of compromise.

Waldeck-Rousseau's 'concentration' ministry, the longest-lived in the history of the Third Republic, replayed a classic drama with which the French were long familiar: the defense of the Republic. That in fact the Republic was in no way threatened was quite irrelevant. Ironically, if there was a genuine threat to the Third Republic in the 1890s it was posed by the *grands bourgeois* themselves who, facing the prospect of what they considered to be revolution by taxation, stood by the dictum enunciated by Adolphe Thiers in the 1870s that: 'Either the Republic will be conservative or it will not *be.*'

This study differs with the conventional view of several aspects of the history of the 1890s. It may be useful to summarize some of these points at the outset.

The period between the Panama scandal and the Dreyfus Affair is generally considered to have been a political doldrums. This study holds that the battle over the impôt dominated the period and produced the most intense political crisis in the history of the Third Republic.

The conventional view holds that anti-Dreyfusards posed a threat to the Republic and that the purpose of Waldeck-Rousseau's 'ministry of republican defense' was to defend the Republic. This study argues that there was no significant threat to the Republic and that Waldeck's purpose in establishing a center 'concentration' ministry was to avoid an homogeneous coalition of the 'left' which might seek 'revolutionary' tax legislation. Waldeck-Rousseau's government, it will be argued, was presented as a 'ministry of republican defense' only in order to promote its own longevity.

Histories of France in the 1890s generally overlook the fact that between 1893 and 1898 the burning political issue in France was the impôt sur le revenu sought by a unified left in the Chamber of Deputies.[11] Consequently the political crisis over the impôt has generally been ignored. For example the historian Jean Marie Mayeur wrote: 'to take but one of the Republics [the Third Republic], the elites were never unanimous [in periods of crisis] – not on the 16 May, not at the time of Dreyfus, nor of the Front Populaire, nor during Vichy.'[12] Mayeur makes no mention of the confrontation between the haute bourgeoisie and Léon Bourgeois' Radical ministry between November 1895 to April 1896; at the time of this crisis the 'elite' – the haute bourgeoisie – stood united virtually to a man, squarely against the Radical ministry seeking the 'revolutionary' impôt. This study focuses on the main political issue of the 1890s, the impôt sur le revenu.

It is commonly thought that the general elections of 1898 did not change the balance of forces in the Chamber of Deputies.[13] In fact, as this study will show (and as bourgeois political leaders at the time realized), the left gained a majority in that election so that Méline's conservative coalition of Moderates and Catholics was no longer viable. To avoid an homogeneous 'left' coalition of the sort which had maintained Léon Bourgeois' Radical ministry in 1895–96, bourgeois leaders decided to seek a center 'concentration' coalition. The result was Waldeck-Rousseau's government of 'republican defense'.

It has been suggested by Herman Lebovics that the defense of the social order in the Third Republic was based on a conservative protectionist alliance of 'iron and wheat' perfected by Jules Méline in the 1890s.[14] While it would be wrong to deny the existence of a protectionist alliance of industry and agriculture, it should be remembered that Méline's 1896–1898 ministry of the right included free traders and protectionists. This study argues that after Méline left office in 1898, the basis of political (not economic) defense by the upper bourgeoisie was a center 'concentration' coalition of Radicals and Moderates whose Moderate

11. Jean-Marie Mayeur, 'Analytical Afterward' in Jolyo Howorth and P. Cerny (eds), *Elites in France: Origins, Reproduction, Power* (New York: St. Martins Press, 1981), p. 250.

12. For example, Michael Burns writes in *Rural Society and French Politics* (Princeton: Princeton University Press, 1984, p. 122) that the Dreyfus Affair was the 'main national event of the epoch.'

13. For example, Herman Lebovics, *The Alliance of Iron and Wheat in the Third French Republic, 1860–1914 – Origins of the New Conservatism* (Baton Rouge: Louisiana State University Press, 1988), p. 185.

14. Ibid., p. 123.

minority could veto any 'revolutionary' legislation favored by its Radical majority.

Sandford Elwitt has suggested that the underlying cause of bourgeois nervousness and fear of revolution in the 1890s was labor strife stemming from the growth of the industrial proletariat.[15] In his opinion the haute bourgeoisie of the 1890s faced, in essence, a labor problem. This study argues that the underlying basis of the bourgeoisie's worry in the 1890s was a *political* problem, with the wealthy 'few' feeling threatened by the non-wealthy 'many' of universal suffrage. Consequently, whereas Elwitt understood the aim of bourgeois paternalism (promoting inexpensive housing, mutual savings societies, worker education, etc.) as opposing revolution by calming labor strife, this study understands it also as a means by which the haute bourgeoisie sought to enhance its moral stature as society's *classe dirigeante* and foster the liberal view that aside from protecting private property, the less government does and spends, the better it is.

This study proposes to recast the history of France in the 1890s and beyond by arguing that the key event of the 1890s was not the Dreyfus Affair, but rather the battle over the impôt sur le revenu. Interestingly, the Dreyfus Affair and the conflict over the impôt were not unrelated. Both were resolved by Waldeck-Rousseau's ministry of 'republican defense', and both, it will be suggested, had their origin in France's efforts to equip its army with the rapid-fire field cannon which would revolutionize warfare in World War I. It was the need to pay for modern weaponry, including rapid-fire artillery, which appears to have motivated Godefroy Cavaignac, the impôt's chief advocate, to push for the tax; and it was the desire on the part of French military leaders to deceive the Germans as to their progress in developing rapid-fire artillery that appears to have motivated the conviction of Captain Alfred Dreyfus of espionage and the maintaining of that conviction after it was clear that he was innocent. Without the injustice against Dreyfus, of course, there would have been no Dreyfus Affair.

If this study's understanding of the history of France in the 1890s is accepted, it does not mean that the traditional story of the period – the Dreyfus Affair, the supposed threat to the Republic, the defense of the Republic – should be discarded. Rather, the traditional story should be understood as being itself part of the history of the period.

The traditional history of France in the 1890s was formulated not by historians looking backwards but by contemporaries writing of their own

---

15. Sandford Elwitt, *The Third Republic Defended – Bourgeois Reform In France, 1880–1914* (Baton Rouge: Louisiana State University Press, 1986), pp. 3, 4, 297.

time. For contemporaries, the traditional story served to explain, with no reference at all to the *fin-de-siècle* crisis of democracy, how France moved from having a Chamber in which a majority of deputies represented the interests of the haute bourgeoisie (Méline's coalition) to having a Chamber with a minority of such deputies (the 'Radical Republic') without jeopardizing the vital interests of the haute bourgeoisie. As such, the traditional story, which served to obscure political reality while protecting the position of France's haute bourgeoisie, is itself part of French history.

The traditional narrative of the 1890s has provided historians with a story so satisfying that they have not felt the need to reconsider it afresh. Once such a reconsideration is undertaken, however, the political narrative recounted in this study readily emerges from a review of the most basic sources of political history – contemporary newspapers, periodicals, pamphlets, books and parliamentary papers. The only aspect of the political narrative recounted in this study which is not readily apparent from contemporary sources is why Godefroy Cavaignac felt such urgency regarding the need for an impôt sur le revenu. The explanation of this aspect rests on an understanding of weapons development shrouded in secrecy in the 1890s.

The appendix of this study challenges the common view that French Army leaders insisted on maintaining the conviction of Captain Dreyfus for espionage for reasons such as anti-semitism and a perverse sense of military honor, reasons which were irrational and unjustifiable. It suggests that there may have been excellent reasons of national defense for maintaining the conviction and that to declare Dreyfus innocent (which he surely was) would have endangered French military secrets of the highest order concerning innovations in rapid-fire field artillery.

The 75mm cannon was a splendid weapon developed by the French Army under deepest secrecy between 1894 and 1896. At the time of its invention it was a decade in advance of similar weapons being developed by other Great Powers. (During World War I, this 75mm rapid-fire cannon was still the finest field artillery piece in existence and arguably saved France from defeat by Germany.) It will be suggested that the need to maintain the secrecy surrounding that weapon led French Army leaders to unjustly convict Captain Alfred Dreyfus of espionage.

Godefroy Cavaignac's name is virtually absent from the pages of French history books. To the extent that Cavaignac is known today, it is for his role in the Dreyfus Affair; as Defense Minister in Henri Brisson's cabinet of 1898, it was Cavaignac who assured the retrial of Dreyfus by revealing that one of the main pieces of evidence used against him was in fact a forgery. Hopefully this study will help extricate Cavaignac from undeserved obscurity by showing that as the driving force behind the campaign for the income tax between 1893 and 1898 it was he, more than any other individual, who set the political agenda for France in that period. It will be argued that although Cavaignac could not publicly acknowledge it at the time, one of the main reasons he favored an income tax was that he saw it as a powerful fiscal tool for raising funds to equip French military forces with modern weapons – including the 75mm field cannon which particularly preoccupied him.

Why did such wide discussion about income tax take place throughout the Western world in the last decade of the nineteenth century? Several contributing factors may be suggested. One was the growth of democratic forces within representative governments. Another was the need for increased government income in a period of economic recession and declining tax revenues. The income tax was viewed by economists as an excellent fiscal tool because it automatically taxed new sources of wealth as an economy developed, and because government revenues could be conveniently increased or decreased simply by adjusting its rates.

An important reason governments needed money in the 1890s was to pay for the arms race taking place throughout the Western world. Innovations in chemicals (smokeless gunpowder), steel production and metallurgy in the 1880s permitted the development of greatly improved cannon in the 1890s. Enormous advances were made in artillery, first on the seas, where ships could carry virtually unlimited weight, and then on land where the size of mobile cannon had to be limited. The great economic expansion (particularly in steel production) since the 1870s provided the basis for the new engines of destruction in the 1890s.[16]

Germany led Europe in technological and economic growth in the 1870s, 1880s and 1890s. It also led the way in acquiring a modern fiscal system, an important feature of which was the introduction of an income tax. With such formidable technological, economic and fiscal equipment, together with her desire for *weltmacht*, it is not surprising that Germany was the power to be reckoned with at the turn of the century. For the British, the German challenge was primarily on the seas and gave rise to the well-known race to build great ships of war capable of carrying the new cannon. For the French, the challenge from Germany was mainly on land and produced the less well-known competition to develop rapid-fire field artillery.

France, the United States and Britain managed to meet their financial

---

16. Clive Trebilcock, 'British Armaments and European Industrialization, 1890–1914', *The Economic Review*, XXVI (May 1973), pp. 254–255.

needs in the 1890s without recourse to an income tax. Helping make this possible was the world-wide revival of prosperity after 1896, which produced increased tax revenues. It would take the surge of military spending in the second decade of the twentieth century to revive the push for an income tax in England, the United States and France.

The Third Republic is commonly known as the 'bourgeois republic'. But historians who study France have honored this commonplace more in the breach than in their observance. With few exceptions (Emmanuel Beau de Loménie and Sandford Elwitt being the most notable), historians of the Third Republic have not focused their attention on its haute bourgeoisie. This study is different. It tries to see the France of the 1890s from the perspective of the members of its haute bourgeoisie: how they thought about society and government (chapter 1); how they interpreted political developments which they believed threatened them with destruction by confiscatory taxation (chapters 2 and 3); how they fought and defeated the Radical ministry which sought the graduated income tax that terrified them (chapters 4 and 5); how their leaders evaluated the various 'revolutionary' threats of the 1890s (chapter 6); how their leaders sought to protect society and civilization as they knew it (chapter 7); and how the bourgeoisie was finally delivered from the 'revolutionary' menace of democracy by the political restructuring directed by Waldeck-Rousseau which I call the 'dreyfusian revolution' (chapter 8).

This study uses the terms 'bourgeois'[17] and 'haute bourgeoisie' perhaps too frequently for the taste of Americans who sense these words to be rather harsh, off-putting and ideological. If these terms were not used, however, the reality of France in the 1890s would be distorted. In those days the haute bourgeoisie stood out clearly as a distinct social class distinguished by its speech, education, dress, ways of living and social interaction. Most important, as we shall see, its members regarded themselves as members of the *classe bourgeoise*, the *classe dirigeante* of France.

---

17. The terms 'bourgeoisie' and 'haute bourgeoisie' refer to a class as does 'proletariat'. 'Bourgeois' and 'haut bourgeois' refer to an individual member of the bourgeoisie as the word 'worker' refers to a member of the proletariat. 'Bourgeois' and 'hauts bourgeois' are the plurals of 'bourgeois' and 'haute bourgeois' as 'workers' is the plural of 'worker'.

—1—

The Haute Bourgeoisie Menaced by Democracy

Léon Say, the haute bourgeoisie's most eminent representative in the government of the Third Republic, died on 21 April 1896. Say died, Robert Mitchell wrote in his obituary for *Le Gaulois*, just when the conservative Republic he had done so much to establish was itself on the verge of collapse.[1] The problem stemmed from the Chamber of Deputies, where a Radical ministry supported by a coalition of Radicals, Socialist Radicals and Socialists was seeking to enact a graduated income tax — an impôt sur le revenu — which, to the French haute bourgeoisie, was the very essence of social revolution.

Mitchell described how he had met Say three months earlier at Cours-La-Reine. Never handsome, Say was looking ill. His face, drawn and faded, was marked by an insurmountable weariness. His skin, slackened by a rapid loss of weight, floated about him like an over-sized garment. He was dying, and clearly he knew it. Mitchell had begun the conversation with the usual opener: 'What do you think of the situation?'

'We are approaching the abyss,' Say had replied. Mitchell was not surprised. Say, he wrote, was one of those who, having founded the Republic, was not pleased with the way it had developed. 'Are you familiar with the story of *The Monster and the Magician*?' Say had continued. 'A sorcerer wished to perfect divine creation by uniting in one new being all the powers distributed in nature. The newly formed creature left its crucible able to fly like a bird, swim like a fish, possessing a marvelous vigor which would assure universal domination to the one who would know how to direct it . . . And suddenly the magician saw before him a monster, an unregulated super-human power, whose first deed was to destroy the one who had given it life.'

Léon Say fell silent; Robert Mitchell had understood. 'If Say had not been a magician,' Mitchell's obituary continued, 'nevertheless he worked in his "laboratory" and played a great part in the work of shaping the structure of the Republic. Having left the Orleanist branch of the

1. *Le Gaulois*, April 23, 1896.

Monarchists which he had at first favored, he had been one of the first to think that it was possible to found in France a republic where the old parliamentarians of 1830 would rediscover their ideal rejuvenated and fortified – a popular state which would respond to liberal and conservative aspirations of the monarchy of compromise [the July Monarchy] and the reformed [Second] Empire. He remained faithful to this conception . . .' and, wrote Mitchell, 'I firmly believe that he died not having realized it . . . Léon Say has died at the very hour of the collapse of the conservative republic he built.'[2]

In the years after the fall of the Second Empire, Say had played an important part in determining that France would be a parliamentary republic: a republic in that there would be a Chamber of Deputies elected by universal male adult suffrage, and parliamentary in that there would be a Senate and President of the Republic as brakes to prevent the Chamber from enacting 'dangerous' legislation. According to the Constitutional Laws of 1875, senators would be elected indirectly by limited suffrage and the President of the Republic would be elected by the combined Chamber and Senate. Say was elected President of the Senate in 1880 after having served as a deputy in the popularly elected Assembly. In 1889, however, foreseeing the crisis of democracy of the 1890s, he returned to the Chamber of Deputies where he believed his influence would be needed.

He was not mistaken. The years that followed witnessed the specter of a Radical ministry seeking the 'revolutionary' impôt sur le revenu to be levied on the wealthiest 14 per cent of France's population. In this graduated income tax France's upper class perceived the opening act of a nightmare of social revolution so frightening that the terror it inspired can hardly be exaggerated.

The Constitution of the Third Republic had been intended to protect the haute bourgeoisie from 'dangerous' legislation. Now, in the spring of 1896, the Third Republic appeared to be turning on its creators. The Chamber of Deputies debated the issue of the income tax in March 1896; close to death, Léon Say served as chief spokesman for the opponents of the tax. But by a small but solid majority, the Chamber had voted in favor of what the haute bourgeoisie considered to be the 'revolutionary' impôt.

The last chance to stop the income tax lay with the Senate. Now, in March 1896, the Senate sought to do what it had never done before – to force from office a ministry supported by a majority of deputies. On April 21, the day Say died, the Senate acted to 'suspend the legislative life of the country'. Henceforth it would refuse to approve any legislation at all until the Radical ministry had departed. The Senate applied the

2. Ibid.

'emergency brake' the day Robert Mitchell published his obituary of Léon Say. It remained to be seen if it would hold.

The Bourgeoisie

A *bourgeois*, in the classic French sense of the term, was a wealthy person who could live on the income of his capital. The *bourgeoisie* was that class of persons which Tocqueville, in the 1830s, had described as 'those wealthy who do not have to work to gain a living'. The Larousse *Dictionnaire Universel* of 1867 defined the bourgeoisie as those persons who could live on the income of their properties, capital, endowments, pensions, subsidies and stocks. The ranks of the bourgeoisie, it wrote, included rich land owners and merchants, chiefs of industry, capitalists, judges and high government officials. Below the bourgeoisie, it continued, was the class which lives exclusively from its labor.[3]

In the 1890s members of the bourgeoisie owned outright the medium-sized industry and much of the large industry of France. Bourgeois shareholders owned giant enterprises such as insurance companies, rails, utilities, banks and some mines. Bourgeois holders of long-term State *rentes* and short-term Treasury obligations owned a great part of the national debt, the single largest area of investment in France.

Statistics produced by the Ministry of Finance indicate the size and distribution of the bourgeoisie. In the 1890s, when an average working man earned about 2,500 francs per year and a deputy in the Chamber was paid 9,000 francs a year, there were 2,680 families in Paris which had annual incomes over 100,000 francs, 5,872 with incomes between 50,000 and 100,000 francs, and 18,160 with annual incomes between 10,000 and 20,000 francs. The provinces, according to the same set of statistics, had a much smaller number of the very richest, with only 641 families having incomes over 100,000 francs. In the lower wealth brackets the provinces made a better showing with 3,817 family incomes between 50,000 and 100,000 francs, 32,649 incomes between 20,000 and 50,000 francs, and 96,781 incomes between 10,000 and 20,000 francs.[4]

The Ministry of Finance's figure of 26,716 Parisian families with annual incomes of over 10,000 francs corresponds nicely with the 1894 edition of the *Tout Paris* directory of 25,000 of the upper crust of the

3. *Dictionaire Universelle du XIX siècle*, vol. II (Paris: Classique Larousse et Boyer, 1867), p. 1126. 'Bourgeois', in the context of nineteenth century France should not be confused with the modern American sense of the word which signifies 'middle class'. In France, to be a *bourgeois* was to be wealthy. As used in this book, the terms 'haute bourgeois' and 'bourgeois' both refer to the members of the bourgeoisie in the classic sense – those wealthy who could live on the income of their capital.
4. France, *Journal Officiel Documents, Chambre des Députés* (1896), p. 59.

capital. The newspaper *Le Temps* recommended this directory to its readers in December 1893, with the New Year close at hand, as rendering 'a real service to all those who belong in any manner to Paris society by helping them prepare their visits, send off calling cards, etc.'

Though the haute bourgeoisie was a well-defined class (that is, its members could recognize who belonged to it and who did not), it was not homogeneous. Differences in levels of wealth, family background, professional interest and religious affiliation delineated sub-groupings of the haute bourgeoisie. Old wealth or new wealth, noble or common origins, financial, industrial, commercial or landed wealth, Catholic, Protestant or Jew; these were significant categories to haut bourgeois Frenchmen of the late nineteenth century. The fundamental unit of the class was the family, as indicated by Emmanuel Beau de Loménie's apt term 'bourgeois dynasties'.

The haute bourgeoisie formed a small society. Particularly among its wealthiest elements, members of the haute bourgeoisie knew each other personally. The wealthiest of the Parisian bourgeoisie in the 1890s resided in sections of the city which had largely been developed since 1848, with the great influx of the provincial upper class. The eighth *arrondissement* was home to the greatest concentration of the wealthiest; within a few blocks of the Parc Monceau lived almost all the *régents* of the Bank of France.

The fifteen régents of the Bank, elected by its two hundred largest shareholders, were representative of the haute bourgeoisie. Among the régents in 1896 were Catholic industrialists such as Henri-Adolphe Schneider (director of the Creusot iron and steel works), Alfred Seydoux (textile magnate) and Charles Balsan (industrialist who held a large interest in the La France Insurance Company); a few Catholic bankers, the most important of whom was Edouard Van Dyck Aynard (head of the Crédit Lyonnais and president of the Lyon Chamber of Commerce and co-founder of many of the great industrial establishments in the Lyon area); and Protestant bankers such as Baron Mallet, Baron Rudolphe Hottinguer (vice-president of the board of directors of the Paris-Lyon-Marseilles Railroad), Charles Goguel, Michel Heine and Edouard Alfred André (head of the great Banque Neuflize). The one Jewish régent in 1896 was the well-known Baron Alphonse de Rothschild.

The French hauts bourgeois were generally 'liberal' in that they favored laissez-faire government and believed that society's problems could best be solved by the action of private initiative and cooperation. They believed, generally, that government involvement in economic and social activity would not only trample the sacred rights of property, but would jeopardize the very basis of French economic and therefore social and cultural well-being. The members of the bourgeoisie believed it was their role to organize and direct the productive enterprise of the country and that they were particularly suited to this by heritage and education. They believed that if government relieved them of their rightful task by controlling or suppressing private capital, both they and society as a whole would suffer. They would lose their wealth and power, and France would lose its organizing brain.

Among the haute bourgeoisie were public leaders who devoted themselves to leading their class and society. Léon Say was the quintessential bourgeois public leader of the first quarter-century of the Third Republic. Descended from an outstanding Protestant family of economists and businessmen, gifted with exceptional intelligence, talent and energy, Say was involved in innumerable leadership efforts. He wrote prolifically and well about economics, politics, and political economy. Married to the granddaughter of Bertin, founder of the *Journal des Débats*, he was the editor of that prestigious newspaper. He was also a Professor at the Ecole Libre des Sciences Politiques, a member of the Academy of Political and Moral Sciences, and a member of the French Academy. His books on political economy were standard texts and still occupy a place on the shelves in the reading room of the Bibliothèque Nationale.

Longtime deputy in the Chamber, Minister of Finance (who arranged through private bankers the payment of the indemnity to Germany resulting from the war of 1870), President of the Senate, Say was also a powerful force in politics and was involved in numerous efforts to 'defend society'. Among the institutions which he helped lead were the Association Libérale Républicaine (a political campaign organization), the Ecole Libre des Sciences Politiques (the school whose purpose was to produce a civil service elite sympathetic to the bourgeoisie), and the Association for Inexpensive Housing (a paternalistic organization which encouraged efforts to give workers the opportunity to own their own homes).

Not unlike other professional callings of the French haute bourgeoisie, public leadership was often a family tradition.[5] Just as there were bourgeois families whose members traditionally pursued careers in medicine, law, the judiciary and the upper levels of the civil service, there were families such as Say's that had a tradition of public leadership. Thus in the 1890s Pierre Leroy-Beaulieu, Pierre Claudio-Jannet, Charles Picot and Pierre LePlay, all of whom were sons of illustrious bourgeois leaders, were coming to be recognized as individuals beginning to play active roles as public leaders.

---

5. Christophe Charle, *Les elites de la république, 1880–1900* (Paris: Fayard, 1987); Pierre Birnbaum, *The Heights of Power – An Essay on the Power Elite in France* (Chicago: University of Chicago Press, 1982).

Bourgeois leaders stressed the social responsibilities of their class and criticized those of its members who devoted themselves exclusively to private affairs. The point they made was that members of the haute bourgeoisie should be leaders of society as well as possessors of wealth. Thus René Stourm, economist and president of the Societé d'Economie Sociale, differentiated between those bourgeois who 'preferred to sit at home without inconveniencing themselves and those who took an active role in leading and defending society'. He noted two senses of the term 'bourgeois'. One, he said, referred to what Victor Hugo had called the 'self-satisfied part of the people, who, at certain periods, had monopolized power, honors and influence, possibly without sufficient concern for others.' The other, Stourm stated, referred to a bourgeoisie which was an honor to France – a *classe dirigeante* – because of its education, work, effort and acquired or inherited intellectual superiority. This bourgeoisie, said Stourm, was a benevolent class by its charity, devotion, love of its neighbor and solicitude for those who suffer: 'a Christian bourgeoisie troubling itself and hastening to do good.' Stourm addressed the members of the Unions for Social Peace as 'social authorities' who had important duties because 'it is normal that those who possess intellectual and moral power must know how to fulfill their social role'.[6]

A wealth of sources expressing the opinions of the haute bourgeoisie of the 1890s are available to the historian. Among them are Parisian newspapers such as the *Journal des Débats*, *Le Figaro*, *Le Temps* and *Le Gaulois* and periodicals such as the *Revue Des Deux Mondes*, the *Nouvelle Revue*, the *Revue Bleue*, the *Revue Diplomatique*, the *Revue de Reform Sociale*, the *Economiste Français* and the *Revue Politique et Parlementaire*. This last publication served as a general forum for bourgeois political discussion. A monthly publication, first issued in July 1894, the *Revue Politique et Parlementaire* was a handsome piece of work published by Armand Colin & Cie. At first each issue had about 140 to 160 pages, but within a few months it ran to about 250 pages.

Members of the haute bourgeoisie also expressed their opinions at the banquets that they organized. In the 1890s when leaders of the bourgeoisie wanted to gain support for an enterprise of social defense, they would invite three or four hundred members of their class to a banquet at the luxurious Hôtel-Continental. These banquets were held in the hotel's sumptuous Grande Salle with its rich red carpets, lavish drapes and wall coverings, expanses of mirrored doors and walls, gilded rococo pillars, magnificent chandeliers and ceilings painted with flowers, cherubs and nymphs. From a dais in front of a large marble fireplace, bourgeois leaders

6. René Stourm, 'Toast', *Reforme Sociale*, II (July 1, 1896), p. 117.

would address the assembled members of their class in order to enlist their support. Often these speeches were reported in the press; sometimes they were reprinted as pamphlets to commemorate the occasion and convey their message to those not present.

Constitutional Ideals of the French Haute Bourgeoisie

The 'parliamentary republic' was the form of government favored by the French haute bourgeoisie to solve the problem of how government should be structured in a regime of universal suffrage. It was this 'parliamentary republic' that Léon Say had helped to establish in the 1870s and which Robert Mitchell claimed, at the time of Say's death in 1896, was near collapse.

Decades before, Alexis de Tocqueville in *Democracy in America* had posed the problem that the 'parliamentary republic' was meant to solve: in a regime of universal suffrage, what form of government would best protect the property and power of the wealthy few from challenge by the non-wealthy many who could be expected to come to dominate the popularly elected assembly?

In 1830, when the vote in France was limited to about 250,000 electors, Tocqueville had traveled to the United States in order to see universal suffrage in action. By visiting America, he believed he was traveling into the future; universal suffrage, he was sure, would eventually come to France. Tocqueville explained that for the few to preserve their position and wealth in a regime of universal suffrage in which the members of the legislature would be chosen by the many, the power of government had to be limited. In the United States, he observed, the power of government was limited by the Federal system which divided jurisdictions between federal (national), state and local levels, by the separation of powers between the legislative, executive and judicial branches of government, and by the absence of a well-developed bureaucracy able to enforce the decisions of the national government.

For France, with its long history of monarchical and Napoleonic centralized bureaucratic administration and almost no tradition of separation of powers, it would not be feasible simply to reproduce the American model. The French solution to the problem of the many and the few would necessarily be different. The haute bourgeoisie of France favored a parliamentary regime as the best means for promoting liberal, limited government protective of private property. Such a regime would have a legislature comprised of two chambers (one of which would be indirectly elected and thereby removed from the direct control of the electorate) and a 'weak' president (whose main function was to designate the individual who would attempt to lead a cabinet supported by a majority of the popularly elected chamber of the legislature). The president of the republic would be elected not directly by universal suffrage but by the two chambers of parliament. The purpose of a parliamentary regime was to limit the government's capacity to legislate and act by shielding it from the direct influence of a powerful executive or legislature elected by the many of universal suffrage.

Parliamentary government had long been favored by the haute bourgeoisie. During the 1789 Revolution, Moderate delegates to the Constitutional Assembly had advocated it. Parliamentary government had been established with the Restoration, and refurbished with a new king in the Revolution of 1830. The Revolution of 1848 had been intended by the bourgeois who promoted it to change the executive by removing King Louis Philippe; but on this occasion the intended little 'revolution' got out of hand and, under the influence of lower-class crowds, led to the establishment of the Second Republic with universal suffrage and a single legislative assembly. This was then followed by the dictatorship of Napoleon III.

Most of the haute bourgeoisie managed to live fairly comfortably under Napoleon III's Second Empire. But by the late 1860s, some of the most powerful members of the class were expressing dissatisfaction with the regime which gave the Emperor more power than they would have wished, and sought to replace it with their favored parliamentary system. Well-known bourgeois attacks on the Imperial system were Jules Ferry's *Les comptes fantastiques d'Haussmann* and Léon Say's series of articles in the *Journal des Débats*, both of which attacked Napoleon III's powerful prefect of the Seine. The thrust towards parliamentary government in the late 1860s largely corresponded with Napoleon III's own intentions, and produced the 'liberal empire' of the last months of the Second Empire.

The constitutional work of Léon Say, whom Robert Mitchell had compared with a sorcerer working in a laboratory, was the joining of the idea of parliamentary government with the idea of universal suffrage. The origins of universal suffrage in France went back to the Revolution of 1789 when the Constituent Assembly abolished all legal distinctions between estates and made France a nation of citizens. The Declaration of the Rights of Man and the Citizen of 1789, which established the idea that political sovereignty belongs to the people, proclaimed that the national sovereignty was 'one, indivisible and inprescriptable' and stated that 'all citizens must participate personally or through their representatives' in the creation of the law.

Under the Restoration monarchy of 1814–30 the right to vote was limited to the approximately 100,000 persons who paid at least 300 francs of direct taxes. The July Monarchy, dating from 1830, reduced property qualifications and thereby expanded the number of eligible voters to about

250,000. With the Revolution of 1848 and the establishment of the Second Republic, universal direct male suffrage was established with about 9 million eligible voters.[7]

Although the Second Republic of 1848 did not last long, the principle of universal suffrage remained. Napoleon III used it to support his regime with nation-wide plebiscites which regularly endorsed his rule. From 1848 on, no French government dared to attack universal suffrage directly and the institution became what Paul Bastid has called a 'religion' of French political life.[8]

In helping to establish the parliamentary republic of 1875, Léon Say had acted in accordance with the lines of thought developed by bourgeois political thinkers in the second half of the nineteenth century as they considered the problem of the many and the few discussed by Tocqueville in the 1830s. Given the fact of universal suffrage (which was accepted by all significant political factions[9]) what kind of constitution would be best for France? How could government be structured so that the few could preserve their property and power against potential attack by government dominated by the many? The problem was posed in terms of the relation between leaders and followers, between elites and masses, between the educated and the uneducated, and between the wealthy and the poor. The composition of the many and the few would vary somewhat according to how the problem was stated, but the constitutional problem remained essentially the same.

The solution on which bourgeois thinkers came to agree was the *parliamentary republic*. This was not a republic in the classical sense, which referred to rule by a single assembly elected by universal suffrage; rather it referred to a regime without a king and with a chamber elected by universal suffrage and a senate elected indirectly, outside the control of the many.

Ernest Renan, a great intellectual light between 1870 and 1890, was a 'reluctant republican'. 'Society', he wrote, 'is a hierarchy . . . an immense organism, which is accomplishing a divine work. The negation of this divine work is the error into which French democracy [the masses] easily falls.' Renan firmly believed that France required the guidance of an elite, but feared that her people had 'learned to conceive social perfection as a sort of universal mediocrity'. Roger Soltau has written that Renan divided mankind into two classes: 'those called to knowledge and thereby to leadership, and those who, while undoubtedly worthy of development,

7. Albert Gigot, 'Discourse', *Reforme Sociale*, VIII (July 1, 1894), p. 26.
8. Paul Bastid, *L'avènement du suffrage universel* (Paris: Presses Universitaires de France, 1948), p. 5.
9. Ibid., pp. 6, 57.

were essentially meant to be led.' Believing in the 'divine right' of the elite, Renan worried that the jealousy of the masses opposed its rule.[10] Renan also presented the problem of the many and the few in economic terms. It was inevitable, he stated, that the elite of society, the 'so-called higher classes', rest on the toil of the many. Arrogant democratic masses motivated by jealousy, he feared, were liable to overthrow property and with it the elites it supported.[11] Renan, stating the problem of the few and the many in its political terms, warned that with universal suffrage and an 'unorganized electorate', France would be condemned to a social leadership 'lacking intelligence, knowledge, prestige, or authority.'[12]

Although Renan would have preferred a liberal, parliamentary monarchy, after 1870 he became resigned to the idea that France would be a 'republic', that is, with universal suffrage and without a king. To achieve the conservative republic he favored, Renan proposed that there be a modified universal vote, a senate, administrative decentralization and a policy of colonization to avoid war between the rich and the poor.[13]

Hippolyte Taine, another leading thinker of the early Third Republic, also believed that society required a ruling class, an intellectual and moral elite, to 'protect the real community against the whims of a passing majority'. In his horrifying (and misleading) picture of Jacobinism, which he claimed incarnated the dogma of popular sovereignty and expressed its essential nature in the Terror of the French Revolution, Taine portrayed what happens when the many succeed in seizing control of government and dominating the few.[14] By 1870 Taine was reconciled to the universal suffrage he had opposed in 1850 but rejected the Jacobin republic with its single legislative chamber. He favored rather two-stage elections 'which would unite the consultation of everyone with the ultimate control of Government by a governing aristocracy'.[15]

Charles Renouvier, generally considered the foremost political thinker of the first twenty years of the Third Republic, believed that the propertied class as a whole should rule France. He favored a republic (that is, a parliamentary regime without a king) which would bring all upper-class

10. Charlotte T. Muret, *French Royalist Doctrines Since the Revolution* (New York: Columbia University Press, 1933), pp. 106, 169.

11. Ernest Renan, *Constitutional Monarchy in France*, trans. from the second French edition (Boston: Roberts Brothers, 1871), p. 20; Roger Soltau, *French Political Thought in the Nineteenth Century* (London: Ernest Ben Ltd., 1931), p. 217.

12. Renan, *Constitutional Monarchy in France*, pp. 26–28; Renan, *La reforme intellectuele et morale*, 5th edn. (Paris: Calman-Lévy, n.d.), p. 115.

13. J.P. Mayer, *Political Thought in France from the Revolution to the Fourth Republic* (London: Routledge & Kegan Paul Ltd., 1949), p. 821; Renan, *La reforme*, pp. 45–58.

14. Mayer, *Political Thought*, p. 82.

15. Roger Soltau, *French Political Thought in the Nineteenth Century*, pp. 237, 243.

elements into the political arena rather than a monarchy which would favor that segment of the upper class closest to the king. Renouvier opposed clericalism and royalism on the right and Jacobinism on the left. The ranks of Jacobinism, he explained, include men from provincial towns and the *sans culotte* proletarian elements of the cities. To him all popular movements were Jacobinism which he, like Taine, identified with mob violence and the direct intervention of the masses into the affairs of government. Rejecting the idea that the people themselves should govern, Renouvier favored a republic with an electoral base of universal suffrage which would be ruled by the propertied classes.[16]

Renan, Taine and Renouvrier were not exceptional in their opposition to a republic in the classic sense. Daniel Halévy observed that 'All the political theorists − who like Victor Broglie, Paradol, Laboulaye and others, had reflected upon and written about the French system for the past ten years [prior to the early 1870s] − demanded a Senate whose main purpose was that universal suffrage, represented by the Chamber, would be held in check by an institution created by another source and imbued with a different spirit.'[17]

The Third Republic was governed by the Constitutional Laws of 1875. The general elections of 8 February 1871 had produced a National Assembly, which was de facto a democratic republic of the sort envisioned in the Constitution of 1793: a single assembly directly elected by universal manhood suffrage with no independent executive. With the constitutional laws enacted in 1875 the de facto republic was transformed by the Assembly's conservative majority, following the lines indicated by bourgeois political thinkers of the 1860s and 1870s, into a parliamentary republic, the so-called Third Republic. As barriers to the power of a potentially Jacobin Chamber of Deputies elected by universal manhood suffrage (which was itself weighted heavily in favor of rural constituencies), the Constitutional Laws of 1875 provided for a Senate and a President of the Republic elected by the combined Senate and Chamber.[18] Senate approval was required to enact legislation approved by the Chamber. The President of the Republic, with the approval of the Senate, was empowered to disband the Chamber at any time and call for general elections.

16. Ibid., p. 243.
17. Halévy, *End of the Notables* (Middletown, Ct.: Wesleyan University Press, 1974), p. 198.
18. John Scott, *Republican Ideas and the Liberal Tradition in France, 1870–1914* (New York: Columbia University Press, 1951), pp. 50, 65, 67–68, 70; J.J. Chevalier, *Histoire des institutions politiques de la France de 1789 à nos jours* (Paris: Librairie Dalloz, 1952) pp. 39–40, 316; Jean-Pierre Marichy, *La deuxième chambre dans la vie politique française depuis 1875* (Paris: P. Pinochet et R. Durand-Auzias, 1964).

Dufaure, the deputy in the Assembly who drafted the constitutional laws of 1875, expressed the prevailing liberal position: 'The Republic? It is above all a Senate!' Besides being elected by a very small number of indirectly chosen electors (for example, in 1895 a senatorial election in the Loire-Inferieure had 994 voters and one in the Sarthe had 888), the Senate over-represented agricultural areas, particularly those of the poorer *départements*, and was therefore weighted toward conservatism.

Prior to April 1896, neither the President of the Republic nor the Senate had succeeded in exercising the full powers specified for them in the Constitutional Laws of 1875 (MacMahon had tried but failed in 1877). Until April 1896 the 'parliamentary republic' had functioned, de facto, as a 'republican' republic in that the popularly elected Chamber had established and terminated all cabinets. This was as intended; the Senate and President were meant to function as emergency brakes to restrain an 'out of control' Chamber, not as daily tools of government. The principle of universal suffrage, in the opinion of 'parliamentary' republicans, should be upheld to as full an extent as possible – up to that point at which bourgeois vital interests were in jeopardy – because employing the Senate and President against the will of the Chamber would be sure to stimulate popular pressure for a pure, single-assembly republic.

In the 1890s, when French bourgeois leaders expressed the idea that liberal government was under attack they sometimes suggested that France stood between the German and English models of society. The English model stood for limited government and respect for private property. The German model, or 'Prussian' as it was commonly called, represented its contrary and placed a heavy hand of state control on private wealth. Bourgeois Frenchmen wanted their society to move toward the English model but feared it was approaching the Prussian.

In the spring of 1896, at the time of Léon Say's death, the parliamentary republic was tested as never before. The Chamber, led by a Radical ministry, had approved the impôt sur le revenu. Now, for the first time in the history of the Third Republic, the Senate would be called upon to turn a ministry out of office.

The Radical Challenge

It was not necessary to look to Prussia for a model of anti-liberal government. The Jacobin idea of government, which had deep historical roots in France, challenged the liberal model and, the haut bourgeois of the 1890s feared, threatened to overwhelm it. The Jacobin ideal joined democracy with the idea that the state, acting through a well-organized bureaucratic administration centered in Paris and reaching out to the smallest towns, could best serve the needs of society.

As Edward W. Fox showed in *History in Geographic Perspective*, the economic basis of the bureaucratic state was France's agrarian society: small, decently prosperous, peasant farms which covered much of the country and engaged a high proportion of her population.[19] Over the centuries, the royal government had succeeded in organizing this agrarian society by replacing feudal landed nobles as the governing agents of the territory. Symbolic of the bureaucratic state were the weekly markets in provincial towns throughout rural France. To these markets peasants brought their surplus production to trade for money with which to purchase goods and pay the taxes and fees of government. The royal government had tapped the wealth produced by the subsistence agricultural sector to fuel the national administration, pay for the seat of government in Paris and Versailles, pay for an army, create an infrastructure of roads and bridges and fund a national debt, the largest in the world.

The Jacobin idea emerged during the French Revolution after the collapse of the royal administration. At that time middle-class lawyers and civil servants organized as members of a network of about two thousand Jacobin Clubs under the direction of strong central leadership acted to restore the functioning of the agrarian-based bureaucratic state.

In the 1890s the haute bourgeoisie felt its control of government challenged by deputies who labeled themselves Radicals and Socialist Radicals. Most of these deputies were educated professionals of the towns – doctors, lawyers, pharmacists, notaries and teachers – who competed on the local level with members of the other educated classes – the gentry and the clergy – for leadership of the mass of rural voters. A minority represented the Parisian lower middle classes.

By the standards of provincial France, Radical deputies were fairly prosperous and well educated. They were not, however, true bourgeois in the classic sense because they were not among the wealthy who could live on the income of their capital. Radical deputies were far outclassed in wealth, education and polish by the hauts bourgeois. Provincial Radicals had little familiarity with the big business and high finance with which the hauts bourgeois were involved. In the context of Paris, provincial Radicals would be virtually invisible save for their presence in the Chamber of Deputies; they counted for little in the higher reaches of the intellectual, educational and cultural worlds. Thus the historian Charles Seignobos described the Radical party of the 1890s as

19. Edward W. Fox, *History in Geographic Perspective – The Other France* (New York: W. W. Norton, 1971) pp. 45–53, 72 ff.

'formed of new men, of obscure provincials, with mediocre culture'.[20]

To an extent, Radicals formed their own social circle in masonic lodges; in Paris the Grand Orient of the Masons on rue Cadet in the ninth *arrondissement* was a gathering place for many Radical politicians in the 1890s. Hence the Radicals were attacked by their home town gentry and clerical rivals as 'freemasons'.

Though not socialists, as their bourgeois opponents often claimed, Radicals had no love for the great industrial and financial bourgeoisie and were willing to accept a degree of government control of business which would be repugnant to the very wealthy. Radicals were not, however, enemies of private property in any ordinary sense; in fact they represented small town and peasant proprietors who were some of its most vehement defenders. The Radicals' Jacobin mentality, which was not liberal in the classic sense, was sympathetic to government intervention in social and economic activity for the greater good of society and less sensitive to what the wealthy believed were the rights of private property.

If the main electoral strength of Radicals in the 1890s lay in the small towns of France, the Jacobin mentality was also traditionally exhibited by the Paris working and lower-middle classes. Living at the center of the administrative state, Parisians characteristically emphasized the democratic and nationalistic (rather than administrative) aspects of Jacobinism. In the French Revolution, Parisian crowds motivated by Jacobin values had played an important role. Similar crowds were active at other times of national crises including the Revolution of 1848 and Commune of 1870. In the 1890s a group of characteristically nationalistic Radical deputies represented Paris in the Chamber.

In provincial towns the state administrative apparatus formed an important part of the economy. The *mairie* (town hall), post office and public school of even the smallest town reflected the presence of the national government. In Paris, however, the national administration was relatively less important as a source of jobs. Thus provincial Radicals particularly valued the administrative system for the patronage it could provide, while Parisian Radicals emphasized democratic and nationalistic values. In the Chamber between 1893 and 1898 Parisian and provincial Radicals shared a Jacobin mentality, inscribed themselves as Radicals and Socialist Radicals, and voted together.

Jacobin values were national and democratic. The democratic ideal insisted on a nation of citizens having equal rights and obligations. The national ideal favored strong, centralized government, be it called royal,

20. Charles Seignobos, *L'évolution de la Troisième République (1875–1914)*, vol. III of *Histoire de France Contemporaine*, ed. E. Lavisse (Paris: Hachette, 1921), p. 185.

imperial or republican, to solve France's problems. During the French Revolution, Jacobin ideals were expressed in the reorganization of local administration, the *levée en masse* which raised an army by drafting all unmarried men between the ages of 18 and 25, and the abolition of the legal distinctions between clergy, nobles and commoners. Jacobins believed that with the fulfillment of their national and democratic ideals, France would be a well-ordered and powerful country able to defend itself and solve the problems it might face. The form of government favored by Jacobins was the democratic republic with a single legislative assembly elected by direct universal manhood suffrage and no independent executive. From the time of the Revolution through the 1890s, this remained *the* design for a republican form of government in France.

Newspapers expressing the Jacobin point of view were generally found in the provinces. Characteristic of these was the widely distributed *Dépêche de Toulouse* and local papers such as the *Républicain de l'Ain*. In Paris, Henri Rochefort's *L'Intransigeant* expressed the nationalist spirit of the lower-middle class of the capital. Parisian upper-class Jacobins, an uncommon breed, could read *Le Voltaire* which described itself in the 1895 *Annuaire de la presse* as 'a newspaper of politics and society: the republican *Figaro*'.

The *Impôt sur le Revenu*: the Main Issue in the Chamber of 1893–98

Tax reform was the main concern of the 1893–98 session of the Chamber of Deputies. Even before the 1893 general elections the Chamber's vote to replace taxes on wine, cider and beer ('boissons' which were staples for the French) with a tax on distilled alcohol signaled that tax reform would be a focus of interest in the months ahead.[1]

Tax reform was widely discussed in the 1893 election campaign.[2] Interest continued strong after the elections. Jean Casimir-Périer, head of the new Chamber's first government, stated in his ministerial declaration that 'fiscal reforms are without a doubt the principle object of the whole legislature. They are, in our eyes, the first and most essential of social reforms . . .'[3] Others agreed. 'Tax reform is on everyone's lips' wrote Paul Leroy-Beaulieu in the *Economiste Français* of December 1893. Observing the widespread popular demand for 'a more equitable distribution of public charges', the *Revue Politique et Parlementaire* reported in August 1894 that 'tax reform is in the air.'[4] Marcel Marion,

1. Pierre Bidoire, *Budget de 1894* (Paris: Guillaumin & Cie, 1894), pp. 3–5.
2. In that year 293 of the deputies elected made a 'general reform and more equitable redistribution of taxes' part of their platforms, compared with 164 who had done so in the general election campaign in 1889. One hundred and ninety-nine of the candidates elected in 1893 called for the reduction or suppression of taxes on 'hygienic drinks' compared with 164 in 1889. 'Suppression of the *octrois*,' another tax reform, was advocated by 108 deputies elected in 1893, compared with 45 in 1889. An *impôt sur le revenu, impôt sur le capital*, or both were called for by 187 winning candidates in 1893, compared with 69 in 1889. In all, the platforms of elected deputies in 1893 contained 787 proposals for tax reform compared with 343 in the previous general elections. (Désiré Barodet, *Programmes et engagements electoraux des députés*, Paris: Imprimerie de la Chambre des Députés, 1894, pp. 228–229.)
3. André Daniel (André Lebon), *L'année politique, 1894* (Paris: Charpentier, 1895), pp. 357–358.
4. Jacques Chastenet, *Raymond Poincaré* (Paris: R. Julliard, 1948), p. 48; *Economiste Français*, Dec. 1893, p. 738; Félix Roussel, 'La vie politique et parlementaire en France', *RPP*, I (Aug. 1894), pp. 312–313. See also 'La Reforme des Impôts,' *Reforme sociale*, VIII (Sept. 16, 1894), p. 423; André Daniel (André Lebon), *L'année politique, 1894* (Paris: Charpentier, 1895), p. 147; André Lebon, 'L'esprit public en France', *Nouvelle Revue* (Nov. 1895), p. 279; Pierre Bidoire, *Les budgets français 1895*, (Paris: V. Giard et

the French financial historian, wrote that never before had there been so many proposals for tax reform as there were in 1894.[5]

The French tax system, which relied excessively on consumption taxes on necessities such as paper, candles, salt, *boissons* (wine, beer and cider), and transportation[6] was criticized for placing a disproportionate burden on society's poorer members and thereby violating Adam Smith's universally accepted maxim that the subjects of a state should support its government in proportion to the income they enjoyed under its protection.[7] It was also criticized as being inefficient, inflexible and incapable of taxing new sources of wealth as the economy developed.[8]

France's so-called direct taxes – the doors and windows tax, the land tax on unimproved property, the tax on personal property and the tax on occupational licenses[9] – which presumably taxed individuals according to their capital or income were widely considered to be unjust. (Strictly speaking, there were no direct taxes in France in the 1890s; what did exist were taxes based on a presumed relationship between certain publicly observable indications of wealth and actual wealth.) The rate of the doors and windows tax was based on the assumption that the homes of the well-to-do had more doors and windows than those of the poor and that real estate values were higher in large cities than small.[10] But, as Paul Leroy-Beaulieu wrote, these criteria did not necessarily indicate the income produced by a particular property. The tax did not sufficiently recognize differences in incomes between families in the poorer and those in the more elegant sections of the same city and, as Leroy-Beaulieu pointed out, it promoted unhealthy conditions because it encouraged the French to cut down on the number of windows in their homes.[11]

The land tax's inequities were described as 'classic'. Since the 1830s, when the tax was established, land values had changed greatly without

E. Brière, 1896), p. 7; Félix Roussel, 'La vie politique et parlementaire', *RPP*, V (Aug. 1895), p. 381; Ferdinand Faure, 'La statistique et la démocratie', *RPP*, III (March 10, 1895), p. 409.

5. Marcel Marion, *Histoire financière de la France depuis 1775*, vol. I (Paris: Rousseau & Cie, 1914), p. 163.

6. Paul Leroy-Beaulieu, *Traité de la science des finances*, vol. I, 2nd edn. (Paris: Guillaumin & Cie, 1879), p. 274.

7. Paul Leroy-Beaulieu, *Traité de la science des finances*, p. 131; Max Boucard and Gaston Jèze, *Elements de la science des finances et de législation financière française*, 2nd edn. (Paris: V. Girard et Brière, 1906), p. 929.

8. Boucard and Jèze, *Elements de la science des finances*, p. 929.

9. Joseph Caillaux, A. Touchard and G. Privat-Deschanel, *L'impôt en France* vol. I (Paris: E. Plon Nourrit & Cie, 1896), pp. 2, 7.

10. Ibid., pp. 38–39; Leroy-Beaulieu, *Traité de la science des finances*, vol. I, pp. 350–352.

11. Ibid.; Paul Cauwès, *Cours d'économy politique*, vol. IV (Paris: L. Larose, 1893), p. 360.

being adequately reflected in the *cadastre* (land valuation registry) and thus in the rates.[12] The personal property tax was criticized for containing injustices that were the result of one hundred years of neglect.[13]

Tax reform in the early 1890s would have required the creation of new taxes to replace inefficient or unfair ones because in that period there were no budget surpluses. Between 1893 and 1896 all political leaders agreed that government finances were very tight. The Moderate Finance Minister Burdeau, in his budget proposal for 1895 (the first budget to be established by the newly elected Chamber), stressed how difficult it would be to avoid a deficit. The Chamber's Budget Committee report for 1895 also indicated a particularly difficult financial situation. In May 1895 Alexandre Ribot, the Moderate Prime Minister then in office, stated that his proposed budget for 1896 'presented itself in particularly difficult conditions'.[14]

The financial squeeze between 1893 and 1895 was due to government expenses climbing slightly while income from taxes declined as a result of the 1893–96 recession. Finance experts and politicians agreed that government spending could not practically be reduced and even had to be increased to pay for existing legislation. Thus in 1891 Godefroy Cavaignac, reporter for the Chamber's Budget Committee, wrote that whatever efforts at economy might be made in the future, the experience of recent years showed that government spending could not be expected to decline. Not only was the state's budget not compressible, he stated, but it would almost certainly expand because 'in a progressive democracy such as France, in a country which seeks to continually develop its effective power to assure its position in Europe, the necessity of new expenses are incessant and ineluctable'.[15]

Peytral, Minister of Finances in the Dupuy cabinet of April to December 1893, explained that the increases in the budget he proposed for 1894 were unavoidable and almost exclusively the result of previous commitments made by the state. For example, the law of 19 July 1889 would increase appropriations for public instruction for 1894 by 2,360,000 francs and the postal and telegraphic administration would require 4,900,000 francs more in order to improve its service and pay its employees, conforming to the frequently expressed intentions of parliament which were already reflected in the 1893 budget. He pointed out that the greatest increases for public works in the 1894 budget were due to the cost of payments on state-guaranteed rail loans stemming from

12. France, *Journal Officiel Débats, Chambre des Députés* (1894), p. 757.
13. Ibid., p. 758.
14. France, *Journal Officiel Documents, Chambre des Députés* (1894), pp. 445, 1502; Ibid. (1895), p. 379.
15. France, Ministère des Finances, *Bulletin de statistique et de législation comparée*, XLVII (Paris: Imprimerie Nationale, 1900), pp. 504, 505.

agreements made in 1883.[16]

Alexandre Ribot, Finance Minister in the cabinet he headed from January to October 1895, explained why state spending could not be reduced: although it might be thought that France's budget could be significantly reduced, Ribot stated, such a view was superficial and mistaken. Of the 3,400 million franc total budget, 1,497 million was devoted to paying the interest on the national debt and 386 million went to the virtually fixed cost of collecting taxes. If the debt service were not paid it would mean state bankruptcy; if money was not spent for the collection of taxes, they would not be collected. Military expenses which accounted for 914 million francs were considered irreducible. Thus, Ribot wrote, of 3,448 million francs in the state budget, 2,797 million were absorbed by expenses which could not be cut. Of the remaining 650 million francs, 195 million went for public education and 131 million for public works. Evidently, wrote Ribot, Parliament did not wish to suppress the 17,000 public schools which had been built over the past ten years and which were 'the honor of the Republican government'. Nor would it want to further reduce appropriations for the maintenance of public works because to do so would eventually have grave consequences for the public fortune itself.[17]

Government spending programs were based on the assumption that government income would gradually increase. From 1886 to 1892 annual tax receipts had risen fairly steadily from about 3,000 to 3,300 million francs. But 1893 saw a decline of about 30 million francs, 1894 a rise of about 50 million francs over 1893, and 1895 a decline of about 25 million francs from 1894.[18]

The Background of the Impôt sur le Revenu in France

The French Parliament had considered proposals for an income tax several times since 1848. Most often the tax had been proposed in periods of financial difficulty, such as 1848–50 and 1871–75, as a means of

16. France, *Journal Officiel Documents, Chambre des Députés* (1891), p. 1677.

17. France, *Journal Officiel Documents, Chambre des Députés*, (1893), pp. 199, 514.

18. France, *Journal Officiel Documents, Chambre des Députés* (1895), pp. 381–382; Paul Doumer, *Projet de loi portant fixation du budget général de l'exercise 1897* (Paris: Imprimerie Nationale, 1896), chart between pp. 161–162; France, *Journal Officiel Documents, Chambre des Députés* (1891), p. 1663; August Moireau, 'Le mouvement économique', *Revue des Deux Mondes*, CXXVII (Feb. 1, 1895), pp. 551–578; Pierre Bidoire, *Budget de 1894* (Paris: Guillaumin & Cie, 1894), p. 31; 'Chronique de la quinzaine,' *Revue des Deux Mondes*, CXXIX (June 1, 1895), pp. 708–710; *Economiste Français*, Jan. 6, 1894, p. 1 and Oct. 20, 1894, p. 490; Charles Seignobos, *L'évolution de la Troisième République (1875–1914)*, vol. VII of *Histoire de France Contemporaine*, ed. Ernest Lavisse (Paris: Hachette, 1921), p. 183.

increasing state revenues. Less frequently, income tax had been put forward as a means to reduce taxes that disproportionately burdened the working classes.[19]

In the mid-1880s demand for the income tax was renewed as a means to achieve democratic tax reform. French academic economists often favored the idea of an income tax because it would offset the regressiveness of existing taxes, it would add elasticity to the fiscal system by allowing government to increase or reduce revenues simply by adjusting the rate on incomes, and it would take into account the increasing industrialization of the French economy by automatically taxing new sources of wealth as they developed. Opposing such a tax were Léon Say's lectures at the Ecole Libre des Sciences Politiques, published under the title of *Democratic Solutions to the Tax Question* (Paris, 1886), and Yves Gyot's *L'impôt sur le revenu* (Paris, 1887), a report made for the Chamber's Budget Committee.

Paul Leroy-Beaulieu, a bitter opponent of the income tax in the 1890s, had to his later embarrassment favored such a tax earlier in his career. In his 1877 *Traité de la science des finances*, he had written that an income tax was an essential ingredient in the fiscal system of a great state and had proposed such a tax to 'redress the inequalities' of existing direct taxes. The income tax proposed by Leroy-Beaulieu in 1877 was similar to the one sought by the Radicals in the 1890s. It would exempt incomes below 2,000 francs, tax those between 2,000 and 4,000 francs at 1.5% or 2% and rise to 3% or 4% for larger incomes. It would produce about one-fifth or one-sixth of total State revenue.[20]

Academic experts who favored the income tax recognized that politically it would be difficult to enact in France. Thus Leroy-Beaulieu wrote in 1877 that such a tax would at first excite lively resistance, but that eventually its justice would be recognized and people would get used to it.[21]

The *Nouveau dictionnaire d'économie politique*, published in 1891–92 and edited by Léon Say and Joseph Chailley-Bert, presented the views of eminent authorities both for and against the income tax. Léon Say

19. Alfred Neymarck, *Finances contemporaines*, vol. V; *L'obsession fiscale – projets ministeriels et propositions dues a l'initiative parlementaire relatif a la reforme de l'impôt, 1872–1907* (Paris: Félix Alcan, 1907), p. 40; Edouard Campagnole, 'Revenu (Impôt sur le)', in Léon Say and Joseph Chailley-Bert, *Nouveau dictionnaire d'économie politique* vol. II (Paris: Guillaumin 7 Cie, 1891–92), p. 741.
20. Paul Leroy-Beaulieu, *Traité de la science des finances*, vol. I, pp. 165, 211–213, 427–429. See also Max Boucard and Gaston Jèze, *Eléments de la science des finances et de la legislation financière française*, p. 628.
21. Leroy-Beaulieu, *Traité de la science des finances*, vol. I, pp. 429, 477. See also Boucard and Jèze, *Eléments de la science des finances et de legislation financière française*, pp. 639–640.

himself was quoted as an opponent of the tax; he argued that to draw up tax rolls and publicly exhibit a list of citizens with the size of their capital and more or less precarious incomes would constitute a political danger of the first order and that to give such lists to government officials would be a political imprudence which sensible men would always refuse to commit.[22] In favor of the income tax, the *Nouveau dictionnaire* presented the views of the eminent liberal French economist Joseph Garnier (1813–81) who was considered to be one of the world's foremost authorities on government finances. Garnier had written that it was not necessary to deny the danger of demagogic theories and appetites, but he stressed that it was also necessary not to exaggerate or misunderstand the conservative moral force which governs the masses which, in moments of anger, respect property more than persons. Garnier claimed that England's experience had shown that confidentiality could be maintained sufficiently by tax officials.[23]

Edouard Campagnole, the author of the *Nouveau dictionnaire d'économie politique*'s article on the impôt, concluded with his own opinion. Such a tax, he believed, established at a level which would provide the Treasury with 150 or 200 million francs, would not present serious disadvantages or great dangers and would offer the undeniable and immediate advantage of permitting the reduction of consumption or other regressive taxes. Besides, wrote Campagnole, an impôt sur le revenu would be a fiscal instrument of great productivity for the years in which the State would be obliged to call on its citizens to increase their tax payments. In all, he held, it would provide 'a fruitful experience with practical results'.[24]

In the 1890s, even vigorous opponents of the impôt admitted that in theory such a tax would be desirable. Thus Edouard Cohen wrote that 'scientifically speaking the income tax is without doubt the best and most equitable tax which could be conceived. In principle, all masters of the science of economics have recognized and proclaimed that it is income which should be taxed because it is continually renewed and that no other element of private wealth lends itself better to the rule of proportionality which is the essential basis of the contribution due from each citizen for the cost of social expenses.' But, continued Cohen, the French had rejected the income tax because of the difficulty of determining personal income without procedures which would violently discontent those who would be required to pay it. Any attempt to create the tax in France, he

22. Campagnole, 'Revenu (Impôt sur le)', p. 736.
23. Ibid. Garnier was one of nine authorities cited in the bibliographical note of the article on 'Taxation' in the *Encyclopedia Britannica*, 11th edn., vol. XXVI (New York: Encyclopaedia Britannica Company, 1911) p. 464.
24. Campagnole, 'Revenu (Impôt sur le)', p. 741.

warned, would run into 'a prejudice more emotional than reasoned' and concluded that the income tax would require arbitrary procedures and had better not be undertaken.[25]

The Radicals in the Chamber of 1893–98 took the impôt sur le revenu as their main issue. The impôt had been a plank in the Radicals' agenda since before the beginning of the Third Republic, since Gambetta enunciated it in his 1869 'Belleville Program.' This agenda included constitutional reform to produce a democratic republic (the Republics of 1793 and 1848) with a single assembly elected by direct universal suffrage, without a senate and without a president, universal lay elementary education, separation of church and state, equality of civil rights and obligations, elections of judges, reduction of the cost of justice, various schemes for social welfare including medical, relief and retirement programs, the eight-hour day, legislation to promote worker safety and limit the labor permitted women and children, nationalization of the Bank of France, the mines and the railroads, and democratic fiscal reforms such as taxes on income and capital in order to reduce the burden on the poorer classes and increase it for the wealthy.[26]

Radicals pursued only some of these goals at any given time. In the late 1870s and early 1880s their primary concerns were amnesty for exiled Communards and equality of military service for all citizens (including the clergy). In the first half of the 1880s free secular elementary education took precedence. With this went a strong dose of anti-clericalism in order to exclude the Church from the national school system. Between 1893 and 1898 Radicals gave priority to democratic tax reform and the impôt sur le revenu. Laid aside were other planks of the Radical agenda including constitutional reform, nationalization of the Bank of France, nationalization of mines and rails and separation of church and state. In the effort to achieve tax reform and the impôt sur le revenu all elements of the left – agrarian, urban and proletarian, Radicals, Socialist Radicals and Socialists – were united.

Godefroy Cavaignac, The Driving Force Behind the Push for the Impôt sur le Revenu, 1893–98

Although tax reform was the main issue in the period and although the income tax had long been included in the Radical platform, it was the

---

25. Edouard Cohen, 'La reforme des impôts', *Reforme Sociale*, VIIII (Sept. 16, 1894), pp. 423, 429, 433, 434. See also *Journal de l'Ain*, March 23, 1893, which expresses a similar idea.
26. Félix Ponteil, *Les classes bourgeoises et l'avènement de la démocratie, 1815–1914* (Paris: A. Michel, 1968), p. 415.

leadership of Godefroy Cavaignac which was responsible for the Radicals placing the impôt sur le revenu at the head of their legislative agenda between 1893 and 1898 and for the decision of Léon Bourgeois to lead an 'homogeneous' Radical cabinet supported by a coalition of Radicals, Socialist Radicals and Socialists. In short, more than any other individual, it was Godefroy Cavaignac who set the political agenda for France between 1893 and 1898.

Godefroy Cavaignac was a political type unique in his time. From birth he was directed first by his mother, who died when he was nineteen, and then by himself to follow his father's footsteps and become a great leader, a president, of France. Descended from a distinguished political family of the highest social class, he upheld the national and democratic ideals of his father, uncle and grandfather. His grandfather, Jean-Baptiste Cavaignac, a strong partisan of the French Revolution, had sat in the Convention and voted for the death of Louis XVI. His father, General Eugène Cavaignac, was a great democratic republican who as a young officer had taken part in the Revolution of 1830. In 1848, as a general in the army, he had been granted dictatorial power and charged with saving the democratic Republic by suppressing anarchic violence in Paris. Once order was restored he surrendered his powers without hesitation. In the presidential election of 1848 Cavaignac was defeated by Louis Napoléon, and after his coup in December 1851 Louis Napoleon had Cavaignac imprisoned for three years in the Chateau of Ham.

Cavaignac's mother, the former Louise Odier, was the daughter of the Protestant banker James Odier whose family was known for its liberal political and tolerant religious views. Louise Odier knew General Eugène Cavaignac as a habitué of her family's salon, and as a teenager she decided to marry the republican hero. It was only with difficulty that she overcame the resistance of the man she had chosen to be her husband; at first General Cavaignac had objected that the difference in their ages would make such a marriage unreasonable. But Louise Odier's unbreakable resolve and deep sincerity overcame the general's objections. 'I told her she was mad,' General Cavaignac recounted to a friend, 'but she refused to listen.' At the time they became engaged Louise Odier was eighteen and Cavaignac was forty-nine. Three years later, after Cavaignac had been released from prison by Louis Napoleon, they were married.

Godefroy was the only child born to the couple. When the boy was four years old General Cavaignac died as the result of a riding accident at his country home at Ourne in the Sarthe. Louise Cavaignac, then 26, undertook to bring her husband's body back to Paris as he had wished, to be buried in the magnificent family tomb sculptured by François Rude in the Montmartre cemetery. Concerned that the Imperial government, fearing an occasion for republican demonstrations, would not permit the republican general to be buried in the capital, Louise Cavaignac decided to accompany her husband as if he were sick; with her husband's body beside her, she had her carriage lifted onto a train bound for Paris. The funeral and burial then took place quietly in the Montmartre cemetery.[27]

At his death, Eugène Cavaignac left his young widow instructions for raising their son:

> Concerning our dear child, I ask you to accept [as husband] only one who would be by his position and character determined to teach my child to respect, by the career he will choose, by his language, his conduct, in short by all his life, the memory of his grandfather, his uncle Godefroy and his father.
>
> In general, you know what I would want done. Raise my son seriously, solidly, with a view to a career which comes from an education at the Ecole Polytechnique, ownership and development of land or an active industry which he could direct. Never, but never, banking or commerce as I have seen them done, ending inevitably, as you know, in the game of speculation, which is to say corruption in all forms, and the overthrow of all moral ideas. If his tastes lead him to follow a military career, if conditions permit it, advise it, but gently. He will find in the army the memory and the protection of his father.[28]

Madame Cavaignac refused to remarry. Henceforth her life would be devoted to raising her son as her husband had wished. She died at the age of 41 in 1872.[29]

As a child Cavaignac was raised at the family chateau at Ourne. At twelve he moved with his mother to Paris in order to attend the Lycée Charlemagne which attracted students from throughout France because it was considered to provide the best preparation for entrance to the Ecole Normale Supérieure and the Ecole Polytechnique, the most prestigious of the state's 'Grandes Ecoles.'[30] At Charlemagne Cavaignac excelled in his studies. When he won the school-wide prize for Greek translation in 1868 the Imperial government hit upon the idea of sending the young Prince Imperial to preside over the distribution of prizes and welcome, it was hoped, the applause of students of Charlemagne. The result would be a sort of public reconciliation between the sons of the two great adversaries, General Eugène Cavaignac and Louis Napoléon.[31]

Cavaignac discussed the matter with his mother and reached a conclusion on what to do at the presentation ceremony. There, as planned, young Cavaignac refused to rise when his name was announced to receive

27. Henriette Dardenne, *Godefroy Cavaignac – Un républicaine de progrès aux débuts de la 3eme République* (Colmar, 1969), p. 21.
28. Ibid., p. 756.
29. Ibid., p. 757.
30. Ibid., p. 211.
31. Ibid., p. 14.

his award. For this he won the enthusiastic applause and bravos of the *lycéens*. As a result of the storm around his refusal to accept the award from the hand of Napoleon III's son, Cavaignac left Charlemagne and completed *lycée* at Louis le Grand. Throughout his life this incident would be used to illustrate his sincere republicanism.[32]

In the 1870 war with Prussia, Cavaignac enlisted in the Army and won a medal for his service. After the war he pursued studies at the Ecole Polytechnique and the Ecole des Ponts et Chaussées, and on graduation he was named state engineer at Angouleme. After returning to Paris to study at the Faculty of Law he was licensed and then, in 1881, named to the high administrative position of *maître des requetes* at the Conseil d'Etat.[33]

In 1882 Cavaignac was elected to the Chamber of Deputies as a republican from Saint-Callais in the Sarthe, and he kept this seat throughout his career in the Chamber. The new deputy quickly came to play the important role for which his upbringing and formal education had prepared him. He became a leading authority on military and financial matters and was highly respected not only for his expertise in these fields but also for his stern and high morality in the tradition of his family. From the time he entered the Chamber, all things pointed to a brilliant future of important leadership.

In the tradition of his family, Cavaignac held national and republican ideals. A democratic regime, he believed, was the best basis for French military strength. He expressed his ideas on this subject in his two-volume scholarly work, *The Formation of Contemporary Prussia*, which appeared in 1891 and 1898 and was awarded the Thiers prize of the French Academy. The thesis of the study was that the French Revolution, by abolishing feudal privilege, centralizing the State and making France a nation of equal citizens, had released tremendous national military energy, enough to defeat the attacking forces of Europe and allow the French army to dominate much of the Continent. In Cavaignac's view, the democratic state was militarily strong because it made citizens of all inhabitants, citizens who would eagerly defend their nation. French society, he argued, had been regenerated by the Revolution, which had opened the democratic era. By proclaiming equal rights, the Revolution had brought into the political life of the nation social elements which had previously stood apart from it and had thereby given the body politic an unforeseen vigor and irresistible force. It had shown for the first time, he wrote, the military power of the masses. As such, it was the model

32. Ibid., p. 24.
33. Ibid., pp. 160–162.

from which Prussia, at the time of the Revolution, had learned.[34]

Cavaignac believed that social justice and equality were the keys to national strength and the basis of the moral superiority of France. He wrote that if it were true that the realization of ideas of social justice is an essential task of civilization, it would be fair to say that in this sense France had been the fatherland of humanity.[35]

Tall and thin, of rather delicate health, Cavaignac's appearance was described as reserved and even somewhat poor. He was an impressive speaker and a hard worker who carried the study habits of his youth — particularly his education at the Ecole Polytechnique — to his work in the Chamber. He was described as 'neither a metaphysician nor a poet but a man who applied himself to successive tasks constructing clear solutions based on concrete detail and was systematic and stubborn in the application of his ideas.'[36]

Cavaignac came to the Chamber as a republican following in the path of Léon Gambetta whom he admired for his opposition to the Second Empire in the 1860s and his organization of the defense of France after the collapse of the Imperial government in 1870. He quickly came to play an important role in the Chamber; in 1885–86 he was Under-Secretary of War in the ministry headed by Henri Brisson, and in 1892 he served in Emile Loubet's cabinet as Minister of Navy and of the Colonies. Elected to the Chamber against a Boulangist in 1889, Cavaignac took an *opportuniste* position which meant that he was willing to postpone social legislation and join in a coalition of Moderates and Radicals in order 'to defend the Republic'.

By the early 1890s Cavaignac had come to reject 'opportunism', which he saw symbolized in the parliamentary corruption and influence peddling of the Panama scandal of 1892–93. In a widely admired Chamber speech, Cavaignac expressed 'with sober eloquence the outraged honesty of the bulk of the French nation' and called for a full exposure and accounting by the politicians involved. The Chamber enthusiastically applauded Cavaignac's speech and took the extraordinary action of having it posted on the official bulletin boards outside every town hall of the approximately 36,000 *communes* of France. After the great impression Cavaignac had made in the Chamber debate on the Panama scandal, wrote the contemporary British observer of France, Edward Bodley, had the presidency of the Republic been vacant in 1893, Cavaignac 'would have

---

34. Godefroy Cavaignac, *La formation de la Prusse contemporaine*, vol. I, 3rd ed. (Paris: Librairie Hachette, 1891), pp. 140, 175.
35. Ibid., pp. 411, 486.
36. *Le Jour*, Jan. 7, 1896.

been called by acclamation to fill it.'[37]

Cavaignac was well-respected even by those who disagreed with his political opinions. In August 1893 the conservative economist Paul Leroy-Beaulieu wrote that Cavaignac was highly knowledgeable about French State finances, and in January 1895 the *Revue Diplomatique* described him as a 'highly honorable statesman of unquestionable talent'. In November 1895, well after he had begun his campaign for the impôt sur le revenu, the *Revue des Deux Mondes* (which vehemently opposed the tax) wrote that he was one of the most studious men in the Chamber.[38] Maurice Barrès, writing in January 1896, expressed the common view that Cavaignac symbolized 'a general purification, the reform of Parliament, of the corps of financiers, and of the administration of the colonies.' He represented, wrote Barrès, 'a conception of government to which honest men would like to return: the general interest placed above private interests.'[39]

Cavaignac was a severe sort of man. Though Jacobin in philosophy, he stood above parties and never did label himself a Radical; until late 1894 he associated with the Moderates in the Chamber and sat at the center rather than the left. Thus in 1893 Radicals denounced him as a reactionary and, when he proposed the impôt in July 1894, the Radical newspaper the *Républicain de l'Ain* described him as a 'Moderate.'[40]

Godefroy Cavaignac was the driving force behind the effort to establish an income tax in the 1890s. At first Cavaignac tried to convince the Moderates in the Chamber to enact the tax; when he failed, he sought to have it passed by a coalition of Moderates and Radicals. Only when this proved impossible did he turn to a 'homogeneous' left coalition of Radicals, Socialist Radicals and Socialists to enact the impôt that he believed was vital for France.

Why did Cavaignac believe that France needed an income tax? The answer was not obvious to his contemporaries, as the *Revue Diplomatique* suggested in 1895 when it wrote that 'it would be for historians to explain the urgency which possessed Cavaignac' regarding the impôt sur le revenu.[41] In a Chamber debate on the income tax in July 1894, Cavaignac claimed that the tax would promote social justice. This, of course, was a standard argument in its favor and there is no reason to believe that he was insincere in expressing it. But, as the *Revue Diplomatique* suggested,

37. John Edward Courtney Bodley, *France*, vol. I (New York: Macmillan Co., 1898), p. 310.
38. *Revue des Deux Mondes*, CXXXII (Nov. 15, 1895), p. 461; *Revue Diplomatique*, Jan. 27, 1895, p. 3; *L'Economiste Français*, Aug. 19, 1893.
39. *Le Jour*, quoting *Le Figaro*, April 7, 1896.
40. *Le Républicain de l'Ain*, July 7, 1894.
41. *Revue Diplomatique*, Jan. 27, 1895, p. 3.

there was probably more to Cavaignac's motives than he explained in public.

In his speeches favoring the tax, which were published in the book *Pour l'impôt progressif* (1895), Cavaignac argued that a campaign for tax reform could unite French democracy, serving as the basis for a disciplined governmental majority that would provide France with strong and stable government and continuity of military command which the country lacked but needed for military strength. Cavaignac argued that progressive government pursuing an impôt would unite the divergent personalities in parliament around a common task and thereby prevent 'weariness, discouragement and confusion' from spreading over France, leading to 'crises of the worst sort'.[42] As the *Revue Diplomatique* suggested, these arguments are rather contrived and are inadequate to explain the fervor with which Cavaignac sought the impôt.

Cavaignac's educational background and experience in government made it certain that he understood the technical advantages of the income tax. He made this clear by his insistence to President Faure in November 1895 that without an impôt sur le revenu it would be impossible to balance the budget.[43] His involvement with military matters in the Chamber also made him aware of the great financial sacrifices that would be needed to insure French military strength in the face of ever-increasing German might. Contributing to his sense of urgency surely was his knowledge that France's historical enemy Prussia had itself adopted a graduated income tax—the income tax that the authority on taxation Edwin Seligman called 'that marvelous engine of fiscal strength'—with the law of 24 June 1891. In *Formation de la Prusse contemporaine*, Cavaignac wrote that Prussia had absorbed the lesson of the French Revolution which, by making every man a citizen, had unleashed tremendous military power. Now, here was Prussia, with the 'fiscal workhorse' of the income tax in place, entering a period in which improved weapon technology opened the way to tremendous growth in military power for those states with sufficient resources and will. It would be perilous, Cavaignac appears to have reasoned, for France not to have the same effective fiscal tool which her neighbor and historic enemy had already adopted.

The key to Cavaignac's sense of urgency about the impôt sur le revenu was his understanding of the cost of equipping France's sea and land forces with modern weapons. The late 1880s and 1890s saw major advances in military technology and great increases in spending for

42. Godefroy Cavaignac, *Pour l'impôt progressif* (Paris: Armand Colin, 1895), pp. 4–8, 11.
43. France, *Journal Officiel Documents*, *Chambre des Députés* (1891), p. 1663; *La Dépeche de Toulouse*, Oct. 31, 1895.

armaments in Europe. The technological basis for the advances in armaments rested on the huge increase in steel production and a corresponding sharp decline in its price, great advances in metallurgy, and the invention of smokeless gunpowder which was three times more powerful than the type previously used. On land the most important result of these advances was the potential for cannon far more powerful and faster firing than had previously existed. From the late 1880s the development of rapid-fire artillery was of the highest priority to the modern armies of the world. The result was a revolution in armaments and the character of land warfare, while on the seas advances in cannon and steel led to the well-known naval race to build ships suitable for carrying the new weapons.[44] Germany, which since its unification in 1870 had experienced a major economic expansion resulting in a sharp growth in wealth and population, led Europe in increasing military spending, and France had to struggle to avoid falling behind its powerful neighbor and traditional enemy to the east.

Godefroy Cavaignac's work in the Chamber of Deputies made him aware of the technical development and financial requirements of modern weaponry. He served as the Budget Committee's reporter for the War Ministry's 1888 budget and naval budget for 1892, and as Minister of the Navy in the Loubet cabinet of 1892 he fought for and won a higher appropriation for naval construction than the Chamber's Budget Committee had been willing to approve. He explained that the funds were needed for new naval artillery which would be the first step in a general conversion of all French ordnance to rapid-fire systems.[45]

In 1895, as reporter of the military budget for the Budget Committee, Cavaignac helped determine the path that the development of France's field artillery would take.[46] At the time, two different systems of improved field cannon were under consideration. One, developed since 1887 by Major Ducros, was an 'accelerated fire' unbraked weapon which increased the rate of fire of the cannon then in service. The other, developed by Captains Rimailho and Sainte-Claire Deville, was a 'rapid-

44. 'Ordnance' in the *Encyclopedia Britannica*, vol. XX 11th edn. (New York: Encyclopaedia Britannica Company, 1911), p. 210; Le Commandant Coumes, *Aperçus sur la tactique de demain mise en rapport avec la puissance du nouvel armement et l'emploi de la poudre sans fumée* (Paris: Librairie Militaire de L. Boudin, 1892), pp. 97, 103.

45. Henriette Dardenne, *Godefroy Cavaignac* (Colmar: H. Dardenne, 1969), pp. 174–187.

46. Rimailho, *Artillerie de campagne* (Paris: Gauthier – Villars, 1924), p. 58.

fire' brake-equipped 75mm cannon of entirely new design.[47] In the spring of that year, together with Georges Cochery (general reporter of the budget) and Paul Doumer (reporter of the budget of finances), Cavaignac observed a demonstration of the two models at the army firing range at Puteaux in order to decide which one should receive an appropriation from parliament for the construction of several batteries for field testing. Present also were General Deloye, director of French artillery, Major Ducros, and Captains Sainte-Claire Deville and Rimailho.[48]

At Puteaux, in the depths of fort Mont Valérian, a firing range had been set up. General Deloye first described Major Ducros's eight years of work to accelerate the fire of the brakeless cannon then used by the army. The Ducros weapon was demonstrated. After each round fired, with its crew standing clear, the cannon rolled backward and then forward to its original position. As the cannon traveled backward, the energy of its recoil was absorbed by compressing a spring which then expanded, returning the cannon to position. Next, Sainte-Claire Deville and Rimailho's 75mm model with a hydropneumatic brake was demonstrated. As this cannon was fired, its crew sat on its motionless carriage while its barrel moved backward and then forward, its 'brake' absorbing the energy of the recoil and returning the barrel to its original position. General Deloye summed up the alternatives: 'In the first case, you have a known quantity, something artless but certain . . . at 3 to 4 shots per minute. With the second there is the boldness of novelty: a more complex mechanism . . . but 25 shots.'

Cavaignac said nothing. Only after the members of the parliamentary group had returned to their carriage and set out towards Paris did he speak. 'Taking everything into account,' he said, 'the financial effort must be applied for the realization of the model which fires at 25 shots per minute.' At first Doumer and Cochery objected to the great cost of replacing the old model cannon with one of entirely new design. The Ducros cannon, they said, would give France parity with Germany and would not be so costly. But Cavaignac cut short their objections. 'The money', he said, 'will be for us to find.'[49]

Until late 1894 Cavaignac directed his campaign for the impôt to Moderates in the Chamber, evidently hoping that the representatives of the upper class would undertake the tax reform themselves. But his efforts

47. Henriette Dardenne, 'Comment fut décidée la construction du canon de 75', *Bulletin Trimestriel de l'Association des Amis de l'Ecole Supérieure de Guerre*, n. 20 (July 1963), p. 68.
48. Dardenne, *Godefroy Cavaignac*, p. 209.
49. Dardenne, quoting letter of Rimailho to Dardenne, *Godefroy Cavaignac*, pp. 209–210; Rimailho, *Artillerie de campagne*, p. 50, 59. Francis Charmes 'Chronique de la quinzaine,' *Revue des Deux Mondes*, CXXXII (November 15, 1895), p. 461.

failed. Then, in late 1894, Cavaignac turned to the Radicals and initiated talks with their leader, Léon Bourgeois, and their financial expert Paul Doumer.[50] In a series of meetings at his apartment on rue Verneuil during late 1894 and early 1895, Cavaignac urged Bourgeois and Doumer to push for the impôt sur le revenu. Also during these discussions, he kept the two Radical leaders informed on the progress being made in the development of the rapid-fire field cannon that preoccupied him.[51]

Léon Bourgeois and Paul Doumer

Léon Bourgeois was leader of the Radicals in the Chamber of 1893–98 and head of the Radical cabinet of 1895–96 which sought to enact the impôt sur le revenu. Born in Paris in 1851, the son of a clock manufacturer, Bourgeois was a man of high intelligence, diverse interests and great energy. Exceptionally amiable, he was a natural conciliator of the differences between men.

Educated at the prestigious Parisian lower school Massin, Bourgeois attended Lycée Charlemagne. After studying at the Law Faculty of Paris, he became secretary of the conference of avocats and would most likely have been highly successful had he remained in the legal profession. But Bourgeois chose to enter government administration where his career advanced rapidly.[52]

In 1888 Bourgeois left administration to enter politics and was elected deputy from the Marne. In the Chamber he sat with the 'Left Radicals'. From the start he was marked for an important role as a leader of the Radicals. Eminently 'ministrable', due to his ability, background and high level of culture, Léon Bourgeois was a type of Radical seldom seen in the Chamber of the 1890s. If he shared the political ideas of other Radicals, he differed from them in his education, polish and experience. Thus the historian Jacques Chastenet described Bourgeois as his contemporaries would have: as a 'man of the left, but well-bred and cultivated.'[53]

---

51. Dardenne, *Godefroy Cavaignac*, p. 211. Rimailho, one of the officers who led the effort to develop France's 75 mm rapid-fire cannon, later wrote (*Artillerie de campagne*, Paris: Gauthier-Villars & Cie, 1924, p.58): 'General Deloye [director of French artillery] found a powerful source of support in the person of Godefroy Cavaignac. From the time that the brake appeared to be close to being perfected, M. Cavaignac, as Reporter of the budget of War, was kept informed regarding the progress of the brake by General Deloye . . . As Minister of War [in the Bourgeois cabinet] he [Cavaignac] supported General Deloye with all his power.'

52. Adolphe Brisson, *Les Prophètes* (Paris: Ernest Flammarion, n.d., probably about 1902), pp. 272, 274.

53. Jacques Chastenet, *Histoire de la Troisième République*, vol. III, *La République Triomphante, 1893–1906* (Paris: Hachette, 1955), p. 78.

Between May 1888 and February 1889 Bourgeois held the position of undersecretary of state in the Interior Ministry of the Floquet cabinet. In March 1889 he replaced Constans as Minister of the Interior in the Tirard government; in that position he played an important role in preparing for the general elections of September 1889. In March 1890 he entered the Freycinet cabinet as Minister of Public Instruction and Fine Arts, being particularly concerned with the reform of university education.

Bourgeois played, at an elevated level, the role of the provincial Radical politician. Appropriately, he took an active interest in public education as president of the League for Education and was a freemason, a member of La Sincérité, a Lodge of the Orient in Reims.[54] As a youth he had detested the Empire; he was anti-clerical and anti-conservative in outlook and held the political ideas of the democrats of 1848.[55]

Léon Bourgeois had a dark complexion and expressive dark eyes. His voice was mellifluous and solemn. A naturally amiable, supple and diplomatic man, it was said that he was a southerner in Toulouse and would be just as easily a Champenois in Reims, Breton in Quimper and Swiss in Geneva. He had a naturally optimistic disposition and outlook on the world. His charm, wrote one observer, 'is irresistible'.[56]

Bourgeois had a taste for activities outside his field of work. As a young man he was an impassioned student of Sanskrit, which he mastered in two years of extra-curricular study. Later he turned his attention to sculpture and became one of the most distinguished amateur sculptors in France. He considered himself an intellectual and was interested in poetry and philosophy.[57] He was also a man who enjoyed the lighter side of life; a widower at an early age, he was considered a bon vivant who liked the company of pretty women. One observer wrote that Bourgeois was a man of the world, and even of high society. He was of 'bon ton', well bred with all the courtesies, tastes, and snobbery of a ladies' man and, if he went to Montmartre (where high society mingled with artists and criminal types at 'cabarets artistique' such as Rudolphe Salis's Chat Noir and Aristide Bruant's Le Mirliton), this writer said, it was because high society went there.[58]

Bourgeois's position as leader of the Radicals in the Chamber was as an arbitrator and conciliator of their various factions. He was generally well thought of by members of all political factions. One contemporary,

54. *Le Grand Orient de France* (published by the Grand Orient de France, 16 rue Cadet, Paris. Imprimerie Beresniak, 18–20 rue de Faubourg-du-Temple, Paris, about 1972), p. 24.
55. Brisson, *Les Prophètes*, pp. 276–277.
56. Ibid., pp. 282, 283, 286.
57. Ibid., *Le Figaro*, March 17, 1896.
58. *Le Matin*, March 17, 1896.

who did not share his political views, said Bourgeois fought for his Radical opinions without faith and without passion, but without difficulty, without fetters and with a lucid skepticism: 'He plays the Radical without being a radical, as certain writers do pornography without being pornographers.'[59] What this contemporary appears to have meant was that although Bourgeois was leader of the Radicals, his elevated level of education, culture, and personal style distinguished him from the typical Radical deputies who were, in the historian Charles Seignobos's terms, 'new men, . . . obscure provincials with mediocre culture.'

Paul Doumer, Finance Minister in the Bourgeois cabinet, should also be mentioned as a Radical leader who promoted the impôt. Born in 1857 Doumer was an ambitious poor boy, the son of a layer of rails, who made good in politics. When he was a young boy his family moved to Paris where his father soon died. At the age of 12 he was apprenticed as an engraver in a medal shop. Ambitious and intelligent, Doumer pursued his education at night. In 1887 he was appointed as a teacher at the College de Mende. He married in 1878 and eventually had 8 children.

About 1880 Doumer entered journalism in Laon under the aegis of his father-in-law. From the outset, he adopted a left, anti-Boulangist orientation. In 1889 he sought election from the Aisne but was defeated by a Boulangist; later, in 1891, he was elected as deputy from the Yonne. He took the role of a militant Radical; in the Chamber he was a protege of the Radical Floquet and chief of his personal staff. Specializing in financial affairs, he was one of the Chamber's authorities in that area. As a deputy, he worked hard and displayed exceptional energy.[60]

Doumer was an attractive man with numerous friends in all political groups. He had, according to contemporaries, a winning open look, a ready smile and an affable way. It was said that the common man came to him as toward a friend.[61]

With Cavaignac as the driving force, he, Bourgeois and Doumer came together to lead the campaign for the impôt sur le revenu during the Radical ministry of 1895–96. The particular character of each would be revealed in the divergent paths each took after the end of the Radical ministry they led.

59. *Le Figaro*, March 17, 1896.
60. *La Petite République*, Nov. 2, 1895; *Le Jour*, profile of Paul Doumer, published about February, 1896.
61. Ibid.

—3—

The Coming of the Radical Challenge

The first homogeneous Radical ministry of the Third Republic took office in November 1895. It was supported in the Chamber by the Radicals, Socialist Radicals and Socialists. Now, for the first time since the Revolution of 1789, France's haute bourgeoisie confronted a government not directed by a sympathetic autocrat or dominated by representatives of the upper class. To them this Radical government, which came to office seeking a graduated income tax, represented the essence of 'Jacobin socialism'.

Radical strength increased steadily in the early years of the Third Republic. In the Chamber of 576 deputies, the number of Radicals rose from about 100 in 1877 to about 200 in 1889. In provincial towns and cities, Radical strength increased as Jacobin politicians — commonly lawyers, doctors, and teachers — gradually replaced the monarchist notables elected in the early 1870s. In Paris democratic forces, decimated in the reaction against the Commune, gradually revived and Radical representation steadily increased. In the modern sector of heavy industry, particularly in the Nord, Socialist strength grew as the number of industrial workers increased.

The Coming of the General Elections of 1893

In the spring of 1893, with general elections scheduled for the fall, French politics revealed two clear tendencies. Social and economic questions were assuming primary concern and the pattern on which majority coalitions in the Chamber was formed was shifting from 'concentration' to a right-left division among deputies.[1]

1. A French cabinet (also called a ministry or government) required support of a majority of deputies voting in the Chamber to stay in office. Two basic patterns of majority coalition were possible. One was a division between left and right with the majority being either of the left (①) or right (②). Coalitions like this were called 'homogeneous.' The other structure, known as 'concentration,' 'republican defense' or 'center' (③).

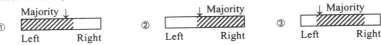

In 1893 leaders of the Radicals (representing the Jacobin idea of government) and Moderates (representing the haute bourgeoisie's liberal ideal of constitutional, limited government) were calling for a right-left division to replace the concentration pattern (composed of a majority of Moderates and a minority of Radicals) on which the Chamber's majority had been organized in the fight against Boulangism. One reason for this was that by 1893 support for the Republic was so widespread that the anti-republican extreme right no longer posed a significant challenge. Another was that the Chamber's 1889–93 concentration coalition had been discredited in the eyes of the electorate because it had failed to enact any significant legislation. Moderates complained that concentration ministries had been weak in the face of labor unrest and had negatively influenced government finances by adopting costly pension and social welfare programs and dangerous schemes of taxation.[2] In the opinion of the newspaper *Le Temps*, concentration had resulted in 'la tyrannie des radicaux sur le gouvernement'. The Moderate political campaign organization *Union Libérale Républicaine* warned that France faced dangers from Radicals and Socialists, and held it was time to abandon concentration and favor a 'liberal republic' against a 'Radical and Socialist republic'. Léon Say, a leader of the Union Libérale Républicaine, called for the end of concentration, which 'was good for the battle against the enemies of the Republic but bad for governing.'[3]

Ralliés (Catholics who had accepted or 'rallied to' the Republic) also advocated a right-left coalition pattern. The rallié leader Piou, looking forward to coalition with the Moderates, denounced concentration and envisioned a political division between men of Goblet's, Millerand's and Lockroy's views (Radicals and Socialists) on the left and Say's and Jonnart's on the right.[4]

By the spring of 1893 Radicals, now spurned by the Moderates, also favored a right-left division in the Chamber in order to prevent Socialists from winning elections by out-flanking them on the left. The Radical

---

In France of the 1890s the right-left or 'homogeneous' division of the Chamber was considered normal for a parliamentary regime. The model for this, of course, was the British House of Commons. The center 'concentration' pattern, it was commonly said, was one of compromise and in order to achieve a coherent legislative program, a 'homogeneous' government supported by a 'compact' right or left majority was essential. In fact, of course, political compromise was needed to form any majority coalition.

2. Daniel, *L'année politique, 1893*, p. 207; *Le Temps*, September 5, 1893; *Journal des Débats*, Jan. 1, 1894, p. 1; Claudio Jannet, 'Les finances républicaines 1889–1893', *Le Correspondent*, CLXXII (July 10, 1893), pp. 3–6; Marcel Marion, *Histoire financière de la France*, vol. VI (Paris: Rousseau & Cie, 1931), p. 157.

3. Ibid., pp. 144, 184.

4. Ibid., pp. 180, 266, 267; Louis Joubert, 'Chronique Politique', *Le Correspondent*, CLXXII (Aug. 10, 1893), p. 584; Ibid., CLXXII (Aug. 21, 1893), pp. 769–771.

leader René Goblet explained that although concentration might have seemed necessary when the Republic was in danger from Boulangism, all clear minds recognized that the moment had come to renounce it. Concentration coalitions, Goblet stated, had created insignificant legislation, left the political world in disarray and produced a feeling of anarchy in the public spirit. Moderate and Radical leaders both favored cooperation with their neighbors at the outer ends of the political spectrum; thus Goblet held that Socialists and Radicals should unite, putting aside questions of pure theory, and Moderate leaders welcomed ralliés to the ranks of republicans.[5]

Not all politicians, however, rejected the concentration pattern of majority coalition. For example Spuller, a Moderate, spoke of 'the ideas common to all republicans' and advocated the continuation of concentration in reportedly eloquent, if vague, terms.[6]

As the 'homogeneous' (left-right) pattern of majority coalition came to be favored in spring 1893, social and economic problems emerged as the main political issues. Questions concerning constitutional revision, the Church's role in education, military service for priests, and the rights of ecclesiastical property were generally set aside. The *Année politique* reported that the constitutional question was raised almost nowhere in the electoral campaign of 1893, and the *Revue des Deux Mondes* stated that the religious question had been set aside and only economic and social questions remained as the focus of future political discussions.[7] What were known as 'social questions' concerned the material aspects of life, particularly those pertaining to society's non-wealthy members. Social reforms, the *Revue des Deux Mondes* explained, had to do with 'the improvement of the condition of the masses'.[8] No one denied the importance of 'social problems': Léon Say acknowledged their existence and Constans, a Moderate leader, stated that the republican party had as its aim the emancipation of the working classes and the improvement of their condition.[9] Socialist Radicals stated that they would be forgetful of their time and themselves if they did not make social reforms their first concern. Socialist politicians, as would be expected, also stressed social concerns.[10]

---

5. Daniel, *L'année politique, 1893*, pp. 180–184; Charles Seignobos, *L'évolution de la 3e République* (1875–1914), vol. VII of *Histoire de France contemporaine*, ed. Ernest Lavisse (Paris: Hachette, 1921), p. 169; Jacques Chastenet, *La République des républicains, 1892–1893*, vol. II of *Histoire de la Troisième République* (Paris: Hachette, 1952), pp. 320–324.
6. Daniel, *L'année politique, 1893*, p. 264.
7. Vte. G. d'Avenel, 'Chronique de la quinzaine,' *Revue des Deux Mondes*, CXVIII (Aug. 1, 1893), p. 708.
8. Ibid., CXIX (Oct. 1, 1893), p. 704.
9. Daniel, *L'année politique, 1893*, p. 193.
10. Ibid., p. 273.

Social reforms included relief for the needy and the unemployed, housing for the poor, support of the sick, disabled and retired, improvement of relations between employers and workers, promotion of industrial safety and public health, promotion of popular savings and credit, and promotion of a more equitable distribution of the tax burden. Politicians proposed various agendas of social reform. Piou, the Rallié leader, favored 'association' to bring together labor and capital, arbitration of conflicts and promotion of retirement funds. Léon Say called for increased justice in taxation and government promotion of cooperatives. Constans advocated what he described as 'practical reforms' to reconcile labor and capital, to aid small farmers with tax reforms and easier credit, to create mutual aid societies and to establish pension funds.[11] The Liberal Left, a grouping of Moderates, favored reforms 'compatible with economic liberty' which would reduce industrial accidents, control child and female labor and promote public hygiene, housing for workers, agricultural insurance, savings and pension plans and medical programs within private companies.

In the election campaign of 1893, Radicals, Socialist Radicals and Socialists called for a reduction of the burden of taxation on the poor and promoted the right of labor to organize. They proposed a variety of measures to aid the urban and rural lower classes. Although some called for abolition of the Senate, separation of church and state, reorganization of the Bank of France and state acquisition of railroads, mines and other large industries,[12] these were not issues which received much attention in the 1893 election campaign.

Moderates defended the rights of property, person and contract. Thus they opposed State acquisition of the Bank of France, railroads and mines and upheld the right of workers not to join labor unions and to work while others were striking.[13]

Both Radicals and Moderates claimed to be the legitimate heirs of the French Revolution of 1789. Moderates insisted that the Revolution was the great liberator and upholder of the individual and his rights of person, property, contract and labor. Radicals claimed the Revolution was the beginning of democracy and they were its continuators, striving for a truly democratic society. Moderates claimed the Radicals were dupes and captives of the Socialists on their left; Radicals accused Moderates of embracing the representatives of the Church and reaction on their right. As would be expected, Moderates and Radicals denied that they

---

11. Daniel, *L'année politique, 1893*, pp. 185–186, 196–196, 267; Ibid., pp. 255–256, ('The program of the Gauche Libérale').
12. Ibid., pp. 181–184, 272–275, 279.
13. Ibid., pp. 144, 183, 193–194, 267.

compromised themselves in seeking alliance with the outer extremes of the parliamentary spectrum.

The General Elections of 1893

The concentration government headed by the Moderate Charles Dupuy set general elections for 20 August and 3 September 1893. The campaign was calm and met with widespread apathy. Of a possible 10.5 million voters, only 7.5 million, a relatively low proportion for France, bothered to go to the polls.[14] The results of the election were not immediately clear. In the fall of 1893 it was difficult to predict how some deputies would vote because party classifications were often vague and more than a few candidates had inscribed themselves in more than one political grouping.

As Dupuy had predicted in May 1893 (on the basis of information available to him as Minister of the Interior), reactionaries did poorly and their number in the Chamber declined from about 120 to 50. Ralliés did less well than the prefects had predicted and won only about 30 seats. Radicals gained a few places and Socialists emerged from the election stronger than ever with about 50 seats.[15] Some bourgeois observers claimed that the election was a great victory for the Moderates; according to the *Journal des Débats*, the elections had produced a block of 311 'republicans of government' (Moderates and ralliés), enough for a solid majority in the Chamber of 576 deputies.[16] The *Revue des Deux Mondes* was confident that a Moderate-rallié majority existed which could adopt a program making no concessions to the Radicals.[17]

But not all bourgeois observers were so sure. The *Nouvelle Revue* of 15 September 1893 suggested that the significance of the elections was unclear and shed little light on the issues which lay ahead. The *Revue Diplomatique*, with its usual keen insight, raised the possibility that the crushing defeat of the reactionaries might promote battles between republicans (Moderates and Radicals) and thereby result in an unstable

14. Daniel, *L'année politique, 1893*, p. 279. According to Léon Muel's *Précis historique des assemblées parlementaires et des hautes cours de justice de 1789 à 1895* (Paris: Guillaumin, 1896), the election of 20 August 1893 had 3.0 million abstentions out of 10.5 million inscribed voters. This compared with 2.6 million abstentions out of 10.7 million inscribed voters in 1889, 2.4 million abstentions out of 10.4 million inscribed voters in 1885, 3.3 million abstentions out of 10.4 million inscribed voters in 1881, and about 2.0 million abstentions out of about 10 million inscribed voters in the general elections of 1876 and 1877.

15. Seignobos, *L'evolution*, pp. 171, 172; 'J.', 'Politique intérieure', *Revue Diplomatique*, Nov. 26, 1893, p. 3; Daniel, *L'année politique*, 1893, pp. 281, 282.

16. Ibid.

17. Vte. G. d'Avenel, 'Chronique de la quinzaine', *Revue des Deux Mondes*, CXIX (Sept. 15, 1893), p. 467.

majority and 'detestable' ministerial instability.[18] In November 1893, the *Revue Diplomatique* expressed doubt that a solid Moderate-rallié majority existed and wondered if it was fitting to abandon concentration and divide the republican party in two in order to install alternating, supposedly homogeneous, majorities of 'whigs' and 'tories'.[19]

The Chamber of 1893–98, Phase I: Moderate Ministries, December 1893–November 1895

Soon after the general elections of September 1893, the Dupuy 'concentration' ministry, which was comprised of a majority of Moderates and a minority of Radicals, left office. During the next two years there would be a succession of three short-lived Moderate ministries, each lacking a solid majority, which sought to pass a budget for 1895 which would include some measure of tax reform. Tax reform, as we have seen, had been advocated by all political groupings in the 1893 electoral campaign. Just how it could be achieved, given the tight financial conditions of the times, was not obvious; there was even the question of whether tax reform was a practical possibility given the current recession. But French politicians of the 1890s would not be the first or the last to promise what others might consider to be the impossible.

In December 1893 Jean Casimir-Périer formed a 'homogeneous' Moderate ministry with August Burdeau as Minister of Finance. Casimir-Périer declared that the tax system should be reformed and the burden more equitably apportioned, and he promised that he would not seek changes which would disturb the wealthy.[20] Burdeau proposed replacing the much criticized personal property and doors and windows taxes with levies on lodgings and domestic servants. He was pleased, he said, that these taxes would completely exempt the poor, give a partial reduction to the 'less well-off classes', and would rely on easily observable external signs of wealth requiring neither 'vexatious inquisition' nor voluntary and therefore fraud-provoking declaration to determine income levels.[21]

Although bourgeois opinion thought well of Burdeau's proposed budget, there was not sufficient support in the Chamber to pass it. In May 1894, after five months in office, Casimir-Périer retired his ministry on

18. Marcère, 'Chronique politique', *Nouvelle Revue*, LXXXIV (Sept. 15, 1893), p. 435; 'J.', 'Politique intérieure', *Revue Diplomatique*, Sept. 9, 1893.
19. Ibid., Nov. 26, 1893, p.3.
20. *Le Rentier*, May 27, 1894; André Daniel, *L'année politique*, 1893 (Paris: Charpentier, 1894), p. 319.
21. Marcel Marion, *Histoire financière de la France depuis 1775* vol. VI (Paris: Rousseau & Cie, 1931), pp. 164, 165; Pierre Bidoire, *Les budgets française 1895* (Paris: V. Giard et E. Briere, 1896), p. 6.

the pretext of a secondary question involving the right of employees of State railroads to unionize. Observers at the time understood that he left office because he lacked the support of a majority which would be able to approve Burdeau's proposed 1895 budget.[22]

After the departure of Casimir-Périer's homogeneous Moderate ministry of the right, the commission to organize a government logically fell to the Radicals who dominated the Chamber's left. President of the Republic, Sadi Carnot, did invite the Radical leader Léon Bourgeois to form a ministry, but Bourgeois declined, claiming that he did not believe he could organize a viable government. (At this time Bourgeois appears to have favored the impossible – a concentration ministry including a few Moderates and a preponderance of Radicals whose chief aim would be to produce an impôt sur le revenu.) Carnot then called on Charles Dupuy to head another Moderate ministry.[23] Dupuy's cabinet, with Raymond Poincaré as Finance Minister, had much the same support in the Chamber as Casimir-Périer's. Its chief task would be to pass a long overdue budget for 1895 that would include some measure of tax reform – the task its predecessor had been unable to accomplish.

Poincaré gave up Burdeau's proposal for a tax on lodgings and domestic servants (which had already been rejected by the Chamber), and proposed instead a mildly graduated tax on inheritances. Though the most conservative of haut bourgeois leaders such as Léon Say and Paul Leroy-Beaulieu viewed this proposal as introducing the seeds of socialism into the French tax system, other bourgeois leaders accepted it.[24] Although the Chamber quickly approved the tax, it was stalled in the Senate until 1898, when it was finally passed.

In July 1894, during Poincaré's term as Finance Minister, Godefroy Cavaignac and Paul Doumer proposed from the floor of the Chamber an impôt sur le revenu to be included in the budget for 1895. In the Chamber debate, advocates of the impôt claimed that it would be a democratic reform and promote justice in taxation. Cavaignac observed that of all issues, tax reform was the one which most occupied public opinion. After describing the injustices of existing taxes, he stated that the impôt he proposed lay between the position which glorified the status quo and dangerous and chimerical socialist utopias. Cavaignac declared that he

22. *Revue Diplomatique*, May 27, 1894, p. 3.
23. *Revue Diplomatique*, May 27, 1894, p. 3; André Daniel, *L'année politique, 1894* (Paris: Charpentier, 1895), pp. 142, 144–145; *Journal des Débats*, May 23, 1894.
24. Marcel Marion, *Histoire financière de la France*, vol. VI, p. 170; Léon Say, 'Budget de 1895 – libéraux et socialistes,' *Revue des Deux Mondes*, CXXV (Oct. 1, 1894), p. 528; *Economiste Français*, Oct. 20, 1894, pp. 490, 491; Francis Charmes, 'Chronique de la quinzaine', *Revue des Deux Mondes*, CXXV (Oct. 15, 1894), p. 949; *Journal des Débats*, July 9, 1894.

wanted France to be a leader in democratic tax reform in order to preserve her leadership of democracy in Europe. After several days of debate, the proposal for an impôt sur le revenu was narrowly defeated by 267 to 236.[25] Poincaré's response to the widespread demand for tax reform was more flexible than Burdeau's had been. In the July 1894 debate on the income tax Poincaré readily acknowledged the shortcomings of the French fiscal system but rejected the impôt sur le revenu because of the 'vexatious, inquisitorial, Prussian measures' which he claimed would be needed to enforce it.[26] One tactic Poincaré used to deflect the thrust for the impôt was to propose a graduated tax on inheritances. Another tactic was to stall the issue by creating an extra-parliamentary committee on *L'impôt sur les revenus* to study the taxation of 'various sources of income' and thereby hopefully relieve public pressure for a tax on total income: which was the essence of the impôt sur le revenu.[27]

In June 1894, after the assassination of President of the Republic Carnot by the anarchist Cassiro, Dupuy resigned as Premier but was called back to office by the newly-elected President Jean Casimir-Périer. In January 1895, having been unable to pass a long-overdue budget for 1895, the Dupuy Moderate ministry resigned after losing a vote on a rail question of secondary importance. Dupuy's ministry fell due to the desertion of the 'Isambert group', which had been organized in June 1894 and included deputies at the margin between Radicals and Moderates.[28] The *Revue Diplomatique* explained that the deputies of the Isambert group who had abandoned Dupuy were not truly concerned with the legal aspects of the rail question on which they had brought his fall; rather, wrote the *Revue Diplomatique*, their intention had been to prepare the way for the arrival of a Radical ministry led by Léon Bourgeois.[29]

The Coming of the Radical Ministry

With the fall of the Dupuy ministry the recently-elected President of the Republic Jean Casimir-Périer, facing his first ministerial crisis, abruptly resigned. The haute bourgeoisie reacted hysterically. 'The first tendency was to cry "desertion" and even "treason". The Moderates were indignant,

25. *Le Temps*, June 22, 1894; France, *Journal Officiel Débats, Chambre* (1894), pp. 1217, 1219, 1291.
26. France, *Journal Officiel Débats* (1894), pp. 830–837; J. Cornély, *Le Gaulois*, July 13, 1894.
27. *Economiste Français*, Oct. 20, 1894; Alfred Neymarck, *Finances contemporaine*, vol. IV, *L'Obsession fiscale, 1872–1895* (Paris: Guillaumin, 1896), p. 367.
28. André Daniel, *L'année politique, 1895* (Paris: Charpentier, 1896), pp. 4, 7; *RPP*, III (Jan. 1895), p. 166; A. Salles, 'Les députés sortants (1893–1898): Votes et groupements,' *RPP*, XVI (April 10, 1898), pp. 69–70.
29. *Revue Diplomatique*, Jan. 20, 1895, p. 2.

discouraged . . .' It was said that in quitting at the first difficulty, Casimir-Périer had failed to fulfill the hopes that rested on him. The *Revue Diplomatique* reported that the former President heard not a single voice raised in his favor.[30]

Le Figaro wrote that, rightly or wrongly, Casimir-Périer had been considered 'our last safeguard before the revolution, our last card.' The *Journal des Débats* discussed the public's concern with the resignation in the midst of 'the terrible perils faced by France – the growing audacity of revolutionary parties, the flabbiness and inertia of the Moderates, and the weakness of the administration.'[31] Casimir-Périer gave his own explanation of why he resigned in his well-known letter to parliament:

I have never hidden from myself the difficulties of the task which the National Assembly has imposed on me. I have expected them . . . The presidency of the Republic, deprived of means of action and control, can only draw on the confidence of the nation for the moral force without which it is nothing . . . For six months [since Casimir-Périer was elected President] there has been a campaign of defamation and injury against the army, the courts, the Parliament, and the chief of state . . . The respect and ambition which I have for my country does not permit me to accept that the best servants of the country, and those who represent it in the eyes of foreigners, can be insulted every day. I am not resigned to equate the burden of the moral responsibilities which rest on me with the powerlessness to which I am condemned.[32]

Contemporaries generally did not accept Casimir-Périer's own explanation for why he had resigned. *Le Temps* noted that a reader of his letter was struck by the inadequacy of the reasons with which he explained his act. The former President had begun by declaring that he had foreseen the difficulties of his task. How then, asked *Le Temps*, could it be that when he found himself confronting the difficulties he had expected, he gave up and quit?[33] The *Revue Diplomatique* wrote that one was forced to attribute Casimir-Périer's decision to motives other than the ones he himself gave, for they were 'truly infantile'.[34]

More plausible explanations of Casimir-Périer's resignation were then offered. *Le Temps* suggested that the President of the Republic, unwilling to ask the Senate for dissolution of the Chamber whose political 'weakness' threatened to render it 'revolutionary', had felt it was his duty

30. Daniel, *L'année politique, 1895*, p. 8; *Revue Diplomatique*, Jan. 20, 1895, pp. 3, 4; *Le Temps*, Jan. 17, 1895, p. 1.
31. Daniel, *L'année politique, 1895*, p. 12; *Revue Diplomatique*, Jan. 20, 1895, p. 4. See also *Le Temps*, Jan. 17, 1895, p. 1.
32. *Revue Diplomatique*, Jan. 20, 1895, p. 3; France: *Journal Officiel Débats, Chambre des Députés* (1895), p. 71.
33. *Le Temps*, Jan. 18, 1895.
34. *Revue Diplomatique*, Jan. 20, 1895, p. 3.

to resign. *Le Temps* suggested that Casimir-Périer evidently thought that the greatest service he could render his country was to sound the tocsin to warn of the danger.[35] The *Revue Diplomatique* suggested that, placed between the alternatives of calling to power the Radical Léon Bourgeois or instituting a cabinet of dissolution in preparation for new general elections, Casimir-Périer had chosen a third way: he had resigned. Charles Dupuy agreed with this view and claimed that Casimir-Periér had left office because he could not face the prospect of calling on Léon Bourgeois to form a Radical ministry.[36]

After Casimir-Périer resigned in January 1895, Félix Faure was quickly elected President of the Republic. His first political act was to invite Léon Bourgeois to form a ministry. Bourgeois undertook to organize a concentration cabinet which would include a majority of Radicals and a few Moderates and would have, as the keystone of its program, the impôt sur le revenu. He held long discussions with Cavaignac, Peytral, Poincaré, Doumer and Cochery, the principal finance experts in the Chamber, and insisted that both Cavaignac and Poincaré be included in any cabinet he might lead. But ultimately, Bourgeois failed to achieve his objective. Realistically, *Le Temps* asked, how could Moderates be expected to accept the fiscal solution of an income tax when they had always been against it and would continue to oppose it with the greatest of energy?[37]

After Bourgeois failed to form a Radical-dominated concentration ministry in January 1985, President Faure sought a conciliatory 'business cabinet' which would be able to pass the long overdue annual budget. For this he called on the Moderate Alexandre Ribot to head a ministry whose purpose would be to avoid hard positions and finally approve a long-overdue budget for 1895. Ribot himself took the position of Finance Minister and presented a vague, non-specific ministerial declaration. In his own words, 'the budget [which had been under consideration for well over a year by three successive ministries] must precede all else.'[38] By the time Ribot took office there was a general impatience to pass a budget for 1895 and, for the moment, the question of tax reform was put off. Now, with Socialists and Radicals no longer blocking the way by insisting on tax reform, a budget for 1895 was quickly approved.[39]

35. *Le Temps*, Jan. 18, 1895, p. 1.
36. *Le Temps*, Jan. 17, 1895, p. 1; *Revue Diplomatique*, Jan. 20, 1895, p. 2; *Démocratie du Centre*, April 9, 1896; Saint Simone, *Propos de Félix Faure*, 3rd edn., (Paris: Ollendorff, 1902), p. 89.
37. Henriette Dardenne, *Godefroy Cavaignac* (Colmar: H. Dardenne, 1969), pp. 436–437; *Le Temps*, Jan. 24, 1895, p. 1.
38. *Revue Diplomatique*, Jan. 27, 1895, p. 3; Daniel, *L'année politique, 1895*, pp. 21, 23.
39. Marion, *Histoire financière de la France depuis 1775*, VI, p. 179.

The Ribot ministry, which had pleased neither Moderates nor Radicals, fell soon after the Chamber resumed its meetings in the autumn of 1895. On 28 October 1895, an adverse vote on a question of secondary interest concerning the Chemin de Fer du Sud gave Ribot the occasion to depart.[40] The coalition that defeated him included the Socialists and Radicals, almost all the 'monarchist' extreme right and the Isambert group at the center between Moderates and Radicals. Once again, wrote the *Revue Politique et Parlementaire*, the crisis was due to a coalition of the parties of the extremes (right and left) and the defection of a part of the Moderates (the Isambert group).[41]

The Chamber of 1893–98, Phase II: The Radical Ministry in Office

After Ribot left office, President Faure again called on Léon Bourgeois to form a government. Now Bourgeois gave up his insistence on a concentration cabinet and resolutely proceeded to organize a homogeneous Radical ministry. Its primary goal would be to establish an income tax.

Cavaignac, the driving force behind the pursuit of the impôt sur le revenu, was to be Minister of War in the Radical cabinet. He was reluctant to have Doumer as a ministerial colleague due to certain information he had regarding Doumer's past associations; Cavaignac's most serious concern was that Doumer had accepted the costs of his election in the Yonne from Gallot, the publisher of the *Piou-Piou de l'Yonne* (*Foot Soldier of Yonne*), an anti-military scandal sheet. Bourgeois, however, held that it was important to include Doumer in the cabinet he was forming. In a meeting arranged by Bourgeois, Cavaignac presented his doubts about having Doumer as a colleague, and Doumer promised that as soon as he had sufficient means he would liberate himself from any obligation to Gallot. This was acceptable to Cavaignac and he then agreed to serve in a cabinet which included Doumer.[42]

With this hurdle overcome, on 1 November Bourgeois formed his cabinet. It included Ricard, Barthelot, Doumer, Mésureur, Guyot-Dessaigne, Vigier, Cavaignac, Lockroy and Guiyesse, all Radicals except for Cavaignac, who was 'above parties'. In the Chamber this cabinet was supported by the Radicals, Socialist Radicals and Socialists, as well as members of the Isambert or *Union Progressiste* group which had formerly

40. Daniel, *L'année politique, 1895*, pp. 173–174.

41. Félix Roussel, 'La vie politique et parlementaire en France', *Revue Politique et Parlementaire*, VI (Dec. 10, 1895), p. 568.

42. Dardenne, *Godefroy Cavaignac*, pp. 443–444.

voted with Moderate ministries. This was the first homogeneous government of the left in the history of the Third Republic.

Bourgeois's ministerial declaration of November 1895 spelled out the government's program. First it would aim to pass a budget for 1896 without the succession of monthly delays which had been the rule since 1893. Next, the government would seek an impôt sur le revenu as part of the 1897 budget. Bourgeois's declaration also called for reforms concerning conflicts of interest, the progressive inheritance tax which Poincaré had proposed, reduction of the tax on wine, beer and cider, laws to promote *mutualité*, insurance and saving, laws promoting pension funds, labor organization and agriculture, and the establishment of a separate colonial army. One thing the Bourgeois ministry did not intend to do was execute an administrative shakeup that would distribute government patronage to its supporters.[43]

Even Bourgeois's political opponents could not but approve of his expeditious handling of the 1896 budget. By 30 December 1895 a budget for 1896 had been approved by the Chamber and the Senate. The next order of business, the impôt sur le revenu, would be more controversial.[44]

The Radical Cabinet Proposes the Impôt sur le Revenu

During its first two months the Bourgeois ministry established itself solidly in office, thereby disappointing opponents such as the *Revue des Deux Mondes* which had predicted it would not survive because it lacked a reliable majority.[45] At first opponents tried to defeat the Radical ministry by driving a wedge between it and the Socialists whose support it required to survive. But the Socialists cooperated with Bourgeois and refrained from challenging the so-called 'anti-anarchist' press laws which they opposed. When police prevented demonstrators from displaying a red flag in the Père Lachaise cemetery during a commemoration of the death of Blanqui and a fracas ensued, socialist deputies did not accuse the ministry of 'police provocation' as they would have if a Moderate ministry had been in office.[46]

The Bourgeois ministry refused to be distracted from its primary objective. Thus it declined to raise questions concerning constitutional revision, the use of secret funds, state support of religion, diplomatic relations with the Vatican and support of French missions in the Far East,

---

43. Ibid., pp. 447–448.
44. Ibid., pp. 450–452.
45. *L'Autorité*, April 7, 1896; Francis Charmes, 'Chronique de la quinzaine', *RDM*, CXXXII (Nov. 15, 1895), p. 463.
46. Daniel, *L'année politique, 1895*, p. 182; *Le Messager*, Jan. 6, 1896.

all which would have divided its supporters.[47] By March 1896 it was clear that the Radical ministry would not be defeated before the Chamber would discuss and vote on the impôt sur le revenu. The tax had been proposed on 31 January by Finance Minister Doumer as part of his budget proposal for 1897. The subject came as no surprise; from early January leaders of the Radical ministry had spoken frequently and strongly in favor of the innovation they intended to propose.

Except for the impôt sur le revenu, most of Doumer's budget proposal for 1897 was anything but radical. It accepted the view that government spending was high and should be reduced if possible. It claimed to be the first budget in ten years to show a real reduction in spending, totaling nearly one million francs less than the figure voted for 1896. Doumer stated that though spending had been vigorously limited, services would function regularly and supplementary credits would not be required.[48] He claimed that the budget he proposed was balanced and that he had been conservative in estimating expected income, systematically refusing to project increases in revenues even when they had been predicted by those responsible for their collection.[49] He was pleased to note that his budget included a new section for the amortization of the national debt. This, he stated, would show in a striking way the will to reduce the national debt. Admittedly the amount proposed for amortization in 1897 was small but, Doumer hoped, it would grow in the future.[50]

The great innovation in the budget proposal was the section calling for a graduated tax on total family income with the exception of that part coming from State *rentes*. Incomes below 2,500 francs would be fully exempt. The portion of income between 2,501 and 5,000 francs would be taxed at 1 per cent, between 5,001 and 10,000 francs at 2 per cent, between 10,001 and 20,000 francs at 3 per cent, between 20,001 and 50,000 francs at 4 per cent, and all income over 50,000 francs at 5 per cent.[51]

According to Doumer's estimates the tax would be levied on approximately 1.5 million of the total of 10.7 million French households. Of these, about 1.3 million families had incomes between 2,500 and 10,000 francs, about 170,000 had incomes from 10,000 to 50,000 francs, 9,800 had incomes between 50,000 to 100,000 francs, and about 3,300 families had incomes over 100,000 francs per year.[52] In each *commune* a committee composed of the *maire*, two appointees of the municipal

47. France, *Journal Officiel Documents, Chambre des Députés* (1896), pp. 45–46.
48. Ibid., pp. 46, 48.
49. Ibid.
50. Ibid., p. 46.
51. Ibid., pp. 51, 55.
52. Ibid., p. 59.

council and two government officials – the *controleur* and *precepteur* of direct taxes – would evaluate incomes for application of the tax. Problems of evaluation at the level of the commune would be resolved by committees which would be formed in each *arrondissement* on a pattern similar to those of the communes. (France's administrative structure included 86 departements, 362 arrondissements and 36,222 communes.)

Doumer explained that the income tax was an expression of the Radical ministry's desire to restructure the French fiscal system. He estimated it would produce 156,900,620 francs, about the same amount that Campagnole had proposed in his article on the subject in the *New Dictionary of Political Economy* and Paul Leroy-Beaulieu had advocated earlier in his career.[53] Most of the revenue from the proposed tax would be used to replace the personal property and doors and windows taxes. Six million francs would be spent on revising the *cadastre* (land registry); bringing this up to date would probably show that land held by the wealthy had generally been under-valued and therefore some of the tax burden could be shifted from the shoulders of poorer farmers.

Doumer's main argument in favor of the impôt was that it would promote justice in taxation. He described the inadequacies of the doors and windows and personal property taxes and presented the graduation of the impôt as a means to counteract the overall regressiveness of existing taxes.[54] Doumer further claimed that the new tax would be in harmony with the principles of the Great Revolution of 1789. He denied that he sought a single tax (which was advocated by socialists) and that he was leading the country along an adventurous and dangerous path of financial innovation.[55] Needless to say, Doumer's words did not sway the impôt's bourgeois opponents.

53. Ibid., pp. 45, 48, 58.
54. Ibid., pp. 48–49.
55. Ibid., pp. 49, 52.

—4—

The Haute Bourgeoisie Battles the Radical Ministry

Haut Bourgeois Opinion Against the Doumer Proposal

From the start of 1896 to 26 March, when the Chamber voted on the question of the impôt, the bourgeois press poured forth a torrent of attacks on the Radical ministry and its 'revolutionary' tax proposal. On 15 January *Le Temps* accused Bourgeois of favoring fiscal reforms which would diminish the inequality of wealth by means of State intervention. From the moment it was agreed that the law should intervene to promote the equality of wealth, claimed *Le Temps*, palliatives such as the inheritance tax and the income tax would not be enough. People would want absolute leveling, the division of property pure and simple through confiscation by a State charged with satisfying all the physical, intellectual and moral needs of its citizens.[1]

On 24 January *Le Temps* warned that to know the total income of each citizen would require inquisitorial investigations contrary to the spirit of individualism, liberty and the dignity of the nation. Categories of citizens would be created and the stability of finances and the security of labor and savings in France would be imperiled.[2] On 30 January *Le Temps* again warned of the dire consequences to be expected from the proposed tax. If it were created, it claimed, political parties would inevitably seek to use fiscal authority as an instrument of rule. To flatter, conquer and enslave the mass of voters, those who wielded the tax would transform it into a means of favoritism for some and reprisal against others. The burden of taxation would be placed on a minority (the wealthy) and this injustice would be called a work of 'apportionment'.[3] Doumer's proposal, wrote *Le Temps* on 1 February, the day after it was introduced, would divide France into two classes of citizens: those who were forced to declare their incomes [those with incomes over 10,000 francs] and those who were

1. *Le Temps*, Jan. 15, 1896, p. 1.
2. Ibid., Jan. 24, 1896, p. 1.
3. Ibid., Jan. 30, 1896, p. 1.

not. The impôt would hurt the middle bourgeoisie whose initiative and devotion had founded the Republic in France, had defended it against the audacity of Boulangism, and continued to protect it against the menaces of invading collectivism.[4]

Shortly before the income tax came to a vote in the Chamber, *Le Temps* stressed that the proposed innovation was more than a fiscal or even ministerial question. It was an issue that put the very life of the nation at risk. It was the kind of 'grave issue', *Le Temps* quoted Bossuet, 'which decides the destiny of peoples and empires.' Its proper resolution was vital for the future of French society and the Republic itself. If the impossible happened and the government's proposal were adopted, the parliamentary and liberal regime would contain the germ of a socialist revolution to which no one could know the end. To *Le Temps*, the issue confronting France was the social question 'in the negative sense of the term'. Enacting the tax would mean that not only the distinction between but also the war between classes would be introduced into the Republic. France, stated *Le Temps*, faced a crisis 'on which the entire future would rest'.[5]

Other bourgeois newspapers were unanimous in their opposition to the proposed income tax. In February and March *Le Figaro* ran a series of long articles titled 'Against the impôt sur le revenu' by Jules Roche, one of the leading opponents of the tax in the Chamber. The financial daily *Le Messager* claimed that the Radical cabinet had declared war against acquired wealth and accumulated savings. The aristocratic *Le Gaulois* opposed the impôt as did, needless to say, the liberal *Journal des Débats*.[6]

Bourgeois periodicals of all shades of opinion also opposed the impôt. The *Revue des Deux Mondes* and the *Nouvelle Revue* attacked it and in the *Economiste Français*, Paul Leroy-Beaulieu decried Bourgeois's tax policy and insisted that the so-called Radical cabinet was actually socialist. The income tax, he wrote, would attack the sacred right of liberty and the confidentiality of private affairs. Leroy-Beaulieu claimed that it defied all French traditions, memories, habits and tastes. It would become

---

4. Ibid., Feb. 1, 1896.
5. Ibid., March 25, 1896.
6. *Le Temps*, March 25, 1896; *Le Figaro*, March–April 1896; *Le Messager*, March 9, 1896. See also Francis Charmes, 'Chronique de la quinzaine', *RDM*, CXXIII (May 1, 1894), p. 229; Ibid., CXXIII (May 15, 1894), p. 229; Ibid., CXXIII (May 15, 1894), pp. 473–475; Léon Say, 'Budget de 1895 – libéraux et socialistes,' *RDM*, CXXV (Oct. 1, 1894), p. 418; Francis Charmes, 'Chronique de la quinzaine', *RDM*, CXXVI (Dec. 15, 1894), p. 947; Ibid., CXXXII (Nov. 15, 1895), p. 463; Ibid., CXXXII (Dec. l, 1895), p. 716; Ibid., CXXXIV (March 1, 1896), pp. 238–239; Marcère, 'Chronique politique', *Nouvelle Revue*, LXXXIV (Oct. 1, 1893), p. 440; Ch. Gehelle, 'Revue financière et économique', *Nouvelle Revue*, XCI (Dec. 15, 1894), p. 442; Marcère, 'Chronique politique', *Nouvelle Revue*, CXI (Dec. 15, 1894), p. 285.

'an instrument of oppression and torture for the rich and well-to-do classes: a true fiscal Terror'.[7] At the left flank of Moderate opinion, in the *Revue Bleue*, Paul Lafitte opposed Doumer's proposed innovation and urged a unified Moderate program of action as the best way to defeat the Radical ministry.[8] In the liberal Catholic *Le Correspondant*, Louis Joubert also denounced the impôt.

Parliamentary Opposition to the Bourgeois Ministry

Within parliament, the Senate and the Chamber's Budget Committee led the opposition to the Radical ministry. The budget committee which was dominated by Moderates at the time, presented a report by Paul Delombre which roundly condemned the proposed impôt. By a vote of 28–5, it adopted the following resolution to be submitted to the Chamber as a whole for its approval:

> The Chamber, shunning all systems based on the declaration of total income, arbitrary taxation and vexatious investigations, invites the government to present a new project for the reform of direct taxes which would permit the equitable taxation of all incomes in their diversity of form and better distribute the charges which weigh on agriculture and labor.[9]

Le Temps considered Delombre's report for the budget committee so important that it printed it as a special supplement to its regular edition. However the budget committee's opposition failed to generate a majority in the Chamber against the Radical ministry.

To buttress its attack on the Radical ministry's tax proposal, the budget committee then called on chambers of commerce and industrial and agricultural associations throughout France to express their opinions on the consequences to be expected from an impôt sur le revenu. Their responses filled a volume of almost 500 pages which was published as a *supplement* to the budget committee's report and distributed to each deputy in the Chamber.[10] The statements in the *supplement* played many variations on the standard themes against the income tax. The Advisory Chamber of Arts and Manufacture of Aubusson wrote that if the impôt were adopted, it would bring to the country the most disastrous

7. *Economiste Français*, Nov. 9, 1895, pp. 502, 601; Feb. 8, 1896, p. 162; March 28, 1896, p. 285.

8. Paul Lafitte, 'La Politique,' *Revue Bleue*, Nov. 30, 1895, p. 673.

9. *Le Temps*, March 8, 1896. p. 1.

10. *Le Petit Temps*, March 14, 1896, p. 2; Paul Delombre, *Rapport fait au nom de la commission du budget chargée d'examiner le projet de loi portant la fixation du budget général des dépenses et des recettes de l'exercice 1897 (Impôt global sur le revenu), Annexe #1831* (Paris: Matteroz, 1896).

consequences. The idea of the Doumer proposition seemed strange, it held, since 'almost all income is already heavily taxed'. It claimed that the tax would be contrary to the 'fundamental principles of French law', inapplicable in practice, ruinous in its consequences and disastrous for the country. It predicted that if it were enacted, the abandonment of the land would follow, menaced French capital would leave the country and the way would be open to ever increasing rates of graduation.[11]

The Chamber of Commerce of Bordeaux claimed that the committees of assessment called for in Doumer's proposal would bring personal interests and political passions to their work. It criticized the excessive snooping into private affairs which it claimed evaluation of income would require; the impôt would produce a vexatious and inquisitorial system repugnant to the temper of the French. If enacted, the Bordeaux Chamber of Commerce warned, the impôt would shake France with a revolution 'at once political, financial and social.'[12]

The Senate conducted the second prong of attack within parliament against Bourgeois's ministry. The Senate's attack on the Radical ministry went through several phases. The first concerned a judicial question. On 11 February 1896, the Senate approved by 156 votes to 53 a resolution stating that the Finance Minister had violated the separation of powers when he replaced an examining magistrate (*judge d'instruction*) he considered insufficiently diligent in investigating possible corruption concerning the Chemin de Fer du Sud.

Proponents of the Senate's position held that the Bourgeois cabinet should resign because according to the letter of the Constitutional Laws of 1875, 'The ministers are jointly responsible before the Chambers for the general policy of the government and individually for their personal acts.'[13] However, supporters of the Radical government argued that all parliamentary regimes had reserved for the popularly-elected assembly the privilege of dismissing ministries and no cabinet had ever resigned because of a hostile vote by the Senate.[14] Léon Bourgeois defended his ministry against the Senate's attack and won, on 21 February 1896, a vote of confidence by 314 votes to 45. Now the conflict was between the Senate and a Radical cabinet expressly supported by a majority of the Chamber.

Following the vote of 21 February, the Senate passed a resolution reaffirming that it had the right to dismiss cabinets and that ministries were

11. Ibid., pp. 38–39.
12. Ibid., pp. 40–41.
13. Jacques Chastenet, *Histoire de la Troisième République*, vol. III, *La République triomphante, 1893–1896* (Hachette, 1955), pp. 88, 89.
14. Ferdinand Dreyfus, 'La crise constitutional', *RPP*, VII (March 10, 1896), pp. 465–466; Chastenet, *La République triomphante*, p. 89.

responsible before both Chambers of Parliament, but that 'in order not to compromise the public peace' it declined to block all legislation and aggravate the constitutional conflict which remained unresolved.[15] Opponents of the Radical ministry hoped that the Senate's opposition would work in two ways. At best Bourgeois would resign when the Senate voted against him. Second best, the opposition of the Senate would undercut support in the Chamber for the Radical cabinet, as deputies who had no stomach for a fight with the 'upper house' and the constitutional revision it implied deserted the government.[16] But the Radical ministry maintained its small but solid majority in the Chamber, and it became clear that its opponents would be unable to prevent the question of the impôt sur le revenu from being debated and voted on by the full Chamber.

Haut Bourgeois Control of the National Debt as a Lever to Influence Government

Alexis de Tocqueville did not mention it as a means to help the few avoid domination by the many in a democratic state; the Constitutional Laws of 1875 which established the parliamentary republic did not refer to it; Taine, Renan and Renouvrier, intellectual lights of the bourgeoisie, had not discussed its role as a lever for the few to use against pressure of the many. Nevertheless, control of the national debt gave the French haute bourgeoisie a powerful tool with which to oppose a ministry which it believed threatened its vital interests. The hauts bourgeois' ability to affect the price of State *rentes* (the securities of France's long-term debt) could be used to influence public opinion against measures it considered to be dangerous, while their control of the short-term State debt allowed them to threaten the government with bankruptcy.

Perpetual and long-term rentes, constituting by far the largest block of French investment, were owned by several million persons. Called 'fundamental' and 'father of the family' securities, rentes offered maximum security. Of them, the economist Paul Leroy-Beaulieu wrote:

> . . . one is sure, regardless of circumstances, to receive every three months the income stipulated. Even the extravagance of the Chambers and the financial waste from which we suffer do not imperil the regular payment of our public debt. It would take a national catastrophe, coming from crushing

---

15. Dreyfus, 'La crise constitutionnelle', pp. 465–466.
16. Francis Charmes, 'Chronique de la quinzaine', *Revue des Deux Mondes*, CXXXIII (Feb. 15, 1896), pp. 947, 955; Charles Braibant, *Félix Faure à l'Elysée* (Paris: Hachette, 1963), p. 22; Francis Charmes, 'Chronique de la quinzaine', *Revue des Deux Mondes*, CXXIV (March 1, 1896), pp. 228, 229, 320, 323; Ibid., pp. 233, 237, 239, 240.

defeats in a great war, to compromise the French rentes. Even then it is probable that they would suffer more in market value than in income.[17]

Rentes were traded on the Paris Bourse through the intermediary of government-licensed brokers called *agents de change*. In each transaction two agents de change would be involved, one acting for the seller and the other for the purchaser. Because rentes were 100 per cent secure, their price reflected the French economy's prevailing interest rate, the closeness to the date of the next interest payment (dividends were paid four times each year so the accumulated interest would add to the price of the rente), and, occasionally, the direct manipulation of the market by powerful financial interests. Because operations of the agents de change were confidential and registration of the owners of State rentes in the *Grand Livre* of the public debt was secret, we can have only a rough idea of the forces influencing the French rente market at any particular time.

Though at first sight this contradicts the idea that State rentes had maximum security, the bourgeois press of the Third Republic often claimed that their price reflected the credit of the State which was determined by the public's confidence in the cabinet in office. In fact, because they were considered 100 per cent secure, in the medium and long range the price of rentes had nothing to do with what ministry was in office.

Though rente levels normally were independent of political conditions, they could be manipulated by financiers in order to influence public opinion.[18] The political efficacy of manipulating the price of rentes was based on the long-observed fact that the general climate of public opinion was affected by the level of the Bourse and, in particular, by the price of State rentes. It was understood that 'the rise or decline of financial securities, has, on the spirits of the public, an extraordinary influence, greater, possibly, than the material interests involved. Without owning financial securities, people are interested in, even impassioned about, fluctuations in the market.'[19] If this observation about the relation between the public mood and the level of the Bourse was apparent in the 1850s when it was first written, it was even more valid in the 1890s when it was quoted because the ownership of State rentes had spread so much more widely throughout the French population.

There were two ways financiers could manipulate the price of rentes;

17. Paul Leroy-Beaulieu, *L'Art de placer et gérer sa fortune* (Paris: C. Delgrave, 1906), pp. 76, 110.
18. Anatole Leroy-Beaulieu, 'Le règne d'argent', *RDM*, CXXXIX (Feb. 15, 1897), p. 896.
19. Legrand, *La Bourse*, pp. 9–10, quoting Alphonse Courtois, *Traité élémentaire des operations de Bourse*.

they could raise and lower their price by buying and selling, and they could cause a major collapse in price through their control of short-term loans which were made for the purchase of 'floating rentes', that is, rentes bought on margin. During the last days of each month all such loans for the purchase of rentes had to be either renewed or called in. If there were a large amount of 'floating rentes', financiers could cause the price of rentes to plummet by calling in their loans. As those who had lost their credit sold the rentes they had bought on margin in order to obtain money to repay what they had borrowed, the market for rentes would collapse.

In the 1890s it was the '3 per cent perpetual' rente which was considered as the barometer of the Bourse. Thus the spirits of a considerable portion of the French population – rente holders and others – could be influenced by raising or lowering the price of the 3 per cent perpetual. As Alfred Neymarck warned in *Le Rentier* in March 1896: 'If tomorrow this confidence [in rentes] declined or disappeared, if rentes, instead of enjoying general favor, were made suspect, what would become of the state . . . How would *rentiers* react if they were menaced with taxes?'[20]

Although trading in rentes was secret, the financial daily *Le Messager* and the newspaper *Le Petit Moniteur Universel* expressed apparently well-informed opinions explaining the movement of rente prices. The presence of René Salles on the staff of *Le Petit Moniteur Universel* may help explain its high level of information. At this time Salles also produced the satirical financial weekly, *La Cravache Parisienne*; later he went to work for the Association National Républicaine as director of its *Bulletin Correspondance* to the provincial press (see below, chapter 7).

Control of the State's short-term *bons du trésor* (Treasury notes) by the hauts bourgeois provided them with a second financial lever with which to influence government. Bons du trésor, with maturities between 6 months and 5 years, were issued to compensate for the uneven flow of tax revenues into the public treasury and make up for deficits in the State budget. The Finance Ministry's Office of the General Movement of Funds administered their sale. After evaluating the flow of government receipts and expenditures, the Office would decide whether to expand or contract the amount of short-term securities in circulation.[21] The director and assistant director of the Office, besides supervising the operation of the Bourse and nominating agents de change, negotiated the sale of bons du trésor.[22] These notes were purchased by hauts bourgeois – banks, large businesses and wealthy individuals – in blocks of hundreds of thousands

---

20. *Le Rentier*, March 27, 1896, p. 9171.
21. Emmanuel Bray, *Traité de la dette publique* (Paris: Paul Dupont, 1895), p. 37.
22. *Almanach National, 1895* (Paris: Berger Levrault, 1895), p. 169.

or millions of francs.[23]

For the state, bons du trésor had both advantages and disadvantages. On the plus side was their flexibility and elasticity; they provided quick and convenient access to large blocks of funds and interest paid on them was generally lower than that on long-term State rentes because of the convenience they offered their purchasers.[24] On the minus side, if funds were not available to reimburse bons du trésor when they fell due and private purchasers could not be found to buy them, the State would find itself in 'serious embarrassment' (that is, bankruptcy) as happened in 1848. For this reason French financial writers stressed that the State should be sparing in its use of short-term credit in order to avoid being too vulnerable to 'embarrassment' in a time of crisis.[25] If the relatively few hauts bourgeois who subscribed to the short-term debt held a common objective, it would be easy for them to exert pressure on a government by threatening not to subscribe to new issues of bons du trésor or renew the ones they held.

In normal times the price of rentes would drop about one franc when a quarterly dividend coupon was detached and henceforth gradually rise until the next dividend payment came due. But from 16 March 1896, the day after the quarterly interest payment had been paid, until late April 1896, just before the Bourgeois ministry left office, the 3 per cent perpetual showed a downward trend from a level of just under 103 francs to just over 101 francs. Its price fluctuated from day to day as if orchestrated to accompany political events.

Whatever the precise mechanism was by which the price of rentes was manipulated in March–April 1896, their decline cannot be explained by any rush to sell among the general population of rente holders. From mid-March to late April, trading on the Bourse was particularly light. The small operators, it seems, had left the field, encouraged by voices of bourgeois finance such as Alfred Neymarck who in April advised readers of his

---

23. For example, subscribing to an issue of short-term treasury obligations to renew a loan falling due September 1896 were the Parisian Gas Company for 7,500,000 francs; the government's *caisses des dépôts et consignations* (bank of deposit and consignation) for 5,450,000 francs; Banque Parisienne for 3,500,000 francs; Eugene Lévy for 4,000,000 francs; Heurotte Sons and Co., for 1,100,000 francs; the Industrial and Commercial Credit company for 4,000,000 francs; and the Panama Canal Company for 4,000,000 francs. Archives nationales françaises, Series AN F30, folder 227 3.(Obligations du trésor a court term . . .1894–1914.)

24. Paul Leroy-Beaulieu, *Traité de la sciences des finances*, 2nd edn., (Paris: Guillaumin & Cie, 1879) vol. II, p. 382.

25. B. Lisle, 'Bons du trésor', in Say and Chailley-Bert, *Nouveau dictionnaire d'économie politique*, vol. I, p. 443; Paul Leroy-Beaulieu, *Traité de la science des finances*, 6th edn. (Paris: Libraire Guillauman & Cie, 1899), vol. II, pp. 337–338, 384–385.

weekly *Le Rentier*: 'Do not buy or sell no matter what the price.'[26]

In a quiet market, day-to-day increases or declines in the price of rentes could be achieved by the trading of a few powerful financiers coordinating their actions. If there were meetings for this purpose it may be supposed that they took place at one of the elegant restaurants in the vicinity of the Bourse.

The Month of Crisis: March 15 to April 21

The conflict between the Radical ministry and its opponents reached a climax from mid-March to mid-April 1896. This 'Month of Crisis' marked a peak of upper-class anxiety in the history of the Third Republic. In no other crisis did the members of the upper class stand as united on one side of an issue as they did against the impôt. In no other crisis did the bourgeois opponents of a ministry threaten as clearly to overturn the Republic. Yet the story of this Month of Crisis is virtually unknown. The result is the common impression that for France 'the middle of the nineties offer a brief period of political calm between the subsiding of the Right and the ascension of the Left.'[27]

Not unlike other traumatic experiences, the crisis of March–April 1896 was forgotten – suppressed or repressed – by the hauts bourgeois who had experienced it most intensely. Others, members of the middle and lower classes, probably could not fully appreciate the intensity of the crisis because they would not understand the haute bourgeoisie's nightmare of leveling by confiscatory taxation. Lacking the street demonstrations and civil unrest which the French traditionally associated with periods of tension and social conflict, the Month of Crisis may not have been particularly eventful for the mass of the French population. The absence of the story of the battle over the impôt sur le revenu in the historical literature of the Third Republic bears witness to how that conflict became a blank space in French historical memory.

The hauts bourgeois had learned from the Revolution of 1848 that it was unsafe to take their protests to the streets. During the Month of Crisis they expressed their anger and anxiety in a variety of other ways: in parliamentary speeches, in articles in the press, in discussions by learned societies, in petitions to the Chamber of Deputies and in that modern version of a gentlemen's street demonstration, a noisy protest at the

26. Arthur Raffalovich, 'Bourse', in Léon Say and Joseph Chailley-Bert, *Nouveau dictionnaire d'économie politique* vol. I (Paris: Guillaumin & Cie, 1891, 1892), pp. 222, 227; Alfred Neymarck, 'L'étiage des cours des rentes 2½ et 3%', *Le Rentier*, March 27, 1896.
27. Guy Chapman, *The Republic of France: The First Phase, 1871–1894* (London: MacMillan & Co., 1962), pp. 16, 368.

Auteuil race track.

The Month of Crisis commenced with the approach of the Chamber debate on the impôt on 15 March, the date of the quarterly payment of dividends on the 3 per cent rente. Bourgeois leaders mobilized public opinion and private finance against the hated ministry that sought the 'revolutionary' tax. The Chamber's debate on the impôt, which began on 21 March 1896, fulfilled the expectations of those who had looked forward to it as a great event in the history of oratorical conflict. Alfred Neymarck, for example, described it as 'highly brilliant,' with partisans and adversaries of the tax showing 'eloquence, energy, and real knowledge'.[28]

Jean Jaurès, the eloquent Socialist deputy, spoke first. In a speech so long that it required an intermission of 25 minutes, he attacked Delombre's Budget Committee report against the impôt sur le revenu and argued that it would promote social justice. The deputies loved to hear Jaurès orate; they enjoyed his classical and literary allusions, laughing at his comparison of the Budget Committee's thoughts with an apt line from Chataubriand. In a display of logic, Jaurès argued that the tax reform proposals presented by the Moderates were contradictory and only intended to divert attention from the impôt sur le revenu. The Budget Committee, he said, had attacked Doumer's proposal on technicalities, leaving it to others such as Paul Leroy-Beaulieu, Georges Michel and Jules Roche to oppose it on grounds of principle. The Socialist orator quoted Lamarck's famous formula that 'the need creates the organ' as a truth of human society to the loud approval of the Chamber's far left, and went on to claim that Doumer's proposed tax would realize the heritage of the French Revolution and promote the principles of humanity. Pointing to the 'feudality of wealth', Jaurès argued that the reform would benefit the lower classes of the cities and the countryside, but denied that Doumer's proposal was a socialistic measure because it affected neither the division of property nor the principle of private property itself. Socialism, he said, would come as a result of the natural evolution of the force of things with the increase of proletarian production. Jaurès then described his dream of the socialist future: 'The time is approaching', he proclaimed, 'when all humanity will achieve social progress for all humanity and no longer for only a minority . . . Nature itself would be appropriated for noble purposes . . .'[29]

Léon Say, consumed by the last stages of the disease which would soon take his life, spoke next. The grand old man of the conservative Republic

28. *Le Rentier*, April 7, 1896, p. 9182.
29. France, *Journal officiel de la République française: Débats parlementaires, Chambre des Députés* (1896), pp. 716–725.

complimented Jaurès on his brilliant oratorical style but claimed to see no practical recommendations coming from his speech. To reject arbitrary taxation as the Budget Committee had done and call for the ministry to propose a just tax on sources of income in their various forms, said Say, was a positive affirmation. He claimed that to enact an income tax would be to follow the star of collectivism and accused Jaurès of having an ideal of justice which consisted of 'developing jealousy and envy and of turning the residents of the countryside against each other'. The income tax, he said, would hurt the small farmer. It violated the principles of the French Revolution. 'Because people do not want to present themselves completely naked before a very fiscal and authoritarian government our forefathers of 1789 sought to get rid of personal taxes,' Say stated, and he accused advocates of the impôt of going toward an excessive and tyrannical centralization.[30]

The bourgeois press appreciated the first day's debate on the impôt. *Le Temps* reported that it had been 'absolutely magisterial . . . It is oratorical jousts such as this of which the parliamentary tribune could be proud.' As usual, bourgeois observers admired the eloquence of Jaurès, star student of the Ecole Normal Supérieure, even if they feared and hated what he advocated. 'Never,' *Le Temps* stated, 'had the words of M. Jaurès been more abundant, full of imagery, more powerful; never had M. Léon Say invested more spirit in the defense of more wisdom.'

Jaurès spoke on a Saturday. On the following Monday the 3 per cent perpetual rente plummeted 60 centimes. As a message from the financiers, this had its own eloquence.[31]

30. Ibid., pp. 729–732.
31. That this relatively large drop in the price of rentes in one day's trading was contrived by a small group of manipulating financiers is suggested by the Bourse's behavior in the face of other contemporary events which affected the public mood more than a Jaurès speech. In early July 1893, after student demonstrations and rioting had torn the Latin Quarter and about 20,000 extra troops had been brought into Paris to maintain order during the closing of the Bourse du Travail, *Le Temps* reported that the Bourse had been 'completely unaffected' by the incidents. In the face of Valliant's bomb in the Chamber of Deputies and the wave of anarchist 'outrages' of February and March 1894 the Bourse had stood firm. Even the assassination of President of the Republic Sadi Carnot, the most horrifying of the anarchist outrages of the 1890s, had not shaken the nerves of French investors. Though the financial world was reportedly 'stupefied' to hear the frightful news and the market experienced a momentary dip, it quickly rebounded and remained firm.(*Le Temps*, July 7, 1893, p. 2; July 10, 1893, 'Semaine financière,' p. 4; *Le Rentier*, July 17, 1893, p. 8332; Ch. Gehelle 'Revue financière,' *Nouvelle Revue*, CXXV (Dec. 15, 1897), p. 82; *Le Rentier*, Feb. 27, 1894, p. 8400; March 17, 1894, p. 8417; June 27, 1894, p. 8519; Ch. Gehelle, 'Revue financière et économique,' *Nouvelle Revue*, LXXXIX (July 1, 1894), p. 208; Artur Raffalovich, *La marché financière en 1895* (Paris: Guillaumin, 1896), p. 3.)
In any case, the 60 centime decline in the price of the 3 per cent perpetual rente after

The Bourgeoisie Battles the Ministry

The Chamber of Deputies renewed its discussion of the income tax on Monday, 23 March. L'Hopiteau, a Radical, supported the measure as a long-overdue act of social justice which would actually help to prevent socialism. He explained that he was one of the numerous farming deputies of the Chamber – a son of a farmer, not the son of a big landowner. Small and moderate merchants and farmers, he maintained, were not alarmed by the prospect of an income tax. L'Hopiteau did not agree with all details of Doumer's project; he suggested that taxpayers should declare their incomes to evaluation committees at the level of the arrondissement rather than the commune, and he also criticized the idea that some persons would be completely exempt from the tax, arguing that in a country of universal suffrage where each elector contributes to the general direction of affairs, each should contribute to its maintenance. He suggested further that Doumer's proposed rate of progressivity did not go far enough.[32]

On Tuesday, 24 March, in an agitated session of the Chamber, the Moderate Jules Méline attacked the income tax, claiming that it would cause a veritable revolution in finances and economics, hurt the small farmer and violate the sentiment prevalent at all levels of the French population, which disliked government snooping into private affairs. Méline warned that approval of the tax would cause the Bourse to decline, and he opposed replacing a tested financial system with an untried one.[33]

Also on 24 March, the 3 per cent perpetual moved up sharply by 25 centimes. This was due, explained the financial daily Le Messager, to the optimism Méline's vigorous speech had inspired in the investing public. But it was more likely that the financiers were not reacting to Méline's eloquence but rather expressing some of their own by orchestrating a rise in the market which was closely watched by the public and the politicians.[34]

The day before the vote on the impôt sur le revenu, on 25 March, Le Temps appealed to the deputies. The vote of the Chamber, it wrote, would determine the direction of the future of French society and of the Republic itself in as much as it was a parliamentary and liberal regime. If the impossible happened and the government's proposal were adopted, Le Temps warned, it would introduce the principle of a socialistic revolution to which no one could know the end.[35]

On 26 March, with the Deputy Dron's proposition, the Chamber voted

the first day of debate on the impôt was not the collapse of rente prices that would have occurred had financiers called in the loans which were used to purchase 'floating' rentes on margin (see below, pp. 77, 78).

32. France, *Journal Officiel Débats, Chambre des Députés* (1896), pp. 735–738, 741.
33. Ibid., pp. 759, 763, 764.
34. *Le Messager*, March 25, 1896.
35. *Le Temps*, March 25, 1896.

on the question of the impôt. By 286 votes to 270 the principle of the tax was approved. Within the Chamber, the impôt and Bourgeois's Radical ministry had withstood the combined attack of the Moderates and the far right.[36] But the issue was not yet settled.

In early April the Senate renewed its attack on the Radical ministry. Doing then what it had declined to do in February, the Senate moved to suspend the legislative life of the country. It began by refusing to vote funds for the French armed forces in Madagascar. Previous legislation had provided credits for the troops in Madagascar through 30 April 1896 and in early April, before leaving for its Easter recess, the Chamber had approved funds for after April. But on 4 April the Senate took up the question and adjourned it by a vote of 155 to 85.[37]

Predictably, the bourgeois press supported the Senate's action and called on the Radical ministry to resign. *Le Temps* deplored the political situation created by the conflict between the Senate and Chamber and warned that if Bourgeois continued to fight the Senate, he would precipitate 'a revolutionary situation.'[38] From the fourth to the fifteenth of April – between the Senate's refusal to vote funds for the French forces on Madagascar and the meeting of the general councils of the departements – the tension of the Month of Crisis reached its peak. On 7 April *Le Temps* reported that recent events had created a state of political nervousness, of discontent, and of fears on one side and hope and audacity on the other, which could explode in the most dangerous way.[39]

One sign of the tension of early April was the anger directed at President of the Republic Félix Faure. Bourgeois opinion was divided in its attitude toward Faure. Though virtually all hauts bourgeois vehemently opposed the Radical ministry, only some blamed President Faure for permitting it to remain in office. Others reserved their venom for Bourgeois and his cabinet. Cassagnac, writing in the reactionary *L'Autorité*, was one of those who attacked Faure: 'This man, elected by the Senate, betrays the Senate. This man elected by the Moderates of the Chamber, betrays the Moderates. He is afraid, he shivers, he trembles, he fears both the bitter reproaches of those he has abandoned and the threats of those who have taken him prisoner . . . He surrenders the Constitution, of which he is the guardian, to the scoundrels of revolution.

---

36. A. Salles, 'Les députés sortants (1893–1898): Votes et groupements.' *RPP*, XVI (April 10, 1898), p. 39; France, *Journal Officiel Débats, Chambre des Députés* (1896), p. 665.
37. Félix Roussel, 'Chronique politique intérieure', *RPP*, VII (May 10, 1896), p. 472.
38. *Le Temps*, April 5, 1896.
39. *Le Temps*, April 7, 1896.

For we are in full revolution.'[40]

Martel, in *Le Petit Moniteur Universel*, addressed an open letter to Monsieur Félix Faure: 'Tranquilly, coldly, after having killed all shame, you are plainly on a revolutionary course; you govern with a ministry which has departed from the constitution, which is outside the law . . .' Martel accused Faure of experiments which could lead the country to an abyss, compromising its institutions and gambling with the very existence of the Republic. 'France', wrote Martel, 'asks itself where do you want to lead it? Do not invoke irresponsibility of office to justify your inertia. You are in the right, within the law, within the constitution; it is your ministers who have departed from it.'[41]

Cornély of *Le Gaulois* was among those who spared Faure their harshest criticism. He disagreed with those who held in early April that President Faure was not doing his job and suggested that once the Bourgeois ministry was appointed, it should be left to live out its life. The only error the President elected by the Moderates had made, Cornély wrote, was to have given power to the Radicals in the first place.

One reason critics of President Faure were probably unfair in their attacks on him was that if he had dismissed the Radical cabinet, dissolved the Chamber and called general elections, an even larger majority of deputies in favor of the income tax might have been elected. It is probably for this reason that *Le Temps* opposed dissolution (which was favored by the Radical Emile Combes and the Socialist Jean Jaurès) as a means of resolving the impasse in which the Senate and Chamber found themselves in April 1896.[42]

Perhaps the key difference between those who insisted that Faure should dismiss the Bourgeois ministry and those who did not was the extent to which they were aware of the plans for the demise of the Radical cabinet which had been made by several leading opponents of the Radical cabinet including Raymond Poincaré, André Lebon, Barthou, de Mackau, de Lamarzelle and Le Prévost de Launey on 4 April over dinner at Durand's restaurant at the place de la Madeleine. René Salles, the satirical journalist, described the occasion as a 'conspiratorial' 'diner historique' referring to the fact that it was at Durand's that General Boulanger had spent his semi-legendary 'nuit historique' while he waited to hear the Paris election results of 1889 but then failed to 'lead the way to the Eluseé'

40. *L'Autorité*, April 6, 1896.
41. *Le Petit Moniteur Universel*, April 9, 1896. See also *Revue Bleue*, April 11, 1896, pp. 449–450.
42. 'La Dissolution,' *Le Temps*, April 2, 1896, p. 1; *The Economist*, March 28, 1896, p. 387.

and attempt a coup.[43]

The sentiment against President Faure inspired, on 5 April, a gentlemen's demonstration at the Sunday races at the Auteuil race track. *L'Autorité* carried the story under a full page headline: 'M. Félix Faure and the Ministry Hooted at Auteuil.'[44] The Presidential prize, created the year before, was the occasion which brought President Faure and seven members of the Radical cabinet to the track, but the spectators at Auteuil greeted Faure frigidly when he arrived shortly after the second race. Evidently not enjoying the atmosphere, the President of the Republic started to leave as the fourth race was about to be run. Just then spectators began shouting 'A bas le gouvernement! Vive le Sénat! A bas Bourgeois!' Gentlemen spectators defiantly tossed calling cards into the air. Unkindly, *L'Autorité* reported that as Faure got into his fashionable landau to leave, pursued by cries against him and the ministry, 'he smiled the falsely easy-going smile of a fat and satisfied bourgeois'. *L'Autorité* noted that the public which had denounced Faure at Auteuil had paid twenty francs for admission and was composed of an elite of bourgeois, sportsmen, and gentlemen, persons who were little inclined to make noisy demonstrations. 'Never', wrote the newspaper, 'had a public so elegant invested such passion in so noisy a demonstration.'[45]

Another symptom of the tension of early April 1896 was the controversy which swirled about the weekly *Journal Officiel, édition des Communes*, informally known as the *Bulletin des Communes*. The *Bulletin*, which included official announcements and an abbreviated account of parliamentary debates, was posted outside the mairies of those towns which could not afford to subscribe to the *Journal Officiel*. The Chamber's Budget Committee (dominated by Moderates at the time), protested at its meeting of 4 April that the *Bulletin*'s most recent issue had unfairly printed a large part of Paul Doumer's Chamber speech advocating the impôt. Georges Cochery, the budget committee's chairman, complained in a note to the Minister of the Interior Jean Sarrien that the Bulletin was a document with an official character which should inform the country on the debates in the Chamber and not, on the contrary, lead it to error.[46] Sarrien presented Cochery's letter to the cabinet, which issued a statement (which did not satisfy its critics) that denied that the *Bulletin des Communes* had been instructed on how to publish Doumer's

43. Frederic H. Seager, *The Boulanger Affair*, (Ithaca: Cornell University Press, 1969), pp. 203–210.
44. *Le Gaulois*, April 5, 1896.
45. *L'Autorité*, April 7, 1896.
46. *Le Matin*, April 5, 1896, p. 3.

speech and insisted that it had done nothing out of the ordinary by making known the views of the government.[47]

The tension of the time was also reflected in the meeting of the Paris Society of Political Economy on the evening of 4 April, the day the Senate refused to approve credits for Madagascar. Its topic, 'The Battle Against Socialism', had been proposed by Anatole Leroy-Beaulieu after illness had prevented Léon Say from leading a discussion on 'Socialism' as originally planned. That the circumstances on 4 April were exceptional was indicated by René Worm's questioning the propriety of the topic and his argument that the Society should not inscribe such a cause on its banner because it was an association for study, not a grouping for combat. But Worm's objection failed to carry.[48]

Leroy-Beaulieu explained that he proposed to discuss the battle against socialism because no topic was more urgent. Economists, he said, could not be indifferent to the dangers which increasingly menaced the country and society. For a long time, he explained, it was believed in France that the job of defending society belonged, above all, to the government, but this was a dangerous error because the government was extending its hand to the Socialists. According to him, the enemy was already in position; soon it might become the master.[49]

The bourgeois press reflected the tension of early April 1896. On 7 April *Le Temps* claimed that France was in the midst of abnormal political circumstances which could not long continue without becoming 'alarming' and 'possibly revolutionary'. There could be no normal and durable government against the will of the Senate, *Le Temps* insisted; for the ministry to persist in a 'war against the Senate' was to follow an essentially 'revolutionary' policy. The Bourgeois cabinet would be greatly mistaken if it imagined that it would suffice to ignore the conflict in order to make it vanish. Recent events, *Le Temps* warned, had created a highly charged political condition of discontent and fear on one side and expectation and audacity on the other which could explode in the most dangerous way.[50] Similarly the *Revue des Deux Mondes* of 14 April reported that the malaise in France was increasing and described the current situation as 'almost revolutionary',[51] and the *Nouvelle Revue* warned that the outcome of the conflict between the Chamber and the

47. *Le Matin*, April 8, 1896.
48. *Economiste Français*, April 18, 1896, pp. 491–492.
49. Ibid.
50. *Le Temps*, April 7, 1896.
51. Francis Charmes, 'Chronique de la quinzaine,' *RDM*, CXXXIV (April 15, 1896), pp. 946, 947, 955.

Senate would be either resignation of the Bourgeois cabinet or 'insurrection'.[52]

The provincial press also expressed the tension of early April 1896. Throughout April the *Démocratie du Centre*, a Moderate newspaper, attacked the Radical ministry and the revolutionary danger it claimed it presented.[53] It insisted that the Senate did have the right to demand that a ministry resign and, if it did not depart it would be taking a clearly revolutionary attitude. The newspaper warned that in accustoming the electorate to scorn either the Senate or Chamber, the bed of dictatorship was being prepared as it had been in 1851 when Louis Napoléon had staged his coup. It worried that 'M. Bourgeois is losing his head . . . is making us enter the path of revolution. What would be the end? An immense unknown, all would agree.'[54]

The conservative Catholic *Journal de l'Ain* proclaimed, after the Senate had for the second time denied its confidence to Bourgeois's cabinet, 'France is in Revolution', and portrayed the impôt sur le revenu as an 'invention more blameworthy even than the famous tax of 45 centimes under which another Republic [the Second] fell.'[55] The *rallié* (Catholic yet accepting of the Republic) *Courrier d'Allier* strongly opposed the impôt sur le revenu and in March it criticized President Faure for delivering France to its worst enemies, the Jacobins. In April it demanded the Bourgeois ministry resign; otherwise the government would be 'in a state of insurrection against the country' attacking the law and the Constitution.[56]

The anxiety of the bourgeois press in early April was a fitting prelude to the meeting of the general councils of the départements scheduled for the week of 13 April, during Parliament's Easter recess. By that time the 3 per cent perpetual rente had declined to about 101 francs, a low for the year, after a brief rally toward the end of March. On 8 and 9 April, for the first time since the rentes began to decline in mid-March, there is some indication that 'sell' orders from the provinces briefly influenced the market. Other than that, downward movement of rentes appears to have been due to the manipulation of financiers in Paris.[57]

On 16 April the Chamber's Budget Committee took the unorthodox step of requesting the general councils to inform it of their deliberations

52. A. Descubes, 'Parlement,' *Nouvelle Revue*, XCIX (April 15, 1896), p. 848.
53. *Démocratie du Centre*, April 6, 7, 8 and 9, 1896.
54. *Démocratie du Centre*, April 5, 1896, p. 1.
55. *Journal de l'Ain*, April 8 and 15, 1896.
56. *Le Courrier d'Allier*, March 1 and 11, 1896.
57. *Le Petit Moniteur Universel*, April 8 and 9, 1896.

and resolutions concerning the impôt sur le revenu.[58] That this was unorthodox is shown by the fact that in 1894, when several general councils had expressed opinions in favor of the impôt sur le revenu, the *Revue des Deux Mondes* had written that the councils knew perfectly well that the law forbade them from taking political votes.[59]

As expected, the great majority of general councils declared themselves against the tax. But a few did support it, and many contained minorities which favored it. Also, as would be expected, the general councils tended to be more circumspect in their opposition than the chambers of commerce and industrial and agricultural associations had been when they had been consulted by the Chamber's Budget Committee.[60] The general council of Allier, for example, adopted by a vote of 16–12 (with the minority comprised of Radicals and Socialists), a vague formula which approved the 'democratic and benevolent' idea of removing overburdening taxes from society's poor and called on parliament to find the means to do this, but opposed the impôt sur le revenu. The general council of the Aube voted 18–4 against the impôt or any other sort of progression in taxation. The general council of the Cher rejected by 16 votes to 7 any tax on total income, but claimed to favor fiscal reforms which would lighten charges on the small taxpayer.[61] The council of the Cote d'Or, after stating that it was absolutely necessary to improve the French tax system and lighten its burden on the agricultural and working population, rejected recourse to the income tax and called for an 'impôt proportional sur les revenus' without superposition, without use of declaration or any vexatious or inquisitorial procedures, and with moderate graduation in favor of small taxpayers, especially those with large families.

A few general councils proposed measures more extreme than Doumer's. Thus the Bouches-du-Rhone (which included Marseilles) voted 20–3 that all taxes should come from a progressive tax on total income, the socialistic single tax.[62]

Moderates in the Chamber claimed that the opinions of the general councils formed a départemental referendum which accurately reflected public sentiment. More correctly, Radicals and Socialists held that the

58. France, Archives nationales françaises, (hereafter cited as A. N.) C5550-22-(#3) (Archives de la Chambre des Députés, VI leg., 1893–1896).

59. Francis Charmes, 'Chronique de la quinzaine', *RDM*, CXXI (Aug. 15, 1894), p. 947; A. N. C5550-22 (#5).

60. André Daniel, *L'année politique, 1896* (Paris: Charpentier, 1897), p. vii; A. N., Archives de la Chambre des Députés VI leg., 1893–1898 C5550 dossier 22.

61. A. N., C5550 22 6 (#10); C5550 22 6 (#14); C5550 22 13 (#18, #19); C5550 22 (#30–32).

62. A. N., C5550 22 (#31).

councils only very imperfectly represented the total French electorate because indirect suffrage gave the wealthy disproportionate weight in those bodies.

Although Radical deputies had legislative objectives (e.g. the impôt sur le revenu) they also wanted patronage and control of governmental administration. Throughout the tenure of Bourgeois's Ministry, Radical deputies pleaded with him to 'purify' the state bureaucracy, but he did not satisfy their requests. Only later, with the Waldeck-Rousseau ministry, (see below, chapter 8) did they obtain the administrative patronage they wanted.

In February, when the Senate had voted against the cabinet, the Radical leader René Goblet asked Bourgeois 'to make his acts agree with his words' concerning the composition of administrative personnel. Also in February Alexandre Brérard, a leading Radical deputy from l'Ain, called on Bourgeois to remove the administration from the hands of clericals, ralliés and monarchists. The prefects in many cities, he claimed, were in absolute agreement with the clerical rural nobility and the old candidates favoring Boulanger and the throne. Brérard was not happy with Bourgeois's cautious moderation in regard to administrative replacements and called on him to act more vigorously, but the Radical prime minister refused.

In mid-March, when it seemed the ministry might founder on the vote on the impôt, Radical politicians called on Bourgeois to remove prefects who 'wage war against progressive republicans', to replace the 'retrograde and often incapable administrators who encumber the prefectures and subprefectures', to favor his friends and stop closing his eyes to the 'astonishing treachery' of certain officials.[63] But in late March, after Sarrien had replaced Bourgeois as Minister of the Interior (Bourgeois took the position of Foreign Minister), Radical politicians were again disappointed in their hopes for administrative patronage. The prime minister's goal was a legislative program headed by the impôt sur le revenu, not a new administrative *seize mai*.[64]

In the days before the Senate reconvened on 21 April, the Bourse exhibited a wait-and-see attitude and the price of rentes remained steady.[65] But the well-informed *Petit Moniteur* explained that a collapse in the price of rentes was possible. In late March it had reported that the ground was

63. *L'Autorité*, Feb. 2, 1896; *Républicaine de l'Ain*, Feb. 8, March 14, 24–25, 1896; *Correspondant Républicaine*, Feb. 16, 1896;

64. *Correspondant Républicaine*, April 13, 1896.

65. *Le Petit Moniteur Universel*, April 20, 1896.

prepared for a long-range decline of rentes through the steady sale of them by the *Caisse des Dépots*.[66] This had produced a 'floating' stock of rentes purchased on credit which was normally renewed at each end of-the-month liquidation of accounts (see above). If the loans were not renewed, the rentes whose purchase they financed would have to be sold. The result would be a sharply depressed market. On 13 April the *Petit Moniteur* wrote that between then and 21 April important decisions would have to be taken in the councils of government with a view to ending the conflict between the Senate and Chamber and the result would be a violent movement of the Bourse in one direction or the other. On 13 April the *Journal des Débats* made the same point, telling its readers that conditions were such that in case of a crisis, the price of rentes could plummet.[67]

The Radical ministry appears to have faced more credit problems than a shaky rente market; there are indications that the government short-term bons du trésor were also under pressure. French financial writers had long explained that in a time of crisis the government would find it difficult to renew bons du trésor which fell due. If ever there was a time of crisis, it was now. Further it may be supposed that the government, particularly its Minister of War Godefroy Cavaignac, was especially concerned with keeping an open line to short-term credit which was expected to be needed to pay for the production of the new 75mm rapid-fire field cannon.

While the Radical ministry was in office, the decision was made to go ahead with full-scale production of the 75mm rapid-fire cannon. An enormous sum of 300 million francs, equal to one-third of the Army's annual budget, would be needed to pay for this. To maintain secrecy, the use of the money would be camouflaged in the budget and the needed funds would be obtained from the sale of short-term bons du trésor which could be arranged with a minimum of parliamentary discussion.[68] (See also below, Appendix) But by deciding to pay for the new artillery with bons du trésor, the Radical ministry left itself open to pressure from the hauts bourgeois who purchased these securities.

66. The law of July 1895 which lowered the maximum size of savings accounts from 2,000 francs to 1,500 francs produced a net withdrawal from these accounts and thereby increased the supply of rentes on the market because a certain fraction of the money deposited in savings accounts was required by law to be invested in the *Caisse des Dépots* which used it to purchase rentes. As savings deposits declined, the Caisse des Dépots sold rentes on the open market in order to reimburse withdrawals.
67. A. P. in *Le Petit Moniteur Universel*, March 24, 1896; *Journal des Débats*, April 13, 1896, p. 3.
68. Henriette Dardenne, 'Comment fut décidé la construction du canon de 75 . . .', *Bulletin Trimestriel de l'Association des Amis de l'Ecole Supérieure de Guerre*, 20 (July 1963), p. 67; France, Sénat, Commission des Finances, archives, Jan. 20, 1896, p. 168; Gabriel Hannotaux, *Histoire de la nation française*, vol. III, *Histoire militaire et navale, Du Directoire à la Guerre de 1914* by Marechel Franchet d'Esperey (Paris: Plon, 1927), p. 436; Dardenne, *Godefroy Cavaignac*, pp. 212, 213.

Even without this particular circumstance, any French government in the 1890s was vulnerable to pressure on the short-term national debt. To apply such pressure, financiers could threaten not to subscribe to new issues of bons or renew the ones they already held. This possibility was noted in 1896 during the Month of Crisis; on 9 March Léon Harmoy, a vehement foe of the impôt sur le revenu, wrote in the financial daily *Le Messager* that the Radical cabinet was entering directly and resolutely into a battle against 'acquired wealth and accumulated savings'. The ministry, he claimed, intended to apply the socialist doctrine and wage war on capitalists, rentiers, and industrialists by using the most effective weapon, the tax. Harmoy called on 'big capital', the country's 'nerve of industrial prosperity', to resist. Two weeks later he wrote that big blocks of short-term obligations were coming due in April and July 1896 and claimed that the amount of short-term debt was not excessive, that the situation of the Treasury was good and that the future held no menace. Save for some unexpected event, he wrote, sufficient funds would be available from lenders. Therefore there was no reason to consolidate the short-term debt and replace it with an issue of long-term rentes. Harmoy did not mention in his later article of 23 March 1896 that the Chamber was about to vote on the impôt sur le revenu; but he and his readers knew very well that it was. It is impossible to imagine that 'big capital', which purchased bons du trésor, would not have seen the enactment of an impôt sur le revenu as a 'menace', an 'unexpected event', which Harmoy had warned could endanger the government's ability to cover its short-term debt.[69]

There is some indication that pressure was exerted on the bons du trésor during the Month of Crisis. In April 1896 4.7 million francs of bons du trésor were issued compared with 13.7 and 15.8 million francs for March and May of that year. This was not the 'big block of short-term obligations' Léon Harmoy had written would come due (and be subject to renewal) in April. The significance of these figures is not conclusive, however, for the amounts of bons sold varied considerably from month to month.

What other evidence would indicate a menace to the State's short-term credit? Did Finance Minister Paul Doumer raise the problem at one of his 7.00 a.m. meetings with André Germain, head of the Credit Lyonnais and great financial power in the 1890s? It would be surprising indeed if financiers had not indicated to M. Delatour and M. de Trogoman, the haut bourgeois heads of the Treasury's Office of the Movement of Funds which

69. Léon Harmoy, *Le Messager*, March 9, 1896, p. 2; Léon Harmoy, 'La Trésorie et l'emprunt', *Le Messager*, March 23, 1896.

arranged the sale of bons du trésor, that they would not be interested in purchasing bons until the Radical ministry had left office.[70]

The anxiety of the haute bourgeoisie during the 'month of crisis' has been completely forgotten. Yet without understanding the 'black hole' of memory sense cannot be made of the subsequent history of France. The Radical ministry which was the immediate cause of the bourgeoisie's anxiety would leave office in April, but the permanent solution to the menace of democracy lay three years in the future, when René Waldeck-Rousseau would form his 'coalition of republican defense.'

70. André Germain, *La bourgeoisie qui brule – Propos d'un témoin (1890–1940)* (Paris: Sun, 1951), p. 42.

The Radical Ministry Leaves Office

La Grande Semaine

'La Grande Semaine' was the headline in *Le Matin* on 20 April 1896, reminding its readers that the conflict between the Senate and Chamber would reach a climax when the Senate would reconvene and take up the question of credits for the French expeditionary force on Madagascar. It was expected that the Senate would again refuse to approve the credits.

The Palais du Luxembourg, where the Senate sat, was animated before the start of the 21 April session. The Senators, 'les bons vieux' (good old boys), expressed their intention to resist the Bourgeois cabinet to the end; they would suspend the legislative life of the country, approving no legislation until the Radical ministry would leave office.[1] The Senate quickly resolved, by 168 votes to 91, that:

> It would not enter into the thoughts of any of us to haggle over the money necessary for the soldiers of France . . . Thus we do not refuse the credits. We are ready to vote them. But not for the present ministry. We propose that the Senate postpone the vote until it has before it a constitutional ministry having the confidence of the two chambers.[2]

But the Senate's reconvening, reported *l'Autorité*, left the Parisian public quite indifferent; if anyone dreamed of 'heroic times, when the popular masses would know how to find their way to the Palais du Luxembourg to impose their will on the Senate, they would be disappointed.'[3]

Two days after the Senate reconvened, Léon Say died of a stomach hemorrhage. Say, whom the Radical newspaper *Le Jour* described as the true head of the conservative party in the Chamber, would not see the outcome of the great test of the parliamentary republic he had done so much to found.[4] It was at this time that Robert Mitchell, in his obituary

1. *L'Autorité*, April 23, 1896.
2. 'La vie politique et parlementaire en France,' *RPP*, VIII (May 10, 1896), pp. 473–474.
3. *L'Autorité*, April 23, 1896.
4. *Le Jour*, Feb. 23, 1896.

for Say, predicted the demise of the 'conservative republic'.

On 22 April, the day after the Senate refused to vote credits for the troops on Madagascar, Léon Bourgeois gathered the members of his cabinet in his magnificent office in the Foreign Ministry. Because no minutes were taken at French cabinet meetings and because their content was treated as secret, the details of the lengthy discussion are not known. But is was reported that the majority of ministers had stubbornly resisted Bourgeois's intention to resign. While the cabinet met, a group of leading Radical deputies came to pledge it their continued support and plead with Bourgeois to stay. The leaders of the 'democratic left', the small Senate grouping which had backed the Radical ministry, also expressed its support. But Bourgeois insisted on leaving office, claiming that if he still held a majority in the Chamber, it was a very slim one which could not be expected to last more than a few days.[5]

At the end of the long meeting Bourgeois announced to the press that:

> considering the refusal of the Senate to vote the credits requested by the government thereby preventing the maintenance and relief of the troops in Madagascar, the ministry has concluded that it can no longer guarantee the direction of affairs. Rather than submit its resignation to the President of the Republic . . . it has decided to request that the Chamber be convoked as soon as possible so that it can inform it of the motives for its decision . . .[6]

The next day *Le Matin* reported what it claimed was the division within the cabinet over whether or not to resign. Opposed were Doumer, Guyot-Dessaigne, Lockroy, Combes and Guieysse; in favor were Bourgeois, Cavaignac, Sarrien, Ricard and Viger.[7]

Shortly before the 2.00 p.m. session of the Chamber on 23 April the scene in front of the Palais Bourbon was animated. More than the usual number of police kept small groups of curious onlookers away from the fence surrounding it. Reporters stood at its entrances, asking arriving deputies what they expected would happen.[8] Inside Léon Bourgeois faced an agitated Chamber. His firmest supporters expressed their disappointment, anger and disgust at his withdrawal in the face of the

---

5. *Le Matin*, April 23, 1896. This appears to be the basis of the claim made by historians that Bourgeois left office because he would have soon lost his majority. It is difficult to take Bourgeois's justification seriously. For one, it is contradicted by the evidence of the solidity of his majority until the time he resigned. For another, it is contradicted by the logic of the situation. If Bourgeois could have left office by the 'ordinary way' by losing a vote in the Chamber he would have done so and thereby avoided the appearance of having been removed by the Senate and the furor it engendered.

6. Henriette Dardenne, *Godefroy Cavaignac* (Colmar: Henriette Dardenne, 1968), p. 275.

7. *Le Matin*, April 23, 1896.

8. *Le Jour*, April 24, 1896; *L'Autorité*, April 25, 1896.

Senate's opposition. While Moderates sat enjoying the spectacle, deputies on the left repeatedly interrupted the Radical premier.[9]

Bourgeois briefly summarized the background of the question of credits for Madagascar while Brisson, President of the Chamber, struggled vainly to maintain order. Lively interruptions directed against the Senate greeted the premier's description of that body's refusal to vote funds. 'The terms of the Senate's decision', said Bourgeois, 'do not permit our cabinet to assure legally . . . from 30 April the functioning of military services indispensable for the defense of the rights and interests of France in Madagascar . . . we believe we are commanded by the demands of patriotism . . .'

'To stay!' called out the Radical Camille Pelletan.

But Bourgeois would not be diverted: '. . . to subordinate all to the interest of the highest question, that of the national security and dignity. No interest of internal politics, whatever its gravity, could, to our eyes, be weighed against this.'[10]

'Then you would have let the monarchy be re-established?' Pelletan called out. The deputies laughed.

Bourgeois continued, stating that the cabinet still had the support of the majority of the Chamber, to cheers from the left. He claimed that he was acting out of patriotism and was not abandoning the doctrine that only the Chamber which was elected directly by universal suffrage had the right 'to make and unmake ministries'. But the justice of his subtle reasoning was lost to many on the left. In fact Bourgeois had resigned at the insistence of the Senate; the Senate had unmade his ministry. Thus the Radical prime minister established for the Third Republic the precedent that a ministry supported by a majority in the Chamber would resign in the face of opposition by the Senate – precisely what was intended by the architects of the 'parliamentary republic' of 1875.

In the Chamber the left met Bourgeois's statement with anger and disgust. 'We have sacrificed everything for you,' said Marcel Hebert, 'and you abandon us!' 'It is capitulation without the honors of war!' declared Paschal Grousset.

Then Ricard, the *garde de sceaux* of the Bourgeois ministry, offered the resolution that: 'The Chamber affirms again the preponderance of the representatives of universal suffrage and its resolve to pursue democratic

9. The source of the account which follows is France, *J. O., Débats, Chambre des Députés* (1896), pp. 727–732.

10. Bourgeois exaggerated the danger to the troops on Madagascar in case the appropriation for their supplies was not approved. As the *Revue Politique et Parlementaire* pointed out, the question was not whether the troops would starve; they had provisions enough. What was at question was whether their support would be legal. 'La vie Politique et Parlementaire en France,' *RPP*, VIII May 10, (1896), pp. 472–473.

reforms.' After some noisy discussion and the defeat by 283 votes to 268 of the Moderate André Lebon's proposal for adjournment, Ricard's harmless proposition was approved by 309 votes to 38.

Finally, at 6.20 p.m., the session was over. Outside the Palais Bourbon the crowd had increased to several hundred, waiting for news from the Chamber. But if any had expected trouble, none occurred.[11]

The Aftermath

The peak of public protest against the Senate's having forced the Radical ministry from office came the next evening at a mass protest meeting at the Tivoli Vaux-Hall on rue de la Douane, near the Place de la République. The Tivoli Vaux-Hall, rather shabby in the 1890s, had seen better days as an orchestra hall in the 1840s, then as the Eden Palace public ballroom and meeting hall. It was there that on 5 March 1871 the statutes of the Commune of Paris were adopted, it was there on 15 January 1893 that the Socialists had decided to ally themselves with the Radicals in the coming general elections. As recently as 3 March 1896 about 2,500 rail workers had assembled at the Tivoli Vaux-Hall to protest legislation by the Senate which denied them the right to strike.[12]

The announced purpose of the Tivoli Vaux-Hall meeting was to protest against the Senate and demonstrate in favor of universal suffrage and the democratic Republic.[13] It had been a long time since Paris had seen a protest meeting as imposing as this one. By 8.00 p.m., when it began, about 8,000 people were packed into the hall and thousands of others filled rue de la Douane outside.[14] The chairman of the meeting asked for calm and silence: 'This meeting must maintain a dignified character; the population of Paris must express its will properly.' But neither speakers nor audience were in a mood to heed the chairman.

Camille Pelletan, the Radical deputy, attacked the 'reactionary provocations' of the Senate and called for constitutional revision. In good Parisian Jacobin tradition, he asked:

What should be done? In former times it was Paris to whom France looked. Paris took the Bastille; it must take it again . . . Paris made the barricades of

---

11. *L'Autorité*, April 25, 1896.

12. Jacques Hillairet, *Dictionnaire Historique des Rues de Paris VI* (Paris: Les Editions de Minuit, 1894), p. 439; *La Petite République*, March 3, 1896; Archives de Police B^A 105 no. 68 (March 2, 1896); Leslie Derfler, *Alexandre Millerand – The Socialist Years* (The Hague: Mouton, 1971), p. 279.

13. Archives de Police B^A 105 no. 69, no. 113 (April 25, 1896).

14. *L'Intransigeant*, April 26, 1896; Archives de Police, B^A 105 no. 69, no. 113 (April 25, 1896); *La Libre Parole*, April 25, 1896; *Le Jour*, April 26, 1896; *Le Gaulois*, April 25, 1896; *L'Autorité*, April 26, 1896.

1830 and overthrew the regime of capitulation in 1870. For some time Paris has been a bit asleep. This heartens our adversaries . . . Paris must awaken and set the example for France . . . We will not act only by force. I do not know if it will be necessary to return to the violent means which bore the Revolution and would be better to avoid because they are unfortunate; but if they be necessary, let none of us fail in our duty.

The audience shouted its approval, acclaiming universal suffrage.[15]

Then the Socialist Jean Jaurès rose to address the meeting. 'Bravo! Vive Jaurès! A bas le Sénat!' yelled the crowd. The enthusiasm of the audience was tremendous, reinforcing each sentence with applause. Jaurès described the two obstacles to constitutional revision: the President and the Senate. Radicals and Socialists, he said, must not settle for a concentration ministry; they must support only a ministry seeking [constitutional] revision. He concluded:

> This is not an empty demonstration this evening. It is not a casual exchange of impressions and indignations. It is the beginning of a serious and formidable battle. The battle may be long and tragic. Let us swear together: for the social Republic — in life and to the death!

'We swear it! We swear it!' responded the crowd.[16]

The meeting was noisy and agitated. One after another, leaders of the left came to the podium to say a few words, trying hard to make themselves heard. But the crowd was impatient and in no mood to listen to speeches. The speakers followed its mood. 'Citizen' Henri Turot (editor of the socialist newspaper *La Petite République*), one of the chairmen of the meeting, declared that it would be silly in the present circumstances to continue to talk platonically. 'The gathering,' he said, 'must take on its true character. It must be an imposing and energetic demonstration of the popular will. It is on the boulevards, in the streets, that we must make our war cry: "A bas le Sénat! Révision!"'[17]

Over the noise of the crowd the chairman tried to read a resolution to be voted on. But he could hardly be heard and the motion was perfunctorily approved as the crowd streamed out of the hall chanting 'Conspuez le Sénat! Révision!'[18]

The crowd intended to demonstrate on the Grands Boulevards, the broad street whose name changes every few blocks, which was the center of Paris theater and cafe life. But rows of police four deep barred the way

15. *Le Jour*, April 26, 1896; *L'Autorité*, April 26, 1896; *Le Matin*, April 25, 1896.
16. Archives de Police B^A 105 no. 69 (April 25, 1896); *L'Intransigeant*, April 26, 1896; *La Petite République*, April 24–26, 1896.
17. *L'Intransigeant*, April 26, 1896.
18. Archives de Police B^A 105 (April 25, 1896); *Le Jour*, April 25, 1896.

from rue de la Douane to the Grands Boulevards. Jaurès and the other deputies were permitted to pass through the ranks of the police, but the rest of the crowd was held back and forced to leave rue de la Douane at its far end, where it runs into quai Valmy along canal St. Martin.[19] Traveling on the streets past those blocked by *gardes républicains* with crossed bayonets, a column of about 2,000 demonstrators tried to reach Place de la République where the Grands Boulevards began. But at rue de Turbigo the demonstrators ran into another force of mounted *gardes*. Now several hundred police arrived from all sides and charged the demonstrators, viciously attacking all they could lay their hands on. It was then that Guerin, editor of the anti-semitic *Libre Parole*, was briefly taken into custody as he protested the brutality of the police. By that time most of the original crowd at the Tivoli Vaux-Hall had dispersed.[20]

Several small groups of young men did succeed in reaching the Grands Boulevards. About 11.30 p.m. a crowd of about 400 gathered in front of the offices of the *Intransigeant* and the *Petite République* at 144 rue de Montmartre, where they chanted 'Vive Rochefort! Vive Jaurès! A bas le Sénat!' At midnight they acclaimed Jaurès who greeted them from the second story balcony of the building. Then the police, with their diminutive chief Louis Lépine in his bowler hat giving the orders, charged and dispersed the crowd.

Another few hundred demonstrators reached the offices of Drumont's *Libre Parole* on boulevard Montmartre. They shouted, 'A bas le Sénat! Vive le Libre Parole! A bas les Juifs! Vive Drumont!' before being attacked and dispersed by the police, who made a few temporary arrests.[21] Then near midnight, about 300 demonstrators led by the deputy Coutant reached the offices of the *Journal des Débats* where they shouted 'A bas les Débats! A bas le Sénat!' for several minutes until they too were dispersed by the police.[22] By 1.00 a.m. calm had returned to the Grands Boulevards, with only several groups of police and gardes républicains remaining to patrol the area.

The Tivoli Vaux-Hall meeting and the demonstrations following it were the peak of popular protest after the fall of the Bourgeois cabinet. There had been no replay of 1848 or 1871. Before the protest meeting Socialist and Radical leaders had not called the Paris masses to violence. At the Tivoli Vaux-Hall meeting itself however, though Jaurès would later

---

19. *La Libre Parole*, April 25, 1896, p. 4; *Le Jour*, April 26, 1896.
20. *Le Gaulois*, April 25, 1896; *Le Jour*, April 26, 1896, p. 3; *La Libre Parole*, April 25, 26, 1896.
21. *Le Gaulois*, April 25, 1896; *La Libre Parole*, April 25, 1896.
22. *Le Gaulois*, April 25, 1896; *Journal des Débats*, April 26, 1896.

deny it, the excitement of the occasion had led to a 'call to the streets',[23] but the result was only several small demonstrations which were easily dispersed by the police. The end of the Radical ministry also inspired an anti-Senate demonstration by students in the Latin Quarter. Years later Joseph Paul-Boncour, a politician active in the twentieth century, would recall the period of the Bourgeois ministry as the only break in the doldrums in the Latin Quarter between the riots following the *Bal de Quatz-arts* of July 1893 (see chapter 6) and the excitement of the Dreyfus Affair in late 1897 and 1898.[24]

After Bourgeois's ministry left office an interesting debate took place between *Le Temps* and the ex-Finance Minister Paul Doumer. On 20 April, just before the Radical ministry departed, *Le Temps* reported that the public credit was weak, pointing as evidence to a decline of 1.5 francs in the price of the 3 per cent rente since Doumer announced the project for the impôt sur le revenu. Soon after Bourgeois resigned, *Le Temps* claimed that with the proposal of the income tax the Bourgeois ministry

> had declared war on capital and had sought to govern against it. Capital, however, had means which were as radical as they were simple with which to defend itself. These were abstention and flight. It had not failed to employ them in rather large measure.[25]

Writing in *Le Matin*, Doumer disagreed and argued that rather than declining, rentes had actually risen significantly during his term as Finance Minister. And yet, continued Doumer, 'with a disarming ignorance or impudence it is repeated that the Bourgeois ministry so alarmed the interests that the level of our state securities was gravely harmed.' He then pointed out that from 2 November 1895 when the Radical ministry took office, to 23 April 1896, when it departed, the 3 per cent rente rose from 99 francs 80 centimes to 102 francs. He affirmed that as Minister of Finance he had done all he could to defend the public credit and had obtained, moreover, the necessary help from bankers and establishments of credit.[26]

Le Temps soon replied to Doumer. The rente, it wrote, had declined 1.5 points from February, between the time the impôt was proposed as

23. *La Petite République*, April 24, 1896; *Le Temps*, April 26, 1896; May 1, 1896; John E. C. Bodley, *France*, 2nd edn., vol. II (New York: The MacMillan Co., 1900), p. 40.

24. *Le Voltaire*, April 28, 1896; *L'Intransigeant*, April 27, 1896.

25. 'Semaine financière', in *Le Temps*, April 20, 1896, p. 4; *Le Gaulois*, April 10, 1896; *Journal des Débats*, May 4, 1896; *Le Messager*, March 2, 1896; *Le Temps*, April 27, 1896.

26. *Le Matin*, May 15, 1896.

part of the 1897 budget and the date Bourgeois left office. Actually, neither *Le Temps* nor Doumer was entirely correct. In fact, the 3 per cent rente had dropped sharply not from the start of the ministry or the end of January when Doumer announced his proposal for an impôt sur le revenu, but from mid-March to mid-April during the 'Month of Crisis'. The ironic thing about the debate between Doumer and *Le Temps* was that it was the bourgeois newspaper which claimed the existence of what would later come to be known as a *mur d'argent* (wall of money), while the Radical finance minister who had been its victim denied it.[27]

The Chamber of 1893–98, Phase III: The Méline Ministry of the Right, April 1896 – June 1898

Jules Méline's 'homogeneous' Moderate cabinet came to office after Bourgeois's departure and remained in office until after the general elections of May 1898. Within six days after the installation of the new cabinet, the 3 per cent perpetual rente rose sharply by about 90 centimes. Clearly, French finance was pleased. Méline's ministry was supported by Catholics and 'reactionaries' of the far right who had refused to vote with the Moderate governments before the Bourgeois ministry. In fact, never before had a republican government been so accepting of and accepted by the deputies of the far right. The Radical ministry with 'socialist' tendencies had done more for 'la réaction', wrote the conservative *Le Gaulois*, than all the conservative opposition of the past 20 years.[28]

Méline's cabinet held office by the slimmest of margins. If it lost its majority, there was the likelihood that another Radical ministry in pursuit of the impôt might take its place. Méline relied on the support of the far right and on some of the Isambert group at the center of the Chambre. At first Isambert had held back his support, but soon his taking a vice-chairmanship in the Chamber in return for certain patronage favors signaled his acceptance of the Moderate cabinet.

Méline's main policy was resistance to 'socialism', by which was meant, in the context of the time, the impôt sur le revenu. His job was to hold the fort against any return of a Radical ministry. Questions which might have divided his coalition were purposely suppressed. Méline's majority included protectionists and free-traders. Disagreements concerning the proper relation between Church and State were left

27. 'Semaine financière,' *Le Temps*, May 18, 1896, p. 4.
28. François Goguel, *La Politique des partis sous la Troisième République* vol. I (Paris: Editions du Seuil, 1946), p. 73; Jacques Chastenet, *Histoire de la Troisième République*, vol. III: *La République triomphante, 1893–1906* (Paris: Hachette, 1955), p. 93; Jules Delafoss, in *Le Gaulois*, April 21, 1896; *Economiste Français*, May 2, 1896, p. 576; *Journal de l'Ain*, April 24, 1896, p. 3.

dormant; fiscal questions which would have divided the majority, such as a tax on rentes which had been proposed by the Moderate Finance Minister Georges Cochery, were purposely not raised in ways which would jeopardize the life of the cabinet. For if the cabinet fell, the way would be open for another dangerous adventure of a Radical ministry.

Other than staying in office, Méline attempted and accomplished little. Because his majority was so small, he could not afford to alienate any of his coalition. To please the Catholics he followed a somewhat pro-clerical policy with administrative decisions rather than legislation, for even reactionary Catholics realized it would be politically infeasible for Méline to offer them pro-clerical laws.[29]

One event which did occur during his tenure was the final approval and production of the 75mm rapid-fire field cannon. Georges Cochery, Méline's Finance Minister, decided to finance production of the new weapon with special loans guaranteed by the obsolete fortifications around Paris rather than ordinary bons du trésor. As it turned out, the prosperity which revived in mid-1896 increased the flow of tax revenues to the treasury and made it unnecessary to sell the fortifications.

While Méline was in office the Radicals concentrated on the issues of the impôt and the government's pro-clerical bias. On 7 July 1896, Doumer proposed the impôt sur le revenu from the floor of the Chamber; it was narrowly defeated by 283 votes to 254. Radicals continued to call for the impôt during the legislative recess in the summer of 1896, and in the autumn of 1896 Cavaignac again proposed the tax in the Chamber. This time it was defeated by 282 votes to 249.[30]

Moderates defended the Méline ministry against the charge that it was pro-clerical. *Le Temps* ridiculed the idea that Méline was at the mercy of the reactionaries and Catholics. Félix Roussel of the *Revue Politique et Parlementaire* wrote that Méline's opponents sought to exploit the terror which, he claimed, the least suspicion of clericalism inspired in the members of parliament. He claimed that the Radicals' cry of 'the clerical peril' only 'masked the poverty of their principles and their dearth of political ideals . . . Anticlericalism', Roussel wrote, 'was the last resource of the opposition; though it had once been an irresistible engine of war, it was exhausted for having been over used.'[31]

29. A. Salles, 'Les députés sortants (1893–1898); votes et groupements', *RPP*, XVI (April 10, 1898), p. 72; *RPP*, X (Nov. 1896), p. 475; *Journal des Débats*, June 11, 1896; *Le Gaulois*, May 4, 1896; Chastenet, *Histoire*, vol. III, p. 97.

30. A. Salles, 'Les députés sortants', p. 79.

31. Félix Roussel, 'Chronique politique intérieure,' *RPP*, X (Nov. 10, 1896), p. 471; A. Salles, 'Les députés sortants (1893–1898)', pp. 39–40; L. Arnaud, 'L'impôt sur le revenu appliqué à Verviers,' *RPP*, X (Nov. 10, 1896), p. 317; *Le Temps*, April 13, 1897, April 10, 1897.

Méline himself denied that his cabinet was pro-clerical and that he governed with the right. His program, he insisted, was clearly republican; the far right voted not for it, but against 'social revolution'. Whether the members of the extreme right would have agreed entirely with this explanation of their support is questionable.[32] In the early days of Méline's ministry Arthur Mayer, director of the far right *Le Gaulois*, had written in response to diehards such as Cassangnac of *Le Verité*, who wanted to refuse any alliance with the Moderates, that the Catholics should support the cabinet 'with pistols on their hips', that is, ready to depart if it went against their interests. Deputies of the far right understood that it would be unwise to cry from the rooftops that the Méline ministry owed its existence to their support. But, warned *Le Gaulois*, if Méline acted in a way that displeased the extreme right, his cabinet's days would be numbered.[33]

32. Félix Roussel, 'Chronique politique intérieure', *RPP*, IX (July 10, 1896), pp. 210–211; Ibid., X (Dec. 10, 1896), p. 700; Ibid., XII (May 10, 1897), p. 462; Ibid., XIV (Oct. 10, 1897), p. 224.
33. *Journal de l'Ain*, April 29, 1898.

−6−

The Threat of Revolution, 1893–98

To even a casual reader the French press of the mid-1890s reveals an unmistakable fear of revolution among the bourgeoisie. What was it they were afraid of? Was it feminism, anarchism, street riots, strikes by workers, or the election of Socialist deputies and city officials, all of which were labeled 'revolutionary'? How can the level of concern inspired by each be gauged? Obviously not simply by measuring the amount of space newspapers devoted to each; some 'revolutionary' movements and events were of more interest or longer duration than others. The seriousness with which the haute bourgeoisie viewed various threats can be gauged by the opinions expressed by bourgeois leaders themselves. These leaders made it clear which threats they feared could succeed and which could not.

Feminism and Socialist Electoral Successes

The feminist movement of the 1890s caused some concern. In April 1895 *Le Temps* worried that the international feminist congress to be held shortly in Paris 'might not be for the best because such occasions are the natural gathering places for revolutionary and eccentric elements.'[1] But bourgeois leaders expressed no concern that feminism threatened to destroy the social or economic order.

Nor, evidently, were they particularly worried by the election of Socialist deputies, mayors and municipal councils. As distasteful as they must have found such developments, bourgeois leaders in the 1890s did not mention them as a serious menace liable to overturn society. The reason is simple: of 576 deputies in the Chamber there were only about 50 Socialists and, given the fact that France was primarily an agricultural country where industrialization was progressing relatively slowly, not many more could be expected in the foreseeable future.

---

1. *Revue Politique et Parlementaire*, I (Sept. 1894), pp. 432–449; Marya Cheligia, 'Le mouvement feministe en France', *RPP*, XIV (Aug. 1897), pp. 271–284.

Anarchist Violence as a Revolutionary Menace

The rash of anarchist *attentats* (outrages) in the first half of the 1890s led some to call that period 'the Terror'. Bombs were the preferred weapon of anarchists who used them to express social protest and revolutionary rage, 'propaganda by the deed'. [2] Bourgeois newspapers such as *Le Temps*, *Le Journal des Débats* and *Le Gaulois* responded to each explosion with horror and indignation and innumerable columns of description and analysis. But did haut bourgeois leaders express fear that anarchist outrages might succeed in destroying their society? Clearly the answer was no.

The period from the winter of 1893 to the spring of 1894 was a season of attentats. In December Auguste Vaillant threw a bomb in the Chamber of Deputies which slightly wounded several spectators and deputies. In February 1894 several bombings shook Paris. In April the *Revue des Deux Mondes* reported an epidemic of anarchist bombings around Paris; at the elegant Fayot restaurant a bomb seriously wounded several patrons including the poet Laurent Tailhade who, a few months earlier, had publicly appreciated Vaillant's bomb as a 'noble deed'.

The crowning attentat occurred on 24 June 1894 when President of the Republic Sadi Carnot, riding in a carriage through a welcoming crowd in Lyon, was stabbed to death by a young Italian anarchist. The enormity of the act, the shock it engendered and its ultimate futility dampened inclinations toward violent 'propaganda of the deed'. After that, attentats became rare.[3]

Though anarchist outrages received extensive press coverage, observers noted that they failed to inspire deep or lasting fear. In the *Nouvelle Revue*, Senator Marcère wrote that the public was only fleetingly concerned with anarchist bombs, and in the liberal Catholic *Le Correspondant*, Louis Joubert noted 'the amazing carelessness' with which anarchists were regarded. 'Society', he wrote, 'forms a sort of spectators' gallery around those who wish to destroy it.'[4] Eugène-Melchior de Vogüé, diplomat and man of letters, compared the wave of attentats in France with a similar one which had swept Russia some fifteen

2. Alvan Francis Sanborn, *Paris and the Social Revolution* (Boston: Small, Maynard, 1905), p. 118. See the *Encyclopaedia Britannica*, 11th edn., vol. I, pp. 916–918, for a good discussion of the distinction between the common usage of the term 'anarchist' and its philosophical meaning.

3. Jacques Chastenet, *Histoire de la Troisième République*, vol III, *La République triomphante*, pp. 61, 63; Jean Maitron, *Histoire du mouvement anarchiste en France (1880–1914)* (Paris: Société Universitaire d'Edition et de Librairie, 1951), Chap. V.

4. Marcère, 'Chronique Politique', *Nouvelle Revue*, March 1, 1894; Louis Joubert, 'Chronique Politique', *Le Correspondant*, Jan. 10, 1894, p. 178. See also J. Cornély, *Le Gaulois*, Feb. 14, 1894.

years earlier. 'What had been observed in Russia then', he wrote, 'was witnessed now in Paris: apprehension, obsessions, bewilderment, a vaguely complicitory feeling among some, exasperated anger among others.' The talk in both countries, Vogüé wrote, included frightened or bantering questions about the bomb of the day, disastrous predictions or skeptical pleasantries, and discussions of the causes and remedies of the problem.[5]

Though the French were shocked by anarchist outrages, bourgeois leaders did not see them as threatening the stability of government or society. The experience of Russia, wrote Vogüé, had shown that formidable jolts of anarchist violence had not led to the great changes which many Russians and almost all of the foreign press had predicted for the country of the 'nihilists'. The attack of 'fever' had passed without killing the patient or even changing it. He expected the same would happen in France.[6]

The absence of hysteria with which France responded to the assassination of President Carnot was interpreted as proof of the Third Republic's solidity and viability. The quick, smooth transition to the presidency of Jean Casimir-Périer, wrote the financial chronicler of the *Nouvelle Revue*, illustrated France's stability and brought 'optimistic tendencies to all markets'. *Le Temps* wrote that the solidarity of the French after the murder of their President demonstrated to Europe and the whole world 'the degree to which the free institutions of France could stand up to the most terrible challenges.'[7]

Labor Conflict as a Revolutionary Threat

Some historians have suggested that labor conflict inspired bourgeois fear of revolution in the 1890s.[8] Labor conflict did trouble the bourgeoisie; between 1890 and 1895 the percentage of workers in France who were organized tripled from 5.6 to 14.8 per cent, and the country experienced serious waves of strikes. 1893 was a bad year for strikes, with about 3,000,000 work days lost on their account; in the autumn of 1893, a wave of major strikes swept the mines of the Nord and the Pas-de-Calais. These

5. Eugène-Melchior de Vogüé, 'Un regard en arrière – Les terroristes russes,' *Revue des Deux Mondes*, CXXII (March 1, 1894), p. 190.

6. Vogüé 'Les terroristes russes', p. 203. See also Francis Charmes, 'Chronique de la quinzaine', *Revue des Deux Mondes*, CXXII (April 15, 1894), p. 948.

7. Ch. Gehelle, 'Revue financière et économique', *Nouvelle Revue* (July 15, 1894), p. 428; André Daniel, *L'année politique, 1894* (Paris: Charpentier, 1955), p. iv; *Le Gaulois*, Feb. 14, 1894; *Le Temps*, June 27, 1894.

8. Sandford Elwitt, *The Third Republic Defended: Bourgeois Reform in France, 1880–1914* (Baton Rouge: Louisiana State University Press, 1986), pp. 3–4.

were reported extensively in the bourgeois press, which viewed them with real concern.

But, although the *Revue des Deux Mondes* worried that the strikes of 1893 were liable to have consequences more dangerous than the 1892 strike at Carmaux, it did not expect them to produce revolution or social collapse.[9] Even the conservative and excitable economist Paul Leroy-Beaulieu did not worry that labor strife seriously threatened the social or political order. 'France', he wrote 'is in a period of strikes', and he advised his readers not to be excessively frightened and lose their heads. From a man like Leroy-Beaulieu, who could make impassioned warnings about social perils when he felt they were appropriate, this was strong counsel against despair.[10]

Nor did the prospect of a general strike (*grève générale*) simultaneously against all employers really worry bourgeois leaders. In July 1893, when the government closed the Paris Labor Exchange (*Bourse du Travail*), *Le Temps* reported that citizen Briant (sic., probably Aristide Briand) advocated a general strike before a meeting of protesting workers who accepted his call and unanimously voted one. But the newspaper evidently was not much troubled by the threat; Briant's speech was that of a theoretician, *Le Temps* wrote, and relegated the story to page two. Two days later *Le Temps* explained why it was not excessively worried by the possibility of a general strike: 'This formidable machine of war', it wrote, 'was not yet ready to be applied effectively.' This new engine of social war which currently receives so much attention, continued the newspaper, was so deadly that it would render useless all means of defense, but 'the idea was not yet ready to be translated into action.'[11]

The Revolutionary Danger of Rioting in the Streets

To the French, the idea of revolution was inseparable from images of barricades and surging Paris crowds which marked the Revolutions of 1789, 1830 and 1848 and the Commune of 1871. In early July 1893 Paris was shaken by several days of rioting by students in the Latin Quarter

9. Vte. G. d'Avenel, 'Chronique de la quinzaine', *Revue des Deux Mondes*, CXIX (Oct. 1, 1893), p. 704; Alphonse de Calonne, 'La grève des mineurs dans le Nord de la France', *Revue des Deux Mondes*, CXX (Dec. 15, 1893), pp. 800, 820; Vte. G. d'Avenel, 'Chronique de la quinzaine', *Revue des Deux Mondes*, CXIX (Oct. 1, 1894), p. 706. See also Fonsèlme, 'Revue des questions ouvrieres', *RPP*, VIII (March 1896), p. 420, 428; Louis Joubert, 'Chronique Politique', *Le Correspondant*, CLXXIII (October 19, 1893), p. 149.

10. *Economiste Français*, April 29, 1893, p. 515; June 24, 1893, pp. 769–771; November 11, 1893, p. 610.

11. *Le Temps*, July 18, 1893, p. 2; 'Les députés socialistes et la grève générale', *Le Temps*, July 10, 1893, p. 1.

and workers at the Place de la République. These were the most serious civil disorders since the beginning of the Third Republic; yet, rather than seeing them as menaces which could overturn society, bourgeois leaders considered them as tests which revealed the essential strength of the Republic.

The student rioting in the Latin Quarter stemmed from the campaign against pornography and the corruption of morals launched the previous year by The League Against License in the Streets which produced a law against outrages to public morals, known informally as the 'Berenger law'.[12] The trouble in the Latin Quarter started on 1 July 1893 after the Correctional Tribunal of the Seine condemned for 'public outrages to modesty' and fined 100 francs each the organizer and entertainers at the university students' *bal des Qat'z-arts* where several female models 'displayed themselves in obscene costumes . . . while guided by no artistic sentiment.'[13]

The next day about 1,500 university students of various faculties rallied at the place de la Sorbonne to protest, 'in the name of art and liberty', the judgment of the Court.[14] Warned of the demonstration, the prefect of police had mobilized two of his central brigades, and no sooner had the students massed, with some beginning to cry 'Conspuez Berenger!' ('Down with Berenger') than the police charged and, with punches, kicks and sabre blows, put them to rout. In the course of the mélée an onlooker was accidently killed by a policeman. Students and much of the Paris press blamed the police for unnecessary brutality, insuring that trouble in the Latin Quarter would continue.[15]

Rioting continued for three days and nights with police and mounted municipal guards battling crowds of students and other demonstrators. By the time it was over the windows of the local police prefecture had been smashed, tree gratings and cobble stones had been torn up, buses and tramcars had been overturned and used as barricades and all the newspaper kiosks on boulevard Saint Michel from rue Racine to the Ille de la Cité had been torched. The scene, reported the newspaper *Le Matin*, was 'the very image of civil war or, sooner, anarchy.'[16]

No sooner did quiet come to the Latin Quarter than rioting commenced in the vicinity of the Place de la République, as a result of the

12. Victor Fournel, 'Les oeuvres et les hommes', *Le Correspondant*, CLXXII (July 10, 1893), p. 340.

13. *Le Matin*, July 1, 1893, p. 3.

14. *Le Matin*, July 2, 1893, p. 3; Paul Robiquet, 'La proposition de loi de M. Berenger sur la prostitution et les outrages aux bonnes moeurs', *Revue Politique et Parlementaire*, I (Aug. 1894), pp. 237–248.

15. *Le Matin*, July 3, 1893, p. 1.

16. *Le Matin*, July 4, 1893.

government's decision to close the Bourse du Travail which was located there. Critics had complained that although it had been established as a meeting place for all workers, unionized or not, the Bourse du Travail had been, with the knowledge and acceptance of the Paris municipal council, 'abandoned to the unions who ruled it as absolute masters', admitting or excluding whom they wished, making it a center for revolutionary agitation and a 'practical school for insurrection'. Recently the Bourse du Travail had been the focus of a rough conflict in which striking cab drivers had attacked others who continued to work.[17]

On 6 July Premier Dupuy announced that the Bourse du Travail would be closed the next day and moved about 20,000 troops into the city, thereby doubling the number normally in the capital. That evening a protest meeting at the place de la République led to overturned kiosks and smashed urinoirs.[18] When the government closed the Bourse du Travail on 7 July, Republican Guards, foot soldiers, dragoons and police guarded its approaches. This did not prevent several hundred protesters from gathering in the streets bordering the place de la République. The protestors extinguished street lamps, again smashed kiosks and public urinals, and burned several carriages and omnibuses. They also set fire to an underground gas main; fortunately, after battling the gas main fire for half an hour, fire fighters extinguished it before it could cause an explosion.[19] Before long troops moved in and dispersed the crowds from the area of the place de la République, thus ending the riots of 1893.

The July riots received heavy coverage in the press. *Le Gaulois*, *Le Figaro*, *Le Temps* and the other bourgeois newspapers devoted innumerable columns to them. From the amount of space the riots received and from the seriousness with which they were discussed, one might think that they were considered to be a grave threat to the social order. *Le Temps* noted how easily a lighthearted student demonstration could change character and become serious because 'in the street all is serious and all can become tragic'. It took only a cry, an injury, a provocative deed, an unintentional push for matters to become grave. 'What had started as a whimsical outing of students,' wrote *Le Temps*, 'had attracted revolutionary elements scattered about the city who took control of the movement and transformed it into a true riot.' The *Revue des Deux Mondes* wrote that the scene in the Latin Quarter had 'all the signs and symptoms of a commencing revolution.' Even the upper-class Jacobin *Le Voltaire*, which had opposed Senator Berenger's censorship campaign used the terms 'particularly alarming' and 'revolutionary condition' to describe the Latin

17. *Le Matin*, July 3, 1893.
18. *Le Matin*, July 6, 1893; *Le Temps*, July 6, 7, 8, 1893.
19. *Le Temps*, July 7, 1893, pp. 1–2; July 8, 1893, p. 2; July 9, 1893, p. 2.

Quarter on 4 July.[20]

Despite the hysterical tone of the press, bourgeois leaders stressed that early July's disturbances did not represent a serious threat to France's social or political order. In an article titled 'Riots and Governments', which addressed the European press and public, *Le Temps* affirmed its belief in the basic stability of the French Republic and complained that the European press too often looked at disorders in France with a magnifying glass while viewing similar events in other countries through the wide end of a telescope. It regretted that nearly a quarter-century of almost absolute calm in the streets had failed to discredit the idea that the established order in France was extremely unstable. The paper scolded the journalist of the London *Times* who had written of 'the eternal danger of mob rule in France' and had declared solemnly that 'no one even a little familiar with French history could ignore the fact that the present troubles could develop into a revolution.' It was inappropriate, wrote *Le Temps*, to cry 'revolution' when what had occurred was only a passing riot.[21]

Bourgeois analysts advanced two reasons why universal suffrage gave France great stability in the face of civil unrest. Because democratic government is elected by all the people and expresses the will of all the people, it has a maximum of legitimacy and moral force and could therefore use almost unlimited physical force to maintain order. Also because all political parties, even the most advanced, could play a role in the political arena, all political parties rejected recourse to brute force, whose use therefore was left solely to declassed and unconnected individuals.

In the *Revue des Deux Mondes* the comte d'Haussonville explained that a proletarian revolution 'in the streets' was not a serious danger in France. If such an insurrection did occur, he wrote, it would not be the first in history and cited revolts in antiquity, the Jacquerie and the Commune. These had never succeeded and they never would wrote Haussonville: society could be damaged in battle, but it would always triumph. He warned that if a proletarian uprising did occur, it would end 'par des chansons', for the new Lebel rifles could be used on the streets of Paris as they had already been employed at Fourmies (where French soldiers had killed ten strikers on 1 May 1891).[22]

20. *Le Temps*, July 15, 1893; *Le Gaulois*, July 4, 1893, pp. 1, 2; To *Le Correspondant* (CLXXII, July 10, 1893, p. 80) the 'barbarous scenes of rioting' of July 1893 were reminiscent of the Commune of 1871. See also *Le Voltaire*, July 4, 1893; G. d'Avenel, 'Chronique de la quinzaine', *Revue des Deux Mondes*, XCVIII (July 15, 1893), pp. 465–467; Marcère, 'Chronique Politique,' *Nouvelle Revue*, LXXXIII (July 15, 1893), pp. 431–432.

21. Ibid.; *Le Temps*, July 7, 1893. See also *Le Gaulois*, July 4, 1894, p. 2.

22. Le comte d'Haussonville, 'L'assistance par le travail, I', *Revue des Deux Mondes*, CXXII (March 1, 1894), p. 57.

Haut Bourgeois Fear of 'State Socialism' and 'Socialist Taxation'

French bourgeois of the 1890s believed that the most serious revolutionary menace was posed by the national government itself. Government, if it were dominated by the many of universal suffrage, could create state socialism (in which the State would produce all manner of goods and services) and a socialized society (in which private wealth would be leveled).[23]

Auguste Burdeau, the Moderate politician, warned that to continually inflate the role of the State would destroy what makes men inventive, enterprising and foresighted. An aggrandizing state, he warned, would reduce individuals to mediocrity in the realm of desires, ambitions, energy and talent. It would replace men motivated by their own interests with quasi-bureaucrats. Léon Say expressed the liberal view in the *Nouveau dictionnaire d'économie politique*: 'We know that the State, in taking for itself too big a portion of the wealth of its citizens; in excessively producing wealth in its own monopoly industries; in transferring too many expenditures from the private to the public sector, discourages the use of individual energy, obliterates the sense of personal responsibility, and leads inevitably to an unfortunate curtailment of the development of the national wealth . . .'[24]

The State budget was the focus of haut bourgeois fears of state socialism and a socialized society. How government spent money would reflect the degree of state socialism; how it taxed would reveal the extent to which it sought to 'socialize' society.

It is impossible to exaggerate the hauts bourgeois' estimation of the importance of the State budget. The budget was 'the driving force which moves the complex and heavy machinery of the modern state'. Violations of the rules of sound budget were the 'cause of great unhappiness for peoples' (including the French Revolution of 1789): 'Good politics is, above all, good finances.' 'The budget', wrote the academician and

23. E. Lavasseur, 'La dépopulation de la France: lettre à Marcel Fournier', *Revue Politique et Parlementaire*, XIV (Oct. 10, 1897), pp. 29–30. See also Léon Say, 'L'impôt sur la rente', *RPP*, IV (June 10, 1895), p. 403.

24. Auguste Burdeau, 'Notes sur le collectivisme', *RPP*, VI (Oct. 10, 1895), p. 3; Edmond Viley, 'Les causes morales et sociales du socialisme contemporaine', *RPP*, V (July 10, 1895), p. 3; Félix Roussel, 'La vie politique et parlementaire en France', *RPP*, VI (Oct. 10, 1895), p. 174; Léon Say and J. Chailley-Bert (eds), *Nouveau dictionnaire d'économie politique*, vol. I, (Paris: Guillauman & Cie, 1891), p. 1076. See also Maurice Hauriou, 'La limitation de l'état', *RPP*, VII (March 10, 1896), p. 557; Félix Roussel, 'La vie politique et parlementaire en France', *RPP*, II (Oct. 1894), p. 183; Joseph Reinach, 'Philosophie de l'assistance', *RPP*, VI (Nov. 10, 1895), p. 226; P.G.C. Jensen, 'Les retraites pour la viellesse au Danemark', *RPP*, VII (Jan. 10, 1896), p. 35.

politician Jules Simon, 'had always to be considered the principal concern of a legislature.'[25]

One way to limit 'state socialism' was to limit government spending. In the 1890s it was a commonplace of bourgeois opinion that the popularly elected legislature possessed an unlimited capacity to spend; that whatever money the government had available to spend, it would spend. Paul Leroy-Beaulieu, in his highly regarded book *The Modern State* (1890), presented the standard view: the only check on the politico-administrative machine of the State is the pressure of financial limitations, and budget deficits are the only curb which can check the ambitions and encroachments of the contemporary State.[26]

Long before the 1890s, Frenchmen had expressed the fear that a democratic government might enact confiscatory taxation. In *Democracy in America*, written in the 1830s, Alexis de Tocqueville had described the danger vividly:

> Let us now suppose that the legislative authority is vested in the lowest order [the situation of democracy]: there are two striking reasons which show that the tendency of expenditures [by government] will be to increase, not to diminish. As the great majority of those who create the laws have not taxable property, all the money that is spent for the community appears to be spent for their advantage, at no cost of their own; and those who have some little property readily find means of so regulating the taxes that they weigh upon the wealthy and profit the poor.

Tocqueville used the term 'poor' to refer to 'those persons who hold no property or those whose property is insufficient to exempt them from the necessity of working in order to procure a comfortable subsistence.'

> In countries in which the poor have the exclusive power of making the laws, no great economy of public expenditures ought to be expected; that expenditures will always be considerable, either because the taxes cannot weigh upon those who levy them, or because they are levied in such a manner as not to reach those poorer classes. In other words, the government of the democracy is the only one under which the power that votes the taxes escapes the payment of them.

25. Estang and Dubois, 'Budget', in Léon Say and Joseph Chailley-Bert, *Nouveau dictionnaire d'économie politique* vol. I (Paris: Guillauman & Cie, 1891–1892), pp. 233, 269; C. Cayle, 'Notes sur la décentralisation', *RPP*, X (Nov. 10, 1896), p. 376; Emmanuel Besson, 'Le control des finances de l'Etat, I', *RPP*, XI (Jan. 10, 1897), p. 96; Jules Simon, 'Le regime parlementaire en 1894', *RPP*, I (July 10, 1894), p. 11; Félix Roussel, 'La vie politique et parlementaire en France,' *RPP*, I (July 10, 1894), p. 103.

26. Paul Leroy-Beaulieu, *The Modern State in Relation to Society and the Individual* (London: Ivan Sonnenschein & Co., 1891), pp. 29–30. See also Boucard and Jèze, *Elements de la science des finances*, p. 289 and Joseph Caillaux, *Mes memoires*, vol. I (Paris: Plon, 1942), p. 185.

In vain it will be objected that the true interest of the people is to spare the fortunes of the rich, since they must suffer in the long run from the general impoverishment which will ensue . . .

May it not be added in perfect truth that in the countries in which they [the poor] possess the elective franchise [in those countries having universal male suffrage] they possess the sole power of making the laws? . . . Universal suffrage, therefore, in point of fact does invest the poor with the government of society.

The disastrous influence that popular authority may sometimes exercise upon the finances of state was clearly seen in some of the democratic republics of antiquity, in which the public treasure was exhausted in order to relieve indigent citizens or to supply games and theatrical amusements for the populace.[27]

What Tocqueville had described as the danger of democratic government threatened, to the way of thinking of the haute bourgeoisie, to become reality in the 1890s. Fear of confiscatory taxation among the haut bourgeois was long and deeply held. Thus when this group reacted against the threat of an impôt sur le revenu with terror and fury, they were responding not just to a current political problem but to a long-contemplated and deeply-impressed nightmare. When Radicals in the Chamber pushed for a tax on total income ranging from one to five per cent, hauts bourgeois warned that if such a tax were approved increasingly higher rates would be voted and the destruction of private wealth would ensue. Society would be leveled and the haute bourgeoisie destroyed. All France would suffer if its 'head', its brains, its organizing force, the haute bourgeoisie, ceased to exist.

Bourgeois leaders claimed that an impôt would violate almost all of Adam Smith's precepts for a sound system of taxation which were universally accepted by French financial experts in the 1890s. Smith had held that 'the subjects of a State must contribute to the support of government, as much as possible, in proportion to their capacities, which is to say in proportion to the income which they enjoy under the protection of the State.' Critics believed that the impôt would tax Frenchmen progressively, not proportionally.[28] (It should be remembered that, as proposed at the time, the impôt sur le revenu would not have been arithmetically progressive but only mildly graduated and would be only one tax in a generally regressive system, and would thereby help restore proportionality in taxation as a whole.)

Adam Smith had held that taxes should be fixed and not arbitrary.

27. Alexis de Tocqueville, *Democracy in America*, vol. I (New York: Vintage Books, 1957), pp. 221–223.

28. René Stourm, 'Impôt', *Nouveau dictionnaire*, vol. II, pp. 1–42; Paul Leroy-Beaulieu, *Traité de la science des finances*, I, 2nd edn. vol. I (Paris: Guillaumin & Cie, 1879), p. 139.

Opponents claimed that the evaluation of income by either State civil servants or locally elected committees would result in arbitrariness; if civil servants evaluated income they would tend to exaggerate values, and if local committees were employed assessments would be influenced by political and personal considerations.[29] Smith had held that taxes should be collected at the time and in the mode presumed to be most convenient for those who pay. Opponents claimed the impôt would be the least convenient of taxes, as it would require inquisitorial and vexatious methods to determine incomes. Whereas Prussians might be able to tolerate the investigations required for an effective impôt sur le revenu, such snooping was inimical to the mores of the French who deeply valued their privacy.[30]

Bourgeois leaders were confident that the dangers of feminism, electoral socialism, anarchism, labor strife and street violence could be dealt with effectively. The same could not be said about the threat of a Radical ministry seeking the 'revolutionary' impôt sur le revenu.

Opponents of the income tax often sought to rally public support by equating 'Jacobin socialism' which sought the impôt with the more vivid threats of labor conflict, socialism and anarchism that were reported extensively in the press. (Then, as today, articles about taxes and government finances did not make for the most exciting reading.) Thus the ex-deputy G. Levasseur warned that 'the socialists and the anarchists both aim to destroy the social structure', but then stated that 'the true, the greatest peril, is the financial ruin of France,'[31] and Georges Picot in his widely praised article and pamphlet 'The Battle Against Revolutionary Socialism', claimed that there was a close relationship between anarchism, socialism and Radicalism. Anarchist outrages, he argued, stemmed from Radical and Socialist propaganda. The Radicals, Picot wrote, were the 'opportunists' of socialism, hated capital, and wanted to spend heavily for all sorts of social welfare. 'The budget and taxes', he warned, 'would carry the weight of Radical schemes.'[32]

Haut bourgeois attacks on the impôt sur le revenu between 1893 and 1898 were intense and innumerable. In September 1893 Paul Leroy Beaulieu stated in his *Economiste Français* that he was not worried about

29. Paul Leroy-Beaulieu, *Traité de la science des finances*, vol. I, p. 139; Stourm, 'Impôt', vol. II, p. 6; Boucard and Jèze, *Eléménts de la science des finances*, p. 649.
30. Paul Leroy-Beaulieu, *Traité de la science des finances*, vol. I, p. 139; Stourm, 'Impôt', p. 6; Boucard and Jèze, *Eléménts de la science des finances*, p. 649.
31. G. Levasseur, *Anarchie et socialism – les partis et le gouvernement* (Paris: A. Charles, 1896), pp. 5, 11. See also Marcère, 'L'esprit nouveau', *Nouvelle Revue*, XCVIII (May 1, 1894), p. 21.
32. Georges Picot, 'La lutte contre le socialisme revolutionnaire', *RDM*, CXXXII (Dec. 1, 1895), pp. 561, 591, 598.

violent revolution; the real danger came from the parliament and lay in the ruination of good finances. The *Revue des Deux Mondes* wrote 'we reject the impôt sur le revenu with all our strength,' and the *Revue Politique et Parlementaire* consistently opposed the tax. Paul Lafitte of the *Revue Bleue*, one of the least conservative of Moderate political writers, rejected the 'progression' which was a key feature of the impôt.[33]

Though haut bourgeois Frenchmen differed as to what would be acceptable in taxation, the overwhelming majority agreed that the impôt sur le revenu was absolutely unacceptable. For example, whereas Léon Say opposed any taxation of State rentes on the grounds that to tax them would be an immoral partial abolition of the national debt, Ferdinand Faure argued that it would be fair to ask owners of rentes to pay taxes on their income just like any other Frenchman.[34] When Raymond Poincaré, the Moderate Finance Minister in the 1894 Dupuy cabinet, proposed a graduated inheritance tax, Paul Leroy-Beaulieu vigorously attacked it for introducing progression into the French tax system.[35] But all leaders of the haute bourgeoisie agreed that an impôt sur le revenu was absolutely unacceptable; it would be the gateway to 'Jacobin socialism' that would destroy their class and civilization as they knew it.[36]

To summarize, the haute bourgeoisie clearly feared revolution in the 1890s. But although articles about revolutionary 'movements' – anarchism and socialism – filled the columns of newspapers and were the subject of ordinary conversation, bourgeois leaders did not in the least fear that they could destroy government or society. Nor did 'revolutionary' events – particularly the anarchist bombings and rioting by students in the Latin Quarter and workers around the Bourse du Travail – threaten, in the view of bourgeois leaders, to overturn the social or political order. To the contrary, the government's ability to deal decisively with these challenges was taken as proof of the solidity of French society and its political institutions.

33. *Economiste Français*, Sept. 16, 1893, p. 354; Nov. 18, 1893, p. 641; 'Chronique Politique', *RDM*, CXXI (Feb. 1, 1894), p. 950; *RPP*, II (Oct. 1894), p. 121.
34. Say, 'L'impôt sur le rent', pp. 402, 422; Ferdinand Faure, 'L'impôt sur le rente', *RPP*, V (July 10, 1895), p. 47.
35. Paul Leroy-Beaulieu, *Economiste Français*, Nov. 23, 1895, pp. 665–667.
36. I have used the term 'impôt sur le revenu' rather than 'income tax' to help avoid confusion between the impôt proposed in the 1890s and the American income tax of our own day. Today's income tax is a tax on all workers. As the hauts bourgeois correctly understood, the impôt sur le revenu was tax on the wealthy. Keeping this distinction in mind should help avoid the mistake of underestimating the danger of the impôt in the opinion of the hauts bourgeois. Gordon Wright wrote that after the creation of the Waldeck-Rousseau ministry Radicals were 'no longer attracted to any social reform more drastic than the income tax . . .' (*France in Modern Times*, third edn., New York: W. W. Norton & Co., 1981, p. 264). In fact to the hauts bourgeois of the 1890s there *was* no reform more drastic than the income tax!

Yet to the hauts bourgeois of the 1890s the threat of revolution was not, as some have suggested, an imaginary 'red scare'. It was real and it was present. The danger of socialism in the 1890s was the danger of 'Jacobin socialism' embodied by the impôt sur le revenu. Sandford Elwitt, discussing the revolutionary threat against which the bourgeois subjects of his book *The Republic Defended—Bourgeois Reform in France, 1890–1914* were defending, wrote: 'Historians . . . will point out that nothing resembling revolution loomed on the horizon of fin-de-siècle France.'[37] But to the hauts bourgeois the impôt sur le revenu was the very essence of revolution. Without understanding this it is impossible to understand the history of France in the 1890s and after. Realizing that to the French bourgeois's way of thinking this was the danger of revolution will make clear what bourgeois leaders were doing to defend their society.

37. Sandford Elwitt, *The Third Republic Defended – Bourgeois Reform In France* (Baton Rouge: Louisianna State University Press, 1986) p. 297.

7

Bourgeois Social Defense, 1893–98

Bourgeois Paternalism

Faced with the threat of 'Jacobin socialism' posed by the Chamber of Deputies, bourgeois leaders of the 1890s sought to defend their class and society. The strategies they considered were meant both to block dangerous legislation and to enhance the moral legitimacy of the bourgeoisie as a *classe dirigeant*. Similar strategies had been considered for similar purposes in the past.

It is useful to survey the ideas for social defense put forward by the haut bourgeois leaders, even if most were not implemented. For one thing, the solutions proposed illuminate the nature of the problems perceived; for another, they reveal the values and ways of thinking of the haute bourgeoisie.

To win support for their plans, bourgeois leaders held dinners for several hundred members of their class at the luxurious Hôtel-Continental, at the place Vendome. By attending those dinners members of the haute bourgeoisie demonstrated their consciousness of class and of social role.

To the bourgeois way of thinking, the wealthy owed their position as a classe dirigeante to the service they provided society. During the Second Empire and early Third Republic, bourgeois moralists explained that the haute bourgeoisie had lost its ascendancy and the liberal regime it had favored (the July Monarchy) because it had failed to serve society adequately. This was similar to Tocqueville's idea that the nobility of the Old Regime had lost its privileged position because it had already ceased its social service. By moving off the land, the argument went, the nobility had deserted the rural masses, its natural charges, and had thereby forfeited its right to lead society. Now in the 1890s bourgeois leaders sought to improve the quality of their class's service to society.

In 1862, Maurice Block had advocated private undertakings to aid society's poorer classes. He reasoned that bourgeois leadership of society was attacked because the bourgeoisie had failed to exercise the responsibilities required of leaders of society. By aiding the poor, Block suggested, the class would gain prestige and social authority, undercut the support of socialism and limit government's activities, cost and need to tax.[1] Similarly in 1896, addressing the members of the *Unions de la Paix Sociale* (League for Social Peace), René Stourm put forward Tocqueville's dictum of 'the great law of work': classes have the influence which they merit, and those which desert their social duties are justly punished by the loss of their ascendancy.[2] Stourm addressed his bourgeois audience as 'social authorities to whom belong the political direction of the country' and noted that in the past (during the July Monarchy) the bourgeoisie 'had perhaps not sufficiently fulfilled its social duties.' He quoted Augustin Cochin's words of 1863: 'If the rich do not work [to serve society], they rob society because they are paid in advance . . . There are', continued Stourm, 'those who are rich, rich not only in material wealth which is secondary for us, but rich from the point of view of morality, rich from the point of view of intelligence and talent.' The members of the audience must have liked what Stourm said for they applauded him well. At the same time they were applauding themselves for being virtuous social servants and not simply rich exploiters.

Many of the bourgeois efforts at self-defense in the 1890s renewed the paternalism for which Frederic Le Play had been the leading advocate during the Second Empire and the early years of the Third Republic. Le Play had sought to alleviate what he described as 'the uneasiness and antagonism which since 1830 has invaded the workshops of the Occident' by improving the quality of bourgeois leadership. He wanted the bourgeois owners of business to re-establish 'reciprocal dependence' with workers by undertaking works of 'patronage'. The appropriate model for the leader of society, he held, was the father of a family. Le Play urged capitalists to act as fathers to their workers, and to be responsible for them beyond the financial obligations demanded of employers by the law. Bourgeois owners of business, he held, should serve as 'social authorities – individuals of exemplary private lives; persons who, among all races and under all social systems, demonstrate a marked tendency towards the good; who, by the example of their homes and their workshops and by their scrupulous practices of the Law of God and Customs of social peace, win the affection and respect of all around them.'[3]

During the Second Empire Le Play had founded the *Societé Internationale des Etudes Practiques d'Economie Sociale*, which aimed to promote the 'rapprochement of divided classes'. With the establishment

1. Maurice Block, *Dictionnaire général de la politique*, 2nd edn. (Paris: Emile Perrin, 1884).
2. René Stourm, 'Toast', *Reforme Sociale*, vol. II (July 1, 1896), p. 115.
3. Frederick Le Play, *La paix sociale après le desastre selon la pratique des peuples prospères* (Tours: Alfred Mame et fils, 1874), pp. 54, 131; Albert Gigot, 'Allocution', *Reforme Sociale*, VII (April 1, 1894), p. 536.

of popular representative government in 1870 Le Play intensified his efforts and founded the Unions de la Paix Sociale. He claimed that the tragedy of the Commune had resulted from the unresolved conflict between French labor and capital. Whatever the validity of this analysis (some would understand the Commune more as an expression of Parisian Jacobin nationalism than of labor conflict), he used the experience of it to promote his ideas. Because the French upper classes had failed to provide effective leadership of society, he claimed, the French people had lost their recognition of natural superiority. The solution was to restore an enlightened 'classe supérieur'.[4]

To enhance the moral authority of their class, bourgeois leaders of the 1890s revitalized their efforts at paternalism. Paul Leroy-Beaulieu, in his book *The Battle Against Socialism*, urged his fellow bourgeois to help the poor. 'Citizens', he wrote, 'must organize themselves against advancing socialism by demonstrating all its falseness and by founding organizations which could serve as obstacles to it.' As an example of what could be done he pointed to the privately promoted low-cost housing, inexpensive restaurants and places for the entertainment and instruction of workers in Lyon.[5]

Bourgeois writers in the 1890s recommended that the State do more to encourage private philanthropy. *The Revue Politique et Parlementaire* wanted the State to promote charity as an activity which respected property and individual liberty. The comte d'Haussonville wrote: 'It is no exaggeration to say that in the view of the State, private charity is today almost an enemy.' Joseph Reinach held that philanthropy in France was excessively limited by laws which controlled associations and taxed private donations; if there was more private charity, he argued, the State would have to spend less on assistance. Reinach praised the Catholic Church as an important vehicle for promoting charity and stated that despite its past shortcomings 'it would long remain the greatest moral force on Earth'.[6]

If charity was one means to aid the non-wealthy, a better way would be to help the poor help themselves. Accordingly bourgeois leaders favored *mutualité* (mutual insurance), associations for cooperative buying, savings banks and programs to promote the construction and

---

4. Le Play, *La paix sociale*, pp. 11–12, 56–60.
5. *Economiste Français*, April 18, 1896, pp. 491–492. Sandford Elwitt's *The Republic Defended – Bourgeois Reform in France, 1880–1914* (Baton Rouge: Louisiana State University Press, 1984) is the most complete study of bourgeois paternalism in the 1890s.
6. *Le Rentier*, Oct. 27, 1894, p. 53. See also Le comte d'Haussonville, 'L'assistance par le travail', *RDM*, CXXII (March 1, 1893), p. 57; Joseph Reinach, 'Philosophie de l'assistance,' *RPP*, VI (Nov. 10, 1895), pp. 214, 219, 224.

purchase of affordable housing. Established in the private sector, often under bourgeois leadership, self-help institutions would, it was hoped, give the less wealthy the means to improve their lives and provide for the future without burdening the State budget. The *Revue Politique et Parlementaire*, which favored government encouragement of mutualité and savings banks and approved of rural mutual aid societies through which citizens could promote their own welfare without turning to the government for aid, described mutualité as a 'union of material and moral interests which were too often pitted against each other by dangerous political ideas.'[7]

In 1894 the Unions de la Paix Sociale, which Le Play had founded in 1870, had about 1,700 members of whom about 500 lived in Paris. Participation in the provinces was concentrated in the areas of greatest commercial and industrial activity. Members included manufacturers, bankers, wholesalers, directors of mines and gas works, engineers, clergymen, lawyers, government officials, members of the *Institut* of France and professors at the University and the *grandes écoles*.[8] Through its meetings and publication of the twice monthly *Réform Sociale*, the Unions de la Paix Sociale sought to promote permanency of employment, savings associations for workers, affordable housing to be purchased by workers, labor rules to protect children and women and Sunday as a day of rest. The Unions also favored stronger local government and more economical national government.[9]

Expanding on the work of Le Play in the 1890s bourgeois leaders established the French Society for Inexpensive Housing (Société Française des Habitations à Bon Marché). The Society was based on the long-held though perhaps questionable belief that social alienation among the poor was due to inadequate housing; if housing were improved, morality of the poor would be improved and social stability would be enhanced.[10] The Society for Inexpensive Housing aimed to encourage private persons and local associations to build salubrious and affordable

---

7. Marcel Fournier, 'Notre programme', *RPP*, I (July 1894), p. 3; Haussonville, 'L'assistance par le travail', *RDM*, CXXIII (May 15, 1894), pp. 393–395; Reinach, 'Philosophie de l'assistance', pp. 220–221, 233, 231; J. Drake, 'La caisse nationale de prévoyance devant le parlement', *RPP*, II (Oct. 1894), p. 52; Louis de Goy, 'Nos sociétés rurales de secours mutuels', *RPP*, VI (Dec. 10, 1895), p. 453; Eugène Rochetin, 'Les assurances mutuelles ouvrières', *RPP*, VIII (April 10, 1896), p. 121; J. Drake, 'Un progrès à faire en matière de prévoyance sociale,' *RPP*, VIII (May 10, 1896), pp. 515–526.

8. *Réforme Sociale*, VII (Jan. 1, 1894), pp. 16–39.

9. Alèxis Delaire, 'Le programme d'action des Unions de la Paix', *Réforme Sociale*, I (June 15, 1881), pp. 396–400.

10. Jules Siegfried at dinner of the Société Française des Habitations à Bon Marché, Feb. 2, 1890, in the *Bulletin* of that society, 1890, p. 10.

housing and to arrange financing with which workers could purchase their own homes. The Society, led by Jules Siegfried, Doctor Rocard and Jules Simon, was located in the eighth arrondissement at 15 rue de la Ville-L'Evêque, the same address as the bourgeois political organization the Association Libérale Républicain (see below).[11] At the Society's inaugural dinner at the Hôtel-Continental, Georges Picot explained the relation between the new undertaking and the problem of socialism: 'In the midst of all the problems which confront the human condition, of all the worries which oppress us, of all the social questions which are so unhappy and obscure, the only one which offers the possibility of a sure solution with no socialistic dangers is the question of the improvement of housing . . . For those who possess capital, the improvement of housing should be the first and chief social obligation.'[12]

Another paternalistic undertaking of the hauts bourgeois was the *Musée Social*, founded in 1894 by the comte de Chambrun. Chambrun, whose fortune came from the Bacarat glass works, was described as one of those 'belonging to the highest classes, who devote their intelligence and activity to the search for solutions to preserve our society from new convulsions.'[13] Not a museum in the ordinary sense of the word, the Musée Social's purpose was to collect information about and promote paternalistic undertakings. The Musée Social was not the comte de Chambrun's only effort to promote social peace; previously he had established chairs for the teaching of 'social economy' (Le Play's answer to laissez faire political economy) at the Ecole Libre des Sciences Politiques and the Sorbonne.[14] In 1898, he would become honorary president of the newly founded 'Federation of Taxpayers Against the Impôt Sur le Revenu'.[15]

The Musée Social had its origin in the Social Economy display at the 1889 Paris Exposition. In reactivating it, Chambrun drew on the aid of Jules Siegfried, Jules Simon and Léon Say. On the board of directors of the Musée in 1898 were familiar names of the haut bourgeois public service elite.[16] At the inaugural dinner for the Musée Social at the Hôtel-

11. Société Française des Habitations a Bon Marché, *Bulletin*, 1890.
12. Ibid., p. 20.
13. *Le Soleil*, Oct. 16, 1897.
14. *La Famille*, March 21, 1898.
15. C. Kergall, *Le suicide de la République — l'impôt sur le revenu* (Paris: Fédération des contribuables, n.d. [1904]). (Marcère was President de la fédération).
16. Among them were Jules Siegfried, Charles Robert (member of the Conseil d'Etat, director of the Union Insurance Company), Emile Cheysson (inspector general of Bridges and Roads, former director of Le Creuzot steel works, professor at the School of Mines and the Ecole Libre des Sciences Politiques), Edouard Gruner (secretary of the Central Committee of Coal Mines), Jean-Honoré Audiffred (deputy and head of the Moderate

Continental, Jules Simon congratulated its founders who from the outset, he said, had rendered a considerable service to humanity. 'You have', he told them, 'refuted a prejudice which some have obstinately tried to spread – which is that the Republic has made many promises to the workers but that they have been only promises.'[17]

Léon Say also addressed the assembled diners. He expressed concern for industrial workers and praised the comte de Chambrun who, he said, 'understood that individual initiative was an untrammeled force for innovation which could achieve what the State, despite its power, could not accomplish.'[18]

Armand Peugeot's address on the same occasion expressed much of the bourgeoisie's conventional thinking about the 'social question'. Never, stated the great industrialist from Valentigney, had the need for good social institutions been so urgent. 'We are witnesses at this moment of a relentless battle between labor and capital, of lamentable strikes which harm the workers at least as much as the heads of industry. In seeing this distressing spectacle, one asks oneself if such antagonism can disappear, if there are grounds for conciliation. I do not hesitate to respond "yes" and need for evidence no more than the results obtained by the business establishments which have created social and paternal institutions.

'Observe what exists in great enterprises like le Creuzot, the mines of Anzin, the spinning works of Seydoux, Agache and Walther Seitz, the bleaching house of Thaoh, the printing works of Mame, Chaix and Colin, in our own factories at Valentigney and Herimoncourt, and in so many other establishments. The most varied sorts of schemes have been developed to ameliorate the conditions of workers in order to attach them to the factories by interest, solidarity and affection. Savings banks; funds for assistance, accidents, and retirement, profit sharing; bonuses; private hospitals; cooperative societies for the purchase of food; real estate societies. These institutions and others which are due to the initiative of employers, have been organized and function smoothly, everywhere reenforcing the lines between workers and those who direct them.

'The creators of these works have understood that to dry up the sources of the antagonism, it is necessary to interest workers in the prosperity of business. Workers and employers . . . cannot be enemies without soon verifying the famous words: "A house divided against itself will perish." It is this idea which penetrates the thought of employers, men who have

---

political campaign Association Nationale Républicaine), Albert Gigot, Georges Picot, and Emile Boutmy, founder and director of the Ecole Libre des Sciences Politiques (*Musée Social, Circulaire*, Serie B, no. 19, June 25, 1898, inside cover).
17. Musée sociale, *Inauguration*, March 25, 1895 (Paris: Calman Lévy, 1895), pp. 2, 3; *Le Matin*, March 26, 1898, p. 1.
18. Ibid., pp. 20, 21.

the heavy responsibility for the direction of businesses and workshops, who are able to make harmony reign between the different factors of production. It is thus that they are able to avoid battles and that peace and prosperity will replace conflict and all the misery which accompanies it.

'Elsewhere the heads of industry have understood this, especially where, accepting the responsibilities of their situations, they have taken the initiative for these beneficial works which have for their aim and result, the making of the personnel of the factory one large family where concord and union reign.'[19]

Bourgeois Efforts to Tame and Restrict the Power of Democratic Government

Forming an Administrative Elite

With the establishment of representative government after the fall of the Second Empire, bourgeois leaders faced the problem of how to defend against the potential danger posed by a powerful, centralized state which would probably be dominated by the many of universal suffrage. One approach was to make sure that the leaders of the State administration would be individuals who shared the values of the bourgeoisie. The other was to limit the power of the State by means of administrative decentralization.

Employing the first approach in 1872, Emile Boutmy founded the *Ecole Libre des Sciences Politiques*. He explained that with the end of the Second Empire the best service he could do for his country, which had just regained its liberties and democratic government, would be to organize an elite, a 'head of the nation', from which the new France would be able to recruit informed and devoted servants. In 1871 Boutmy described the problem faced by the bourgeoisie: 'The classes which have an acquired position and the leisure to cultivate their intellect, the classes which until now had held the preponderance of political power, are now menaced. They had established their first line of defense in the heights of birth and wealth; they had for this laws and customs. But the customs have been everywhere betrayed, the laws abandoned. The upper hereditary chamber has been abandoned in France [this was before the creation of the Senate in 1875]; elsewhere its prerogatives decline. The electoral property qualification has disappeared in France; in all the countries of Europe it tends to decline. The peasant excludes the great land owners, the descendant of old local aristocracy, from his municipal council. The worker considers it axiomatic that his vote be the contrary

19. Ibid., pp. 30, 31.

of his employer's. In this ruin of the exclusions which assured them power, in this decline of the sentiments which assured them moral influence, the classes which represent acquired situations seriously risk seeing themselves excluded from the *pays legal* from which the greatest number had been so long excluded. This would be excessive revenge, but it would leave me rather indifferent, if, in striking at men, it did not attack the vital conditions of all progressive societies; the empire of spirit and government by the best.'

It would be folly, Boutmy held, for those menaced to believe that they could use laws to maintain their position. 'Privilege', he wrote, 'is no more; the masses hesitate not at all.'[20]

Constrained to accept the electoral rights of the most numerous, those who call themselves the 'higher classes' could conserve political hegemony only by invoking the right of the most capable. It was necessary, wrote Boutmy, that behind the barrier of upper-class prerogatives and traditions the democratic flood runs into a second rampart made of 'striking and useful merits, of superiorities whose prestige impose themselves, of capacities which could not be bypassed without madness.'[21]

In 1872 Boutmy founded the Ecole Libre des Sciences Politiques (commonly referred to as Sciences Po) with the cooperation of well-known haut bourgeois leaders. Hippolyte Taine, a friend of Boutmy's, contributed with a long article in the *Journal des Débats*, and Guizot praised the school as an undertaking 'almost as difficult as it is necessary to accomplish.'[22] Boutmy's call for the creation of a new school of political science in the spring of 1871 was well received by haut bourgeois leaders and resulted in the formation of a *societé anonyme* of two hundred members who invested five hundred francs each.[23]

It was no accident that Boutmy and the bankers who provided the main financial backing for the new school were Protestants; Boutmy himself wrote that the Protestant religion, more than the Catholic, tended to give men the ability and taste for self-government. Protestantism, he stated,

20. *L'Ecole Libre des Sciences Politiques, 1871–1881* (pamphlet) (Paris: Typographie Georges Chamerot, 1889), pp. 11–13.
21. Ibid., pp. 12–13.
22. Pierre Rain, *L'Ecole Libre des Sciences Politiques* (Paris: Fondation Nationale des Sciences Politiques, 1963), pp. 14–15.
23. Among the school's strongest supporters were Edouard André (a Protestant banker who for many years would preside over its administrative council), Jacques and Jules Sigfried (enormously wealthy Protestant merchants of le Havre), P. Hely d'Oissel, Adolphe d'Eichthal (Protestant banker) and Emile Menier (Pierre Rain, *L'Ecole Libre des Sciences Politiques, 1871 – 1881*, Paris, Typographie George Chamarot, 1889, p. 16).

was the religion which suits a people born for action.[24]

Although the leadership of Sciences Po remained predominantly Protestant, the school was open to all members of the haute bourgeoisie. In a sense its mission may be understood to have been to help introduce the Catholic bourgeoisie to the art of self-government. Sciences Po welcomed both Catholic and Jewish students and faculty; on its staff, for example, were the Catholic Claudio-Jannet and the Jewish financier Raphael-Georges Lévy. In the 1890s, most of the faculty of the Ecole Libre des Sciences Politiques belonged to the Societé d'Economie Sociale founded by Le Play. Many were members of the Academy of Moral and Political Sciences, and its board of directors was comprised of illustrious leaders of the haute bourgeoisie.[25]

Sciences Po sought to avoid the excessive specialization which Boutmy believed characterized the education provided by the *grandes écoles* such as Ponts et Chausées and Polytechnique and the excessive theorizing of which he accused the University. As a private school, Sciences Po was able to choose its faculty and students and control its curriculum outside the influence of government; government which, in Boutmy's opinion, would likely be more and more dominated by the democratic masses. Teachers at Sciences Po would be drawn from the world of business and therefore avoid some of the anti-bourgeois tendencies of university professors. Students would generally be sons of the hauts bourgeois. Admission to Sciences Po would not be brutally competitive (as it was for the Ecole Normale Supérieure and Polytechnique) and would put a premium on the sorts of knowledge and training the sons of the wealthy acquired naturally in their upbringing. Because work would be at a gentlemanly pace, the school would serve to educate sons of the bourgeoisie who lacked the talent or inclination for hard work required for entry into the Ecole Normale Supérieure or Polytechnique.

By the 1890s, Sciences Po had reached maturity as an institution. With a high faculty-to-student ratio and a student enrolment of three to four hundred, it appears to have achieved Boutmy's aim of producing an administrative elite for the Republic. In 1896, Léon Aucoc, chairman of its administrative council, noted that more than seven thousand young

24. Among them were Hely d'Oissel, Emile Boutmy, Alfred André, Edouard Aynard, Jean Casimir-Périer, comte Chaptal, Griolet, L. de Sugur, Jacques Siegfried, C. de Varigny, and W. H. Waddington. The Improvement Committee in 1893 included the comte de Chambrun, Glasson, Claudio Jannet, Paul Leroy-Beaulieu, Georges Picot, A.Ribot, and Léon Say .(Ecole Libre des Sciences Politiques, *Année Scolaire, 1883–1894, Organisation et programme des courses* (Paris, E. Pichon, [1893], pp. 7–8)).

25. Emile Boutmy, *Essai d'une psychologie politique du peuple anglais aux XIXe siècle* (Paris: Librairie Armand Colin, 1901), p. 78.

men had passed through the school since its founding and that many of them occupied high positions in important branches of the State administration.[26]

Sciences Po came to have a near monopoly on filling the highest positions in government administration. Between 1900 and 1934, 113 of 117 appointments to the Conseil d'Etat, 202 of 211 *candidats reçu* by the Inspection des Finances and 246 of 280 of those who entered the Ministry of Foreign Affairs had attended Sciences Po.[27]

Administrative Decentralization

The Ecole Libre des Sciences Politiques was intended as a means of controlling the power of the central government by producing an administrative elite to run it. Administrative decentralization was intended to decrease the power of the central government, which the many of universal suffrage threatened to dominate. The 1890s witnessed intense bourgeois efforts to promote administrative decentralization.

The idea that administrative decentralization could help solve the problem of democracy was not new in France. In the 1830s, looking ahead to the coming of universal suffrage in France, Alexis de Tocqueville had viewed the United States as the country where 'the principal of the sovereignty of the people . . . spreads freely, and arrives without impediment at its most remote consequence.'[28] In *Democracy in America*, in the chapter on the 'Causes which Mitigate the Tyranny of the Majority in the United States', Tocqueville indicated the advantages of administrative decentralization as a means to limit the power of government. Whereas the United States did have a central government, he wrote, it did not have centralized administration:

'In America, with its weak central administration, the majority, which so frequently displays the tastes and propensities of a despot, is still destitute of the most perfect instruments of tyranny . . . The majority has become more and more absolute, but has not increased the prerogatives of the central government. However the predominant party in the nation may be carried away by its passions, however ardent it may be in the pursuit of its projects, it cannot oblige all the citizens to comply with its desires in the same manner and at the same time throughout the country. When the central government which represents the majority has issued a decree, it must entrust the execution of its will to agents over whom it

26. Rain, *Ecole Libre*, pp. 38, 49.
27. Rain, *Ecole Libre*, p. 90, quoting from the school's brochure for 1934–35.
28. Alexis de Tocqueville, *Democracy in America*, vol. I (New York: Vintage Books, 1957), p. 57.

frequently has no control and cannot perpetually direct. The townships, municipal bodies, and counties form so many concealed breakwaters which check or part the tide of popular determination. If an oppressive law were passed, liberty would still be protected by the mode of executing that law.'[29]

Administrative decentralization was advocated by bourgeois leaders in the 1890s as a means to defend against 'Jacobin socialism'. Decentralization, they reasoned, would counteract the tendency of the Chamber of Deputies to expand the functions of the State, increase its cost, and seek 'socialistic' taxes. Also, it was hoped, decentralization would stimulate conservative provincial elites to be more actively involved in local affairs and thereby regain for them some of the influence with the voters which they had lost to the professional politicians of the Third Republic. The idea of decentralization was not new to France; during the Second Empire liberal Orleanists had advocated it, and after the end of the Empire in the 1870s decentralization had been actively discussed and, as the historian Robert Gooch has written, its cause 'presented the most hopeful appearance in the course of its history'. But decentralization was not then realized.[30]

From 1890 the movement for administrative decentralization was revived. In 1890 several proposals for it were put forward, though none were acted upon. In 1891, *Le Temps* published a series of articles favoring decentralization by the rising Moderate politician Paul Deschanel. In early 1895 the Moderate Ribot ministry formed an extra-parliamentary committee on decentralization led by Minister of Commerce André Lebon.[31] But the most important effort in promoting such reform in the 1890s was the campaign of the League for Decentralization founded and led by Emile de Marcère, vice-president of the Senate and political chronicler for the *Nouvelle Revue*.

Marcère's understanding of the political situation was typical of the hauts bourgeois of the 1890s. By early 1893 he had warned against the danger of 'Jacobin socialism', which would 'show the people the state's power and wealth and tell them it was all theirs ... What tempting allurement', he wrote, 'for workers who do not sufficiently suppress their lusts.' Marcère proposed that conservatives and liberals join together to

---

29. Ibid., pp. 281–282.
30. René Waldeck-Rousseau, *Pour la République* (Paris: Charpentier, 1904), p. 298; R.K. Gooch, *Regionalism in France* (New York: The Century Company, 1931), p. 58.
31. *Le Temps*, Sept. 9, 1893; André Daniel, *L'année politique, 1894* (Paris: Librairie Charpentier, 1895), p. 369; Gooch, *Regionalism*, pp. 58–59; Paul Deschanel, *La décentralisation* (Paris: Berger-Levrault, 1895); France, Presidence du Conseil, *Resumée des travaux de la Commission extra-parlementaire de décentralisation, fevrier 1895 – juillet 1896* (1896).

defend their own interests and those of France.[32] He explained that socialism was distinguished by the suppression of the individual and his absorption by the State. The socialists were very clever, he wrote, and had prepared a dangerous tactic: they would seek to enlist as many as possible for the accomplishment of their wicked work. If they tried to despoil by taxation, they would extend the categories of exemption in a way as to increase their own clientele.[33]

In February 1894 Marcère wrote about the 'sad results of centralized power', and claimed that the sentiment of personal independence, which was closely related to the possession of local liberties and dear to the hearts of the well-born, was the great motive force for decentralization. Of all the tasks the Republic had to accomplish, he insisted, none was more necessary than administrative decentralization if France was not to become progressively weaker, going from tyranny to violence, from anarchy to caesarism.[34]

In May 1894, in line with conventional bourgeois thinking, Marcère warned that socialism was spreading and preparing an era of revolution in which France could perish. Economic questions mixed with violent passions presented themselves. Finances, he wrote, were the nerve of everything: credit, the state budget, taxes. In this area false and reckless ideas were developing which could promote the work of social dissolution favored by so many.[35] 'Socialists', he claimed, 'wanted to turn society upside down; they intended to proceed deliberately to level it and would use the tax to achieve their goals. If they had their way, the state would become the arbiter of wealth, the master of property.'[36] Marcère's solution to the problem was decentralization.

He began his campaign for decentralization in the spring of 1895. The *Nouvelle Revue*'s 'Political Chronicle' was dropped as a regular feature and replaced by a 'Chronicle of Decentralization' and 'The Provinces'. The aim of the new features was evidently to help remedy the situation criticized by Marcère, in which the provinces participated in politics only during election periods.[37] Typical of the *Nouvelle Revue*'s 'The Provinces' was an article entitled 'In Franche-Comté' which reported on a senatorial election in the departement of le Doubs and discussed the problem,

32. Marcère, 'Chronique Politique', *Nouvelle Revue*, LXXIV (March 15, 1893), p. 426.
33. Marcère, 'Chronique Politique', *Nouvelle Revue*, LXXIV (Oct. 1, 1893), pp. 438–440.
34. Marcère, 'Chronique Politique', *Nouvelle Revue*, LXXXVI (Feb. 1, 1894), pp. 658–659.
35. Marcère, 'L'esprit nouveau', *Nouvelle Revue*, LXXXVIII (May 1, 1894), p. 21.
36. Marcère, 'Chronique Politique', *Nouvelle Revue*, XCI (Dec. 15, 1894), p. 852.
37. Marcère, 'Chronique de la décentralisation', *Nouvelle Revue*, XCV (July 15, 1895), p. 380.

evidently of some local concern, of what should be done with a statue of Cardinal de Granvelle that stood in Besançon. Pieces such as these were both presented as evidence of the vitality of provincial sentiment and intended at the same time to stimulate that sentiment. Hopefully, they would help counteract the idea that the provinces were only the devoted servants of Paris with no political life of their own.[38]

In March 1895 Marcère founded the Ligue de la Décentralisation. At the time, *Le Temps* reported, propositions for administrative decentralization were coming from all sides.[39] The League's organizational meeting took place at the Grand-Hôtel in Paris; present were about 100 men connected with diverse factions of Parliament and the press. Marcère and Maurice Faure, the deputy who had called the participants together, presided. Secretaries for the evening were Mm. A. Arman de Caillavet (a Le Havre shipper and husband of Anatole France's mistress) and Gaston Guignard (a deputy from Maine et Loire). After an eloquent speech in which Marcère described the growth of the idea of decentralization in France, provisional statutes were adopted and a committee was named to elaborate a program of action and prepare for a national congress.[40]

Advocates of decentralization believed that it could win support across the political spectrum and thereby out-flank existing political divisions.[41] Thus Senator Marcère, a Moderate, was president of the League and Léon Bourgeois, leader of the Radicals in the Chamber of Deputies, was a vice-president. Promoters of decentralization sought to enlist the support of a broad spectrum of leading Frenchmen not directly involved in politics. In 1895 Paul Bourget, playwright and member of the French Academy, expressed his support for decentralization; the question he wrote was vital and of interest to all, even the most distant from political activity (as he described himself). He explained that he favored decentralization on social and artistic as well as political grounds.[42]

In July 1895 the *Revue Politique et Parlementaire* claimed that a broad ground-swell was building in favor of decentralization and that the press, 'usually more ready to follow than to lead, had made a chorus and sung

38. E.L. 'Les provinces – en Franche-Comté', *Nouvelle Revue*, XCVVII (Dec. 15, 1895), p. 831.
39. *Le Matin*, March 6, 8, 1895; *Le Temps*, March 5, 1895.
40. *Le Matin*, March 8, 1895.
41. Félix Roussel, 'La vie politique et parlementaire en France', *RPP*, VI (April 10, 1895), p. 180; 'Décentralisation', *Nouvelle Revue*, XCIX (April 1, 1896), p. 621; Henri Charriaut, *Enquête sur la décentralisation* (Paris: Nouvelle Revue Internationale, 1895), which shows a wide spectrum of political opinion regarding decentralization; *L'Autorité*, Jan. 27, 1896; *RPP*, IV (April 1895), p. 180.
42. Paul Bourget, 'Décentralisation' (1895), in *Etudes et Portraits*, vol. III (Paris: Plon Nourit, 1906).

in copious columns the merits' of such reform.[43] It was the subject of numerous books published in 1895.[44] Decentralization had wide support in the bourgeois press. The *Nouvelle Revue* led in promoting it. Paul Leroy-Beaulieu's *Economiste Français* favored it, claiming that it would counteract the Jacobin doctrine which was incarnated in centralization and would promote social solidarity by involving provincial elites in local administrative affairs. *Le Temps* gave extensive favorable coverage to the campaign for decentralization. The reactionary newspaper *L'Autorité* favored it, as did the *Revue Bleue* which saw it as a means of economizing on the cost of government.[45] The *Revue Politique et Parlementaire* devoted many pages to articles favorable to decentralization.[46]

In December 1895 Marcère reviewed the benefits of decentralization: 'By nature a democratic regime is extravagant and tends to multiply beyond measure the number of jobs in the public service.' Administrative centralization was 'a marvelous medium for developing the "microbe" of government spending.'[47] Decentralization would promote concord and more intimate union between all the members of 'the great French family' and help prevent the perils to which an excess of public spending exposed France.

The League claimed as its objective the substitution of a system of liberty, 'the very essence of democratic government, for the (Napoleonic) institutions of the year VIII which are its negations.' Wanting to give to local councils jurisdiction over all local matters and the budgets they would involve, it held that the proper role of the State was to make and execute laws concerning the army, the navy, diplomacy, public finances, justice, police and all that was of 'national interest'. Other functions would

43. A. Salles, 'Les conseils généraux et la décentralisation,' *RPP*, V (July 10, 1895), p. 101.

44. Among these books were *Decentralization* by Paul Deschanel; *Today and Tomorrow, Decentralization and Revision* by Leopold Marcellin; *Decentralization* by le comte de Lucay (based on lectures he had given at the Catholic Institute of Paris); and *A Proposal for Administrative Decentralization* by J. Ferrand.

45. Georges Michel, 'La décentralisation administrative,' *L'Economiste Français*, Aug. 3, 1895, pp. 142–143; *Le Temps*, Jan. 18, 1896, 'Un bon exemple', *Le Temps*, March 9, 1896, p. 2; 'Organisation politique et la décentralisation', *Le Temps*, June 20, 1897; Paul Lafitte, 'La politique', *Revue Bleue*, Aug 3, 1895, p. 129; *Le Matin*, May 8, 1896; *L'Autorité*, Jan. 27, 1896.

46. Maurice Hauriou, 'Décentralisation par les établissements public', *RPP*, IV (April 10, 1895), pp. 56, 57, 59; Marcère, 'Lettre sur la décentralisation', *RPP*, IV (April 10, 1895), pp. 1–5; Léon Aucoc, 'Les controverses sur la décentralisation administrative – étude historique, II', *RPP*, IV (May 10, 1895), pp. 227–254; Richard della Volta, 'La décentralisation et les finances des administrations locales en Italie', *RPP*, IV (Oct. 10,1895), p. 82; Maurice Hauriou, 'La limitation de l'état', *RPP*, VII (March 10, 1896), p. 559.

47. Marcère, 'Chronique de la décentralisation', *Nouvelle Revue*, XCVII (Dec. 15, 1895), pp. 831, 832; 'Décentralisation', *Nouvelle Revue*, XCIX (April 1, 1896), p. 621.

be reserved for local government. Thus, evidently, education and social welfare would be outside the concern of the central government and their costs eliminated from the national budget.[48]

The League intended to organize meetings in provincial cities and publish a bulletin on decentralization. Reflecting its strategy of promoting decentralization across lines of political division, the League's board of directors included a sprinkling of Radicals such as René Goblet and Léon Bourgeois as well as Moderates such as Senator Marcère, Paul Bourget, the comte de Lonjuinais, Georges Picot, Boudenoot, Denys Cochin, Jean Dupuy and Léon Say.[49]

Proposals to Reduce the Power of the Chamber of Deputies

Because the 'problem of democracy' arose as a result of the many coming to dominate the Chamber of Deputies, proposals were made to reduce the Chamber's power. In July 1894 Jules Simon argued that most of France's ills came from the Chamber of Deputies and proposed that the Senate should have a greater role in creating the budget.[50] Eugene d'Eichthal and Th. Ferneuil also recommended that the Senate's role should be strengthened to 'reestablish the balance between the public powers' which they claimed had been destroyed by an excess of 'parlementarisme' (power of the Chamber of Deputies).[51]

To reduce the relative power of the Chamber, Jules Simon proposed that the Conseil d'Etat's role in the legislative process be increased. Created by Napoleon I, the Conseil d'Etat had over the years served two functions. One was as high court in the system of administrative justice; the other was in drafting and implementing legislation. In periods of a strong executive (for example under the two Napoleons), its administrative function of drafting and implementing legislation was predominant. Under parliamentary regimes it had functioned primarily

48. Marcère, 'Chronique de la décentralisation', *Nouvelle Revue*, XCVII (Dec. 15, 1895), pp. 831–834; 'Chronique Politique,' *RPP*, VII (Jan. 1896), p.205. The stated aims of the League for Decentralization were to simplify and perfect the administrative machinery of the State without hurting the national prosperity; to realize considerable economies by reducing the number of administrative personnel; to promote freedom of association; to increase the powers of local assemblies in the management of their interests; and to develop private initiative and to encourage the flowering of all provincial artistic, literary, financial and political forces whose seeds exist but which were enervated by inaction.

49. *Le Messager*, Jan. 22, 1896, p. 3; *L'Autorité*, Jan. 1896; *Le Petit Temps*, Jan 18, 1896, p. 3.

50. Jules Simon, 'Le régime parlementaire en 1894', *RPP*, I (July 1894), pp. 7, 8, 11–12.

51. Th. Ferneuil, review of *Souveraineté du peuple et gouvernement* by E. d'Eichthal in *RPP*, IX (July 10, 1896), p. 177; *Economiste Français*, Feb. 9, 1893, p. 161.

as an administrative court. (Administrative law in France provided a means for private citizens to sue the State and thereby served to protect citizens from the power of government. Therefore as an administrative court the Conseil d'Etat helped limit the power of the State.)[52]

By the 1890s the Ecole Libre des Sciences Politiques had become almost the sole source of candidates to the Conseil d'Etat. Because *conseillers d'etat* were not responsible to an electorate and were carefully selected and trained in an educational system dominated by liberal hauts bourgeois, Simon believed that increasing the role of the Conseil d'Etat in the legislative process would serve to oppose the negative influence of Jacobin representatives of the 'many' on government.[53]

Some in the 1890s argued that the president of the Republic was an underdeveloped resource for defending against dangerous legislation. The idea of having the president of the Republic utilize more fully the powers nominally granted him by the Constitutional Laws of 1875 was a retreat from the weak-president precedent established in the *seize mai* crisis of 1877 which curbed the power of President MacMahon. Whereas at the time of the seize mai a 'strong' president stood in the way of haut bourgeois domination of government, in the 1890s, with the Chamber coming to have a Radical and Socialist majority, a strong president elected by the combined Chamber and Senate could help block 'dangerous' legislation coming from the Chamber.

One way to increase the power of the president of the Republic was to enhance his prerogative in choosing who would be invited to head a government. Another was to have the president (with the consent of the Senate) dissolve the Chamber in order to block dangerous legislation. In June 1895, several weeks after Jean Casimir-Périer had resigned as President of the Republic, the Moderate politician Ferdinand Dreyfus urged that the presidential powers provided for by the Constitutional Laws of 1875 be more fully utilized. The president of the Republic, he wrote, was almost a constitutional king of limited tenure and the power to call general elections conferred on him the power of a suspensive veto. That power, Dreyfus wrote, should be used to defend the 'vital interests of the country' against the 'caprices of universal suffrage'.[54] Suppose, asked Dreyfus, the legislature voted military service of six months (it was then

52. David Thomson, *Democracy in France Since 1870*, 4th edn. (New York; Oxford University Press, 1964), p. 99; Vincent Wright, 'L'épuration du Conseil d'Etat' (July 1879), *Revue d'Histoire Moderne et Contemporaine*, XIX (Oct.–Dec. 1972), p. 650.
53. Simon, 'Le régime parlementaire en 1894,' p. 13; 'Le Conseil d'Etat', *Journal des Débats*, Jan. 5, 1894.
54. Ferdinand Dreyfus, 'A propos de la présidence de la République', *RPP*, I (Aug. 1894), pp. 195–196.

three years), religious persecution, or a tax which was clearly inquisitorial. Would not the president of the Republic present a living barrier to preserve national independence, liberty of conscience and the inviolability of the hearth? In a menacing situation the president could provide at least a temporary safeguard, 'to permit a call to an intoxicated majority to sober up'.[55]

Proposals For Electoral Reform

Universal male suffrage was the source of the danger of 'Jacobin socialism'. Though bourgeois leaders dared not frontally attack this 'axiom of French political life,' in the 1890s some did make proposals intended to defang universal suffrage by 'organizing' the electorate and moving it a step away from the direct control of government.

In the 1870s Ernest Renan had discussed the danger of an 'unorganized electorate' in a regime of universal suffrage. In the 1890s this discussion was revived.[56] Charles Benoist pointed to the problem in his book *The Organization of Universal Suffrage* (first published in 1895 as a series of articles in the *Revue des Deux Mondes*). While a modern state must be based on universal suffrage, Benoist acknowledged, France had long attempted the impossible by trying to construct a State from 'ten million unstable grains of sand' (the voters of universal manhood suffrage) with no apparatus and no system to organize sub-groups of voters. With inorganic suffrage, he warned, 'class warfare threatens to become a chronic problem'.[57]

Raoul de la Grasserie recommended several stages of occupational representation in order to avoid the direct influence of atomized democratic voters on government. Maurice Hariou, a political theorist, proposed that individuals be represented politically as members of corporate groups; he suggested that 'positive society' be encouraged to organize itself, with complete liberty of association, into constituent groupings which would be represented in the legislature.[58]

---

55. Ibid., p. 108. See also Félix Roussel, 'La vie politique et parlementaire en France', *RPP*, III (Feb. 10, 1895), p. 371.

56. Th. Ferneil, 'Nos moeurs parlementaires d'après une étude recente', *RPP*, VI (Oct. 10, 1895), p. 135; Edmond Viley, 'Les causes morales et sociales du socialisme contemporaine', *RPP*, V (July 10, 1895), p. 6.

57. Charles Benoist, 'L'organisation du suffrage universel', *RDM*, CXXX (July 1895), pp. 2, 13, 24; Ibid., Aug. 1, 1896, pp. 540–541.

58. Raoul de la Grasserie, 'De la représentation professionelle', *RPP*, V (Aug. 10, 1895), p. 278; Maurice Hauriou, 'La limitation de d'état', *RPP*, VII (March 10, 1896), pp. 557–558. See also Th. Ferneuil, 'La crise de la souveraineté nationale et du suffrage universel', *Revue Bleue*, Dec. 7, 1895, p. 705; 'Un reforme urgente', *Revue Bleue*, Feb. 16, 1895, p. 193.

The compulsory vote was proposed in the 1890s, based on the presumption that widespread abstentions permitted an active and organized minority of voters to constitute an electoral majority and a real tyranny likely to have revolutionary consequences. The assumption underlying this way of thinking was that most of those who abstained from voting were satisfied with the status quo. Félix Moreau proposed the obligatory vote as a way to prevent 'tyranny by a minority', and Paul Lafitte claimed that the Chamber of Deputies as it was constituted in 1895 did not accurately reflect the sentiment of the country and that making voting compulsory would help remedy this.[59]

Bourgeois Efforts to Obscure Class Lines and Expand the Ostensible Ranks of the 'Bourgeoisie'

During the Second Empire some had argued that the haute bourgeoisie had lost the political dominance it had enjoyed under the July Monarchy because the class was too small to successfully resist pressures applied against it. Two approaches were proposed to deal with this problem. One was to argue that in the France of the Third Republic there was no bourgeoisie. The other was to claim that the bourgeoisie was a large and open class capable of including almost everyone.

Following the first strategy, A. Vavasseur equated class with caste and argued that because the Great Revolution had done away with hereditary castes there was no longer a bourgeois class. The 'classe bourgeoise,' he claimed, had disappeared, dissolved with the nobility and clergy in the Revolutionary crucible which made equal citizens of all Frenchmen. Vavasseur wrote that under the Restoration after Napoleon I and the July Monarchy of 1830 to 1848, the bourgeoisie had become an electoral caste of those who paid enough taxes to have the right to vote. But, he argued, with universal suffrage established by the Revolution of 1848 there were 'no more castes, no more ruling class: and if the bourgeoisie is still spoken of, it is by a habit of language which corresponds to no precise idea.'[60]

Reflecting this approach in the 1890s, the eminently bourgeois newspaper *Le Temps* rarely if ever used the word 'bourgeoisie' in its columns. Also reflecting an effort to deny the existence of the class was the difference between the articles on 'bourgeoisie' in the 1867 and 1900 editions of the Larousse *Encyclopedia*. The Larousse of 1867, published during the Second Empire, wrote at length of the class of rich capitalists

59. Félix Moreau, 'Le vote obligatoire', *RPP*, VI (Jan. 10, 1896), p. 39; Paul Lafitte, 'La crise du suffrage universel', *Revue Bleue*, (Dec. 7, 1895), p. 705; 'Un reforme urgente', *Revue Bleue*, (Feb. 16, 1895), p. 193.
60. A. Vavasseur, *Qu'est ce que la bourgeoisie?* (Paris: Albert Fontemoing, 1897), pp. 7, 10.

of nineteenth-century France. It defined the bourgeoisie as the wealthy who lived from the income of their capital, the 'feudality' of the modern financial, industrial and commercial sectors of the French economy. In the Larousse *Encyclopedia* of 1900, however, the 'bourgeoisie' was described benignly as the 'social category which includes persons of independent income, or those who earn a good livelihood and maintain a certain standard of living and style of life'. Whereas the 1867 Larousse article on the 'bourgeoisie' filled more than two large pages of small print, the 1900 article on the same subject covered only one-ninth of one page and was mostly devoted to a discussion of the bourgeoisie of the Old Regime.[61]

Though bourgeois Frenchmen might have wished that the name and public awareness of their class would disappear, it did not. Vavasseur acknowledged this when he wrote that then (in the 1890s), as always, it was the fashion to attack the bourgeoisie. 'Today', he wrote, 'it is invective and outrage which are used; the bourgeoisie is denounced to the indignation of the public. It is stigmatized for its greed, its egoism. For certain publications the denunciation of the bourgeoisie has become a daily cliche; menace follows insult: the day before the judgment day it will be subject to spoliation and death. The slogan of these publications is: "The bourgeoisie – there is the enemy."'[62]

The second strategy for dealing with the problem of the haute bourgeoisie being too small a minority of the total population was to ostensibly increase the size of the bourgeoisie and claim that the class was constantly expanding and open to whoever worked hard, planned ahead and saved. Following this approach, during the Second Empire Maurice Block had advised the bourgeoisie 'to enlarge its nucleus, to open its ranks', and in that way assimilate into itself those who did not yet belong to it. To achieve this, Block suggested, there could be no better means than to expand public education and favor the creation of the common wealth by the application of sound principals of political economy. By developing public education, he argued, the strata of society (*les couches sociales*) which did not yet participate in intellectual life and, as a result, 'contributed only confusion to the formation of public opinion', would lead 'the members of their contingent to the bourgeoisie and raise them above the narrowness of opinions inherent in private interests.'[63]

---

61. *Larousse du XXe Siecle*, vol. I (Paris: Larousse,[n.d.]), p. 818.
62. Vavasseur, *Qu'est ce que*, p. 1.
63. Maurice Block, *Dictionnaire général de la politique, deuxième edition, tirage de 1884* (Paris: Emile Perrin, 1884), p. 244.

The early decades of the Third Republic witnessed the development of a large number of *petit* and *moyen* 'bourgeois' who had certain interests and attributes in common with the true capitalistic bourgeoisie. Education was one means to expand the ranks of the so-called 'bourgeoisie'. Another was to increase the number of Frenchmen who owned the kinds of financial securities in which the hauts bourgeois invested their money. Under the Third Republic the number of owners of State rentes and popular securities such as railroad and utility shares increased greatly. Bourgeois publicists frequently pointed to the expansion in the number of French owners of securities to prove that property was undergoing a continuous process of division (*morcellement*). They claimed that French society was not composed of a small 'financial feudality' and a great mass of proletarians, but rather included a very large class of haut, moyen and petit bourgeois who shared common interests.

Among the publicists who stressed the supposed expansion of the bourgeoisie were Paul Leroy-Beaulieu and Alfred Neymarck. Neymarck, president of the Societé de Statistique and member of the Societé d'Economie Sociale, was a leader in this enterprise. In 1869 he founded *Le Rentier*, a political and financial journal costing six francs a year in the 1890s and addressed to a wide audience of savers. Over the years Neymarck frequently repeated the idea that the bourgeoisie was a large and expanding class; in a typical article, based on a paper he had presented in 1896 to the Statistical Society of Paris on the subject of 'The Distribution of Stocks and Shares', Neymarck explained that the 80 billion francs worth of French securities were divided into a tremendous number of titles whose incomes belonged to millions of small holders. 'There is no financial feudality,' he wrote; 'there is only a thrifty financial democracy . . . One can only affirm that there is no aristocracy of holders of shares . . .'[64] Also in 1896, Neymarck described the evolution of ownership of State rentes in the nineteenth century. In 1830, he stated, there were 125,000 owners of rentes, there were about 550,000 in 1869 and a minimum of two million in 1896, with an average income from their holdings of well under 400 francs.

Neymarck exaggerated the number of owners of rentes because his figures failed to take into account multiple holdings by individuals. Moreover, by stressing the relatively modest average income from rentes, he ignored the great difference between big and small holders. What bourgeois publicists such as Neymarck obscured was the fact that a small holder of rentes was not a bourgeois or 'rentier' in the classic sense, a wealthy person who could live on the income of his capital. By classifying as 'rentiers' all owners of rentes, Neymarck distorted the original meaning

64. *Le Rentier*, July 17, 1896.

of the term, blurred the dimensions of the bourgeoisie and sought to help protect a class whose small size contributed to its vulnerability.

Bourgeois Political Organization for Class Defense

From 1895 haut bourgeois leaders prepared for the general elections scheduled for the fall of 1897 (later postponed to spring 1898), thus continuing a practice established since the earliest years of the Third Republic.[65] The Union Libérale Républicaine and the Association Nationale Républicaine were the haute bourgeoisie's main campaign organizations.

The Union Libérale was founded in 1889 to oppose the Floquet ministry's proposal for general reform of all taxes and the efforts of the Radicals to limit the power of the President of the Republic and abolish the Senate.[66] In the early 1890s its leaders included Henri Barboux (a lawyer in the Court of Appeal, member of the French Academy and former president of the Society of Comparative Legislation), Léon Say and Georges Picot. By late 1894, facing the prospect of an homogeneous Radical ministry, the Union Libérale renewed its activity.

In a letter to its adherents dated 1 January 1895, Henri Barboux described the danger posed by 'the Radical party, strongly united, if not by the conformity of doctrines at least by the shared hate of all which supports moral authority in a civilized society and all which assures the reign of law . . .'[67] For the present, wrote Barboux, the Union would continue its vigorous six-month campaign to enlighten the public on current issues. (This campaign was led by Léon Say and Georges Picot.) Later, Barboux continued, it would help organize the electorate for the coming general elections.

In 'The Battle Against Revolutionary Socialism', published first as an article in the *Revue des Deux Mondes* and then as a pamphlet, Georges Picot expressed the thinking behind the Union Libérale: a political party was needed to oppose the combined Radical, Socialist and anarchist 'assault on society' which was the salient feature of the current political situation. The political party, Picot stated, would be a 'conservative party' of men of goodwill concerned with the suffering of others and not just an organization to protect menaced wealth. In a democratic regime, he

65. Sandford Elwitt, *The Making of the Third Republic – Class and Politics in France, 1868–1884* (Baton Rouge: Louisiana State University Press, 1975).
66. Marcel Fournier, 'L'organisation du parti progressiste', *RPP*, XIII (Nov. 10, 1897), pp. 237, 238.
67. Comité de l'Union Libérale Républicaine, 'Lettre du comité de l'Union Libérale Républicaine a ses adhérents, Sancère 1895', signed Henri Barboux (Paris: Jan. 1, 1895), pp. 2, 6.

explained, guarantees rest not on the varying tendencies of ephemeral cabinets but on the organization of solidly established parties which serve the needs of the nation.[68]

From December 1895 the Union Libérale issued a weekly *Correspondance Politique*, which it distributed to newspapers throughout France. Its purpose was to provide provincial newspapers with articles and editorials to be reprinted without attribution. The new *Correspondance* drew an angry reaction from the directors of the *Correspondance Républicaine*, a bi-weekly Radical publication which was also directed to the provincial press as a source of articles to be reprinted. The directors of the *Correspondance Républicaine* warned their readers that there had recently appeared under the title of 'Correspondance' a publication in all aspects of its appearance – paper, format, typeface and make-up – identical to their own and which addressed itself to republican newspapers of the *départements*. They warned their subscribers that 'the new forgery could create a distressing confusion' and reserved the right to establish in court its fraudulent character.[69]

At a banquet held at the Hôtel Continental in January 1896, the leaders of the Union Libérale sought to mobilize their adherents. Georges Picot and Léon Say attacked Léon Bourgeois's Radical ministry then in office, and called for the end 'to the discouragement which afflicts French society' and for action to elect a liberal majority in the next general elections.[70] By March 1896 the Union Libérale had announced a broad-ranging program which included political lectures in the départements by leaders such as Paul Leroy-Beaulieu, Georges Picot, Léon Say, Yves Guyot and Félix Roussel, publication of the *Correspondance Politique* to provide articles to provincial newspapers, creation of local committees, distribution of publications and brochures for the masses, support of liberal republican candidates to parliament, and publication of a monthly bulletin to be sent to its supporters.[71]

The other important political campaign organization of the haute bourgeoisie in the mid-1890s was the Association Nationale Républicaine organized in 1888 from the fusion of the Association Républicaine du

68. Georges Picot, 'La lutte contre le socialisme révolutionnaire', *RDM*, CXXXII (Dec. 1, 1895), pp. 591, 617–618, 620.
69. *La Correspondance Républicaine*, Jan. 16, 1896, signed Alph Bertrand, the director of *La Correspondance Républicaine* and E. Stahl, it administrator. *La Correspondance Républicaine* was founded in 1871 under the auspices of the 'republican left' of the National Assembly. Its office was at 28 rue de Varenne, Paris, and it was issued Monday and Thursday. See also *Journal des Débats*, April 20, 1896.
70. *Le Messager*, Jan. 15, 1896, p. 3; *L'Avant bourse*, Jan 15, 1896; *Le Matin*, Jan. 15, 1896, p. 2.
71. *Le Journal des Débats*, April 20, 1896, p. 2.

Centenaire de la Revolution (created for the occasion of the Exposition of 1889) and the Comité National Républicain (founded in 1887). Active in the general elections of 1889 against the combined monarchist-Boulangist challenge to Opportunist dominance, it had distributed through its members, local committees, newspapers and candidates nearly 2 million brochures representing about 20 different titles.[72]

Between 1889 and 1894 Maurice Rouvier and Jules Ferry led the Association; in 1894, Jean-Honoré Audiffred, deputy from the Loire, became its president. By 1896 the organization showed signs of renewed activity. In May it began to publish a *Bulletin Correspondance* which provided provincial newspapers with articles and editorials for re-publication without attribution. (In return the more than 800 newspapers which received it by 1897 were requested to make an 'exchange service' with René Salles, the director of the *Bulletin Correspondance*.[73] Presumably this 'exchange service' helped provide the Association Nationale Républicaine with a detailed picture of political conditions throughout France.)

Bourgeois Self-Fortification: Improving the Quality of Bourgeois Youth

Faced with what they perceived as a challenge by the many, bourgeois leaders of the 1890s sought to defend their class by improving its quality as a *classe dirigeante*. One way of doing so was to promote paternalism; another was by attempting to overcome what appeared to be serious deficiencies of bourgeois youth.

It was normal in France for the older generation of bourgeois to have doubts about the adequacy of the youth to fill their shoes, but in the 1890s the problem seemed particularly acute. In the opinion of those attuned to such matters, educated youth suffered from 'moral phylloxera,' from neuroses (*nevrosité*) and atrophied wills. Youths were considered to be rebellious and contemptuous of authority.[74] *Lycéens*, it was said, manifested a 'mad aspiration toward a free life, a scorn of all authority,

72. Among the pamphlets distributed in 1889 were *Boulanger as Soldier, The Caesarian League, The Political Comedy – Assault of the Pretendants, The Educational Achievements of the Republic, The Finances of the Republic, Agriculture and the Republic, The New Colonies of the French Republic* and *The Trial of General Boulanger Before the High Court* (*Le Petit Moniteur Universel*, March 9, 1896; Felix Roussel, 'Chronique politique intérieure,' *RPP*, VII, (Feb. 10, 1896), p. 415).
73. *Bulletin Mensuel de l'Association Nationale Républicaine*, Feb. 1896; *Le Petit Moniteur Universel*, May 5, 1896; *Bulletin Correspondance de l'Association Nationale Républicaine*, March 11, 1903.
74. Edouard Maneuvrier, *L'Education de la bourgeoisie sous la République* (Paris: Librairie Leopold Cerf, 1888), p. 8.

an unhealthy aspiration of the oppressed being who ardently desires to escape his oppression.' These scorners of authority, it was feared, would themselves be unable to exercise authority.[75]

Those who said that French youth suffered from weakness of will (*volonté*) had a fairly clear idea of what they meant. They conceived of the 'will' as a human faculty comparable to the 'mind.' If the mind is the faculty of understanding, the volonté is the faculty of doing. One's 'will' might be strong or weak, healthy or diseased. A sound 'will' was considered an adjunct to a good 'mind'; both were essential for proper action and success in life.

By the 1890s the idea that the volonté could be unhealthy was well established in France. Théodule Ribot, professor of comparative and experimental psychology at the College de France, had published *The Diseases of the Will* in 1884. A small book which would be popular in the years after its publication, *Diseases of the Will* described healthy and morbid states of the volonté. 'To will', Ribot wrote, 'is to act . . . volition is a transition to action,' the normal volonté is able 'to choose in order to act'. Ribot discussed 'abnormalities of the will' (conditions in which defective and irresistible impulses impaired the will), 'caprices of the will' and the 'extinction of the will'.[76]

Bourgeois youth appeared to have adopted anti-bourgeois values expressed in fin-de-siècle entertainments and literature. The literary hero of the fin-de-siècle was 'anti-bourgeois' in the sense of being opposed to 'bourgeois values' of discipline and hard work, simplicity in dress, moderation in the expression of the passions, willingness to delay satisfactions, and concern more with doing than with experiencing sensations and displaying the self. Anti-bourgeois themes were expressed in the entertainments, styles and activities of the bourgeois themselves. Members of the upper classes were depicted in fin-de-siècle literature as over-refined, over civilized hot-house varieties either incapable of action or drawn to all manner of bizarre behavior. Heros of literature were described as having substituted dilettantism for action, as powerless and incapable of defending their civilization, as bored, passive, dandyish and lacking in will. Some used drugs, opium, hashish and morphine. Male and female roles and traits were blurred and confused. In short, the subjects of fin-de-siècle literature could be understood to suffer from deficiencies of the will.

Contributing to the pessimism of the fin-de-siècle (and perhaps the

75. Ibid., pp. 63, 64, 66, 68.
76. Théophile Ribot, *The Diseases of the Will*, authorized translation from the 8th French edn., 4th enlarged English edition (Chicago: Open Court Publishing Company, 1915), pp. 27, 28, 86, chap. V.

fundamental cause of it) was the long-term decline in domestic interest rates in France from about 5 per cent in 1870 to 3 per cent in the 1890s. Paul Leroy-Beaulieu observed that this decline was a profound change, 'the greatest of social changes, which would gradually produce more important effects in Europe especially on her middle and upper classes.' The situation of capitalists and rentiers, he wrote, 'is gravely threatened by the gradual decline [since 1870] in the income from capital.' As understood by thinkers such as Paul Leroy-Beaulieu, the decline in French rates was the result of the decline in the demand for capital which resulted from a 'natural law of civilization' whereby low interest rates were taken as a sign of advanced development.

The great economic expansion of 1820–70 and especially that of 1845–65, Leroy-Beaulieu held, was an exceptional and completely transitory era during which man had transformed all means of commerce and industry, producing more change in those twenty years than in the previous twenty centuries. By the 1870s, he continued, France had built her great capital ventures – her canals and railways – and barring an enormously destructive European war, there was simply no fresh area for major investment within the country to stimulate the economy and increase the demand for money. Leroy-Beaulieu argued that between 1850 and 1875 interest rates in France had been kept artificially high due to the great capital consumption of the American Civil War of 1860 to 1865, the Austro-Prussian war of 1866 and the Franco-Prussian war of 1870–71. As a result, the natural and inevitable decline in interest rates had been postponed until after 1870.[77]

Adam Smith had observed that a stagnant economy produces low wage rates, low interest rates and a melancholy mood in all strata of society; hence France's fin-de-siècle pessimism. He had also observed that a stagnant economy tends to produce a static level of population; hence France's population problem in relation to Germany's, which led Jacques Bertillon to warn in 1897: 'In fourteen years Germany will have twice as many conscripts as France. Then this people which hates us will devour us. The Germans say it, print it, and will do it.'

Pessimism in the fin-de-siècle was not limited to characters in novels. A writer in the *Nouvelle Revue* observed that: 'the modern soul is exhausted, tormented, anxious. Disappointed by sciences, deceived by philosophy, irritated by literature, it feels profoundly unhappy and troubled . . . The man of our time deliberately damns existence, he lives

---

77. Paul Leroy-Beaulieu, *Traité théorique et pratique d'économie politique*, vol. IV (Paris: Guillaumin, 1896), pp. 140ff., 223. See also Gaston Saugrain, *La baisse de taux de l'intérêt; causes et conséquences* (Paris: Larose, 1896); Clement Jugler, *La baisse de taux de l'intérêt* (Paris: Imp. de Chaix [1892]).

without acting, he submits without murmur to inexorable necessity, his ideal is nothingness.'[78]

Educated youth was the segment of the population most effected by the pessimistic mood of the fin-de-siècle and most effected by the power of pessimism to corrode the will and the ability to act.

Concern with the problem of action was expressed in the graduation addresses to lycéens in 1894. At Lycée Lakanal, Ferdinand Brunetière of the *Revue des Deux Mondes* spoke of 'the need for action which is the very law of humanity'. At Charlemagne, the illustrious author and critic Jules Lemaître criticized the 'amiable dilettantism, witty or morbid, of the present generation' and attacked the egoism which would lead one to sit comfortably in a corner with two or three friends and ignore the rest of the world. At Lycée Juilly, Ollé Laprune, the eminent lecturer at the Ecole Normale Supérieure, proclaimed 'the duty to act, a duty more imperious than ever in the troubled times in which we live'.[79]

Concern with willing and acting did not stop with lycée commencement speeches by famous men; books were also written. In *L'Action*, a long philosophical work, Maurice Blondel[80] described 'the state of spirit well known among aesthetes who delight in their own dreams, love illusion, say that all is illusion and resign themselves to accept only what is given them . . . sacrificing action — some to science, some to art but removing all value from art and science because they see uncertainty or nothingness as the end of each.'[81] Blondel sought to counteract this mood with philosophical and metaphysical reasons for action. He claimed that action is 'a call and an echo of the infinite from which it comes and to which it goes.'[82]

Educated youth's rebelliousness and weakness of will was commonly blamed on the French system of secondary education. Critics of secondary education in the 1890s worried that lycées over-developed the minds of students, stuffing them with information aimed at passing the examinations for the baccalaureate and entrance to the grandes écoles, and did not sufficiently develop their wills and their capacity for action. Critics claimed that French lycées relied excessively on external constraints and, as a result, produced young men deficient in internal

78. Paul Bourley, 'L'evolution morale contemporaine', *Nouvelle Revue*, LXXXVI (Jan. 15, 1894), pp. 62, 68.

79. *Le Correspondant*, CXL (Aug. 25, 1894), pp. 823–826; Ferdinand Brunetière, review of *L'education de la volonté* by Jules Payot, *RDM*, CXXI (Jan. 1, 1894), p. 238.

80. Maurice Blondel, *L'action, essai d'une critique de la vie et d'une science de la pratique* (Paris: F. Alcan, 1893).

81. Henri Joly, 'L'action, le caractère et la volonté', *Le Correspondant*, 140 (July 25, 1894), p. 245; J. Angot des Rotours, 'Vouloir et Agir,' *Réforme Sociale*, VII (April 1, 1894), pp. 532, 533.

82. Angot des Rotours, 'Vouloir et Agir', p. 533.

discipline.[83] According to Edouard Maneuvrier, lycées provided insufficient moral education appropriate for citizens, resulting in the destruction of initiative, energy and the spirit of duty. Writing in 1899, the eminent French educator Octave Gréard described the milieu of the lycées as poor for the development of character; a dry, inflexible rule, he wrote, broke the spirits of youth and bent them under a yoke, and a formal discipline enveloped the student in a network of prohibitions which at once irritated and annihilated his will.[84]

Reformers in the 1890s put forth numerous proposals for improving secondary education, and looked to England for their model. Discussing the current polemic on educational reform in 1898, Gréard observed that the French had long had their eyes fixed on Germany but now they turned toward England. English 'public schools' (actually private and very expensive) such as Harrow, Eton, and Rugby provided the models for physical and moral education. Sports and the tutorial system summarized the reforms to be pursued.[85]

Edouard Maneuvrier was one of those who advocated the English approach in educating the sons of the bourgeoisie. In *The Education of the Bourgeoisie Under the Republic* he wrote 'it is the bourgeoisie which governs France', and proposed how members of the class should be educated so they would be prepared for living in a democracy. He explained the need for educational reform in terms of class defense. The bourgeoisie, Maneuvrier observed, was beginning to be afraid; some educated young men were among those who spoke of destroying the bourgeoisie, of 'pasting them to the wall'. Each day in the press, in public meetings, even in the assemblies of parliament, he wrote, the masses were being taught to confuse equality with leveling.[86] Maneuvrier proposed his educational reforms in the belief that there would be a social question as long as there were people who were poor and miserable. 'All the disinherited,' he wrote, 'ceaselessly tossing about on their bed of unhappiness, would be instruments and victims of mad or ambitious leaders who would promise them the end of their troubles and call on them to create, by iron and fire, a new order in which they would be the masters.'[87]

Maneuvrier claimed that the French system of education was suitable for an aristocracy but not a democracy. The bourgeoisie, he claimed, had

83. Maneuvrier, *L'éducation*, pp. 8, 64–68.
84. O. Gréard, 'De l'éducation morale et physique dans les lycées,' *Revue Bleue*, (July 20, 1889), p. 66.
85. Ibid., pp. 68–69; Max Leclerc, *L'éducation des classes moyennes et dirigeantes en Angleterre* vol. I (Paris: A. Colin , 1894), pp. 33–40.
86. Maneuvrier, *L'éducation*, pp. 5, 7.
87. Ibid., p. 383.

only one way to escape the worst destiny and that was to take courage and reform itself by education so that it would merit authority by meriting respect. He proposed to help the young 'understand, will and act' (*comprendre, vouloir et agir*) and recommended that the French adopt the 'sentiment of sport', so powerful among the English but hardly known in France, which he claimed promoted individualism and competitiveness. 'The English', he wrote, 'enthusiastically acclaim young champions, while we distribute crowns of gilded paper to our laureates of the great competitive examinations, heroes of French oratory and analytic geometry.'[88]

The Education of the Middle and Ruling Classes In England, by Max Leclerc, was published in 1894 in response to a competition sponsored by the Ecole Libre des Sciences Politiques. In his preface to the book Emile Boutmy, the director of the school, had admiring words for the products of the English 'public' schools; they had a high level of physical energy which made them relish the sustained and strenuous activity essential for economic and political success, and they learned to command after having long learned to obey.[89]

Leclerc observed that in England education (upbringing, moral and character development) and instruction (subject matter) were so thoroughly mixed together that the English language had one word – 'education' – to express both. He described at length the relationship between the English master and his students, explaining the difference between the English term 'boys' and the French 'éleves' in speaking of students. The English master, he wrote, spoke of 'my boys' as a father would speak of his sons. This, he claimed, was the external sign of a fundamental difference between the two systems. To the French teacher the child was most often only a student; for the English master, the student was like an adopted son.[90]

Leclerc explained how the system of monitors in English public schools promoted internal discipline. A boy learned to obey student monitors, and then to exercise authority when he became a monitor. External authorities such as the *maitres-repetiteurs* and *surveillants* of the French lycées, were unknown in English schools.[91] Leclerc also claimed that sports produced strong and supple bodies and trained young men in perseverance, tenacity, sang froid and discipline – traits which would be

88. Ibid., p. 307.
89. Emile Boutmy, 'Avant-propos' in Max Leclerc, *L'éducation des classes moyennes et dirigeantes en Angleterre* (Paris: A. Colin, 1894), pp. x–xi; Max Leclerc, 'L'éducation en Angleterre – Education physique et morale', *RDM*, CXXI (Feb. 15, 1894), pp. 882–905.
90. Leclerc, *L'éducation*, vol. I, pp. 33, 80.
91. Ibid.

preserved off the playing field.[92]

Edmond Demolins was the most radical Anglicizer among French educational reformers of the 1890s. Earlier in his career Demolins had been a disciple of Frederick Le Play and had directed *Reforme Sociale*, the publication of the Unions for Social Peace founded by Le Play. But he had come to reject Le Play's paternalistic, characteristically Catholic approach to dealing with social problems and, as director of the periodical *Science Sociale* which he had founded, had adopted an ideal of pure individualism and completely free competition. At the same time Demolins turned his efforts from pacifying the relations between labor and capital to educating the sons of the haute bourgeoisie.

Between 1893 and 1898 Demolins published a series of books in which he presented his educational ideals, described the English models on which he believed French reform should be based, and presented the school which he proposed to found. Demolins wrote that the times required men who could stand independently on their own feet. French education, he argued, was excellent for the preparation of government officials, men who were at home in the massive bureaucracy of the State. But what France needed were men of independence, initiative, will, energy and virility, men who could act effectively in a modern private enterprise economy. The challenge to France in the 1890s, he claimed, came from the Anglo-Saxons – the English and the Americans – and not the Germans on whom France had fixed her attention in the past. The competition would not be military as it had been with Germany, wrote Demolins, but economic and colonial. To compete with the Anglo-Saxons, the French would have to learn from them.[93]

The Ecole des Roches, which Demolins founded in 1899 and named after the chateau which housed it, was located near Verneuil-sur Avre in the Normandy countryside, about two hours train ride from Paris. It was financed by members of the haute bourgeoisie.[94] The goals of the Ecole

92. Ibid., pp. 37–40.
93. Edmond Demolins, 'Le devoir present,' *La Science Sociale*, XVIII (Feb. 1894), pp. 104, 107; Edmond Demolins, *Comment élever et établir nos enfants?* (Paris: Firmin-Didot & Cie, 1893), pp. 47–48; *A quoi tient la supériorité des Anglo Saxons* (Paris: Firmin-Didot, s.d. 1898).
94. Among its sponsors were Vicomte de Glatigny, Alfred Firmin-Didot (the publisher), the Vicomte Ch. de Cahen, Paul Lebaudy (a deputy and millionaire in the sugar business), Pierre Lebaudy (brother of Paul Lebaudy), Jules Siegfried (senator, former cabinet minister, immensely wealthy ship-owner and merchant of Le Havre), Marc Maurel (ship-owner of Bordeaux), Edouard H. Krafft, Oliver Benoist, Olivier Sen (industrialist of Le Havre), Raverat, Edmond Marey and P. Lebouteux (a farmer and graduate of the Institute of Agronomy) (Edmond Demolins, *A quoi tient la supériorité des Anglo Saxons*, (Paris: Firmin-Didot [1898], p. xi). Many of the sponsors were from French port cities whose business orientation was outward, toward the Atlantic – and England. Two of them, Paul and Pierre Lebaudy, had recently experienced a tragedy of

des Roches were reflected in its motto: 'Ecole Nouvelle. Bien Armée Pour la Vie.' The school which Demolins founded and directed for many years, still exists and is known for the broad and excellent education it offers its students. Its description of its aims would please Demolins: 'The Ecole des Roches has always had for its calling the promotion of emotional and moral equilibrium of adolescents, to form characters.'[95]

If educated youth expressed anti-bourgeois cultural values and acted in ways reminiscent of characters in fin-de-siècle novels, they also exhibited anti-bourgeois tendencies in the economic, social and political sense. Some were attracted to socialism, others to anarchism.

The bravest and perhaps most important bourgeois effort to oppose socialistic tendencies among educated youth was the anti-socialist campaign in the Latin Quarter and other university centers led by Anatole Leroy-Beaulieu. In 1894 Leroy-Beaulieu organized the Comité de Defense Sociale[96] as an offshoot of the Unions for Social Peace. A statement issued by the Comité de Defense Sociale sought to explain the inroads socialism was making among educated youth. Unnecessary to mention said the statement was the natural rebelliousness of youth; but in addition there were the current feelings of solicitude toward the downtrodden, the passion for social questions and the propaganda of the enemies of the family, property and society who offer lectures and courses and who agitate among the educated youth who are only too willing to

faulty upbringing in their own family when Max Lebaudy, a young relation, died after having dissipated himself and squandered, in two years, several million francs of his inheritance (*Le Matin*, March 14, 1896; Emmanuel Beau de Loménie, *Les responsibilités des dynasties bourgeoises*, vol. II, Paris, Editions Denoel, 1947, p. 273).

95. Demolins, *L'éducation nouvelle*, p. viii. The fullest description of the Ecole des Roches which I know of in English is in M. B. Betham-Edwards, *French Men, Women, and Books* (Freeport, N.Y.: Books for Libraries Press, 1967). *Guide National de l'Education Privée* (Paris: Le Centre National de Documentation sur l'Enseignment Privée, 1971), p. 1.

96. By the time it began its activities, its organizers had changed its name to 'Comité de Defense et de Progrès Sociale.' Evidently they did not want to be labeled diehard conservatives. Among the Comité's members were the haut bourgeois public leaders Albert Gigot (president of the Society of Social Economy, Director of the Forges d'Alais and former prefect of police), E.-D. Glasson (member of the French Institut and professor at the Faculty of Law in Paris), Claudio Jannet (professor at the Free Law Faculty of Paris), Dr. Rocard (president of the Academy of Medicine and retired Inspector General of the Navy's Health Service), Georges Picot (permanent secretary of the Academy of Moral and Political Sciences of the Institute, honorary president of the Unions of Social Peace of the Nord), Henri Beaune (former official of the court in Lyon and honorary president of the Unions for Social Peace of the South East), A. Gibon (former director of the Commentry Steel Works and honorary president of the Unions for Social Peace of the Centre), Gaston David (*avocat* and honorary president of the Unions for Social Peace of the South West) and A. Delaire, editor of *Social Reform* ('L'oeuvre nouvelle, Comité de defense sociale,' *Reforme Sociale*, VIII, (Oct. 16, 1894), p. 565).

listen. The Comité called on students to come in large numbers to hear the speakers it would present, with the intention of fighting false ideas and unhealthy utopias. The threat of socialism was great and growing, claimed the Comité. It jeopardized property and individual effort – the very bases of prosperity and civilization – in France and throughout the Occident on both sides of the Atlantic.[97]

At meeting after meeting Anatole Leroy-Beaulieu and his friends brought their message to the Latin Quarter and other university centers. Though most members of the audiences they faced were friendly or at least tolerant and polite, each session had its determined minority of hecklers and disrupters. When the Jew Raphael-Georges Lévy addressed the students in February 1896 (before the Dreyfus Affair became a big public issue), a group of about thirty violent cane-swinging anti-semites turned out to disrupt the meeting, destroying lecture room furniture and wounding several members of the audience.

It would be easy not to take seriously the concern of bourgeois elders with the problems they perceived in the youth of their class. If the student of history is not sensitive to the concerns of the hauts bourgeois it would be easy to dismiss their worries about rebelliousness, weakness of will and socialistic tendencies among their sons as the product of excessive paternal fretting about spoiled rich boys. Understandable as this might be, it would be a mistake if the aim is to understand the French haute bourgeoisie. Even if the fin-de-siècle educational concerns of the bourgeoisie had produced no tangible results at all – no Ecole des Roches, no anti-socialist campaign in the Latin Quarter, no English 'public school' style athletics – it would still be necessary to be sensitive to these concerns if the ways of thinking of France's 'classe dirigeante' are to be understood.

Several conclusions emerge from a survey of bourgeois efforts at social defense in the mid-1890s. The intensity and diversity of those efforts indicate that for the haute bourgeoisie this was a period of considerable anxiety. The various bourgeois approaches to social defense had essentially the same objectives: to strengthen the haute bourgeoisie as a classe dirigeante and block 'Jacobin socialism' threatened by a Chamber

97. Among the lectures presented by the Comité were Anatole Leroy-Beaulieu on 'Why we are not Socialists', George Picot on 'The Use of Liberty and Social Duty', Eugène Rostand on 'Social Progress and Individual Initiative', Paul Desjardins on 'The Duty of Primogeniture', Emile Cheysson on the 'Role and Duty of Capital', Wagner on 'The Social Duty of Youth', Albert Gigot on 'Worker Insurance and Socialism', Daniel Zolla on 'Agriculture and Socialism', Raphael-George Lévy on 'The Diffusion of Wealth in France', Mabillieau on 'The Benefits and Limits of Cooperation', and Eugène Rostand on 'Socialist Solutions and Bureaucracy'.

dominated by the many. The efforts of bourgeois leaders – Jules Simon, Emil Cheysson and Léon Say, to name a few – were directed toward numerous enterprises in which the bourgeoisie – liberals and conservatives, protectionists and free-traders – united to defend society as they knew it.

As it would turn out, the threat of 'Jacobin socialism' would be defeated in 1899 by Waldeck-Rousseau with the political restructuring which I call the 'dreyfusian revolution'. One outcome of the dreyfusian revolution would be a sharp decline of interest in approaches to social defense which were no longer considered to be of urgent necessity.

8

The Dreyfusian Revolution Resolves the
Fin-de-Siècle Crisis of Democracy

The conventional narrative of French history from 1898 to 1899 focuses on the Dreyfus Affair, presenting it as a discontinuity which interrupted the normal course of politics. In this chapter the history of those years is recast by focusing on their political narrative and by showing how, when the 'dreyfusian revolution,' the political restructuring directed by Waldeck-Rousseau, is properly understood, it represents a clear continuity with the years before and after it.

The 'dreyfusian revolution' is sometimes understood to refer to the emergence of a division of deputies between those who believed Dreyfus was innocent and those who believed he was guilty, which evolved into a situation where anti-clericalism became the salient division between deputies. This is incorrect. Rather, the essence of the dreyfusian revolution was the creation by Waldeck-Rousseau of a concentration coalition composed of a majority of Radicals and a minority of Moderates.[1] One outcome of the dreyfusian revolution was that henceforth Radicals would constitute the majority of deputies supporting ministerial coalitions; another was that henceforth Radicals would exercise first claim to feed at the trough of government patronage. A third was that henceforth the Chamber of Deputies would no longer threaten the vital interests of the haute bourgeoisie.

Though the term 'Dreyfusard revolution' is sometimes used for what I call the 'dreyfusian revolution', I will use the term 'dreyfusian' because it makes the useful distinction between 'Dreyfusard' (one who believed that Dreyfus was innocent and campaigned for the reversal of his conviction), and the political restructuring which produced the change from Méline's 'homogeneous' coalition of the right to Waldeck-Rousseau's center 'concentration' coalition of republican defense which was produced by politicians who were not, generally, Dreyfusards.

The dreyfusian revolution occurred in June 1899 when Waldeck-

---

1. Generally whether a deputy believed in the guilt or innocence of Dreyfus had nothing to do with whether he supported or opposed Waldeck-Rousseau's ministry.

Rousseau formed his 'ministry of republican defense'. It followed the most intense periods of the Dreyfus Affair, the first half of 1898 when the conviction of Captain Dreyfus was the subject of public controversy outside the political arena and the year from mid-1898 to mid-1899 during which the Affair was a focus of attention in the Chamber of Deputies.

The dreyfusian revolution is usually depicted as representing a change in political direction. In one sense this is not incorrect; it did entail a sharp change in the personnel constituting the majority coalition in the Chamber (most deputies who had been part of Méline's majority – Moderates, *ralliés* and conservatives – would be excluded from Waldeck-Rousseau's coalition). But for Waldeck-Rousseau himself and for the French haute bourgeoisie the new coalition represented a clear continuity of political purpose. In the general election campaign of 1898 Waldeck had fought against the impôt; the government which he organized in June 1899 would continue to reject the impôt sur le revenu.

Waldeck-Rousseau, Leader of the Dreyfusian Revolution

René Waldeck-Rousseau was the chief engineer of the dreyfusian revolution. (I have purposely not described him as its 'architect'; the credit for that accomplishment, I suspect, should be shared by, among others, Poincaré, Millerand and Joseph Reinach). He was characteristic of a type of Third Republic political leader who, coming from a comfortable but not haute bourgeois background and recruited by haute bourgeois sponsors, shuttled between a highly lucrative career as a lawyer representing haute bourgeois clients and a politician representing haut bourgeois interests.[2]

Waldeck-Rousseau was born in Nantes in 1846. His father, an avocat, was a local republican leader in the Revolution of 1848, had briefly gone into hiding as a *proscrit* following Louis Napoléon's coup of 1851 and had returned to politics in the crisis of 1870 to proclaim the Republic in Nantes on 4 September. Waldeck-Rousseau himself, educated for the bar, was elected to the Chamber of Deputies in 1879. He was Minister of Interior in Gambetta's 'grande ministère' of 1881 and Jules Ferry's cabinet of 1883–85, where he suppressed the system by which government posts were obtained through the patronage of local deputies and, it was said, 'gave proof of great administrative powers'.

In 1886 Waldeck-Rousseau began to practice law before the Paris bar. From 1888 he turned away entirely from participation in politics and

2. Alexandre Millerand and Raymond Poincaré were other important *avocat* politicians who served in the Third Republic. (See Francis Delaisi, 'Les Financiers et la Démocratie,' *Crapouillot*, Nov. 1936, p. 23.)

devoted himself to his practice as avocat for some of the wealthiest hauts bourgeois of France. He wanted, he said, to earn enough not to have to worry about the future. Possibly contributing to Waldeck-Rousseau's decision to devote himself fully to what would be an enormously lucrative law practice was the fact that in 1888 he married the widow Marie Durvis, the sister-in-law of the famous Dr. Charcot. Described as 'jeune, brilliante, agitée, très mondaine', Waldeck's new wife (with whom he had been having relations for several years before she became a widow) brought to the marriage a considerable fortune and a young son. As an avocat Waldeck-Rousseau's annual income was several hundred thousand francs at a time when an average laborer earned 2,500 francs a year and a deputy in the Chambre was paid 9,000 francs.

Elegantly dressed in British suits, Waldeck-Rousseau was an impressive speaker with an imposing presence. Contemporaries described him as having impassive, unmoving features, a slightly troubled expression and a gaze reminiscent of a jelled fish in aspic. Poincaré, who was himself noted for his imposing presence, recalled that as an avocat opposing Waldeck in court for the first time, he felt like a poodle in the presence of a statue.[3] Far more reserved and less talkative than was typical of a Frenchman of his position, Waldeck-Rousseau gave an impression of strength without divulging the content of his mind.

In 1894 Waldeck-Rousseau re-entered politics, having been recruited by Jean Honoré Audiffred, deputy from the Loire and head of the Association Nationale Républicaine. He was provided with a 'safe' Senate seat in the Loire for which he did not have to campaign. From the moment he re-entered politics it was clear that he was expected to play a major role. In the *Revue des Deux Mondes* of October 1894, Francis Charmes devoted two pages of his 'Chronique' to Waldeck-Rousseau's return to politics. Charmes pictured him as a man above the fray, without the image of a professional politician greedy to retain office at any cost; in all things, he wrote, Waldeck-Rousseau stood above the ordinary. Charmes observed that the press had treated his election as an important event: 'even before he was elected, the new Senator had been designated for an important role.'[4]

3. Jacques Chastenet, *Histoire de la Troisième République, La république triomphante, 1893–1906* (Paris: Hachette, 1955), pp. 155–156.

4. Francis Charmes, 'Chronique de la quinzaine', *RDM*, CXXV (Oct. 15, 1894), pp. 951–952. In February 1895, when it seemed a Radical cabinet might be formed, the *Revue Diplomatique* suggested that after a brief attempt at pure Radicalism, there would be an antidote of Waldeck-Rousseau (*Revue Diplomatique*, Jan. 20, 1895, p. 3). See also *Le Gaulois*, March 10, 1896; *Revue Diplomatique*, Feb. 24, 1895, p. 2; Barnave, 'Chronique politique', *Nouvelle Revue*, XCIII (March 1, 1895), p. 181; André Daniel, *L'année politique, 1895* (Paris: Charpentier, 1896), p. 53.

After Waldeck had run unsuccessfully for President of the Republic after the resignation of Casimir-Périer, the *Revue Diplomatique* suggested that perhaps it was for the best that he had not been elected because 'in a period of uncertainty and transition' such as it claimed existed at the time, 'a man of conciliation and neutrality' [such as Félix Faure, who had been elected President] would offer a smooth surface to the polemicists. 'Besides, the militant eloquent and energetic Waldeck-Rousseau remains a useful reserve to be employed in case of a serious crisis of social danger.'[5]

Between 1894 and 1898 Waldeck-Rousseau was one of the chief spokesmen for the Moderates. His speeches were extensively and favorably reported in the bourgeois press. In that period he expressed standard bourgeois opinions concerning the danger of revolution. He spoke against 'collectivism' and 'an all powerful State' but stated that he did not believe that France faced a danger of violent collectivist revolution. What Waldeck did warn against as a serious threat was the impôt sur le revenu, which he described as a 'socialist doctrine' which violated the principles of the French Revolution. He warned against 'the revenue service being used as a tool for leveling wealth by the inequality of tax burdens', against 'taxation used as a legal instrument in the battle between classes', and against the 'impôt progressif et global sur le revenu'.[6]

Waldeck-Rousseau was chief Moderate organizer for the general election campaign of 1898. He was honorary chairman of the executive committee of the Association Nationale Républicaine,[7] had helped found in 1894 the Association des Gambettistes which sought to promote the Moderate cause in each *arrondissement* of Paris[8] and helped organize in 1897 the Comité National Républicain de Commerce et de l'Industrie, a joint project of the Association Nationale Républicaine and the

5. *Revue Diplomatique*, Jan. 20, 1895, p. 3; *Le Temps*, Feb. 5, 1895, p. 1; Nov. 17, 1895, p. 1; Nov. 18, 1895, p. 2; Félix Roussel, 'Chronique politique intérieure', *RPP*, IX (Sept. 10, 1898), p. 643; Ibid., X (Nov. 10, 1896), p. 472; Ibid., XI (March 10, 1897), p. 696; Ibid., XII (May 10, 1897), p. 462; René Waldeck-Rousseau, 'Discours prononcé au diner de la Revue Politique et Parlementaire du 18 juin 1897', *RPP*, XIII (July 10, 1897), pp. 5–13; Félix Roussel, 'Chronique politique intérieure', *RPP*, XIV (Nov. 10, 1897), pp. 464, 470, 471.
6. René Waldeck-Rousseau, 'Les républicains du gouvernement et le programme radical', speech given Oct. 25. 1896, in *Pour la République* (Paris: Charpentier, 1904), p. 296; Waldeck-Rousseau, 'Le déclin du radicalisme', speech given at Reims, Oct. 24, 1897, in *Pour la République*, p. 381; *Pour la République*, pp. 261–270, 330.
7. Pierre Sorlin, *Waldeck-Rousseau* (Paris: Armand Colin, 1966), pp. 368–369.
8. René Waldeck-Rousseau, *Discours*, (at the Hotel-Continental, 24 Feb. 1897) (Paris: Association Nationale Républicaine, 1897), p. 4; René Waldeck-Rousseau, papers at Bibliotheque de l'Institut, MS 4575(10); Marcel Fournier, 'L'organisation du parti progressiste', *RPP*, XIV (Nov. 10, 1897), p. 239.

Association Générale des Commerçants et Industriels, whose purpose was to support the Méline ministry and prepare for the coming general elections 'by organizing a strong propaganda campaign against socialist and collectivist doctrines which menace the principles of the French Revolution – namely individual liberty, individual property, and the right to work.'[9]

To launch the Comité National Républicain de Commerce et de l'Industrie, Waldeck-Rousseau addressed a gathering at the Hôtel-Continental. The coming general elections, he stated, would be 'of decisive interest and of exceptional gravity'. Basic questions would be raised 'which could determine the future of republican government and even of the country . . . The essential principles of the French Revolution would be challenged by a dangerous demagogy.' Waldeck-Rousseau explained that he was not alluding to what is known as the 'collectivist peril . . . that was not now a real threat.' He did not fear, he said, 'even a partial realization of the collectivist chimera . . . calls for the nationalization of the land and State acquisition of all means of production were only banners deployed to attract crowds.'[10] What was to be feared, he told his bourgeois audience, was a 'disguised socialism, at certain times official – and fiscal.' One of the gravest events of recent years, he said, 'had occurred when, not a private person, not even a minister, but the president of the council of ministers himself [that is, Léon Bourgeois], had formulated and expressed the opinion that the tax should be a means to re-establish equality in the battle between those who possess more and those who possess less.' All socialism, stated Waldeck, 'is revealed in this formula'.

Waldeck-Rousseau explained the danger of the impôt in terms of the many and the few: 'We live in a country of universal suffrage, in a country, therefore, where the number makes the law, and if anything is the guarantee of liberty, it is that the law cannot be against some without being turned immediately against all. The day the greatest number would be able to impose its will, its arbitrariness, its caprices on the smallest; when the most numerous could displace the burden of public charges and make them press on only one group of society, then would be reached the most detestable and abominable of tyrannies.' Waldeck-Rousseau said that he insisted on these ideas in speaking of the coming general elections because in various and diverse formulas more or less precise, more or less daring, more or less prudent, the progressive tax would very certainly be an issue.

9. Paul Deschanel, 'Discours', March 2, 1898 at the Grand-Hôtel, Paris (Paris au siège de la Comité National Républicain de Commerce et de l'Industrie, 1898).
10. René Waldeck-Rousseau, *Discours*, Feb 24, 1897 (Paris: Association Nationale Républicaine, 1897), p. 4.

'The menace', he stated, 'is formidable. Therefore it is essential to prepare for the coming political battle whose results could be decisive.'[11]

He described the work of propaganda which would be required in the months ahead and called upon the assembled businessmen to support it with their money. Brochures by the hundreds of thousands would have to be distributed. Speakers would be sent throughout France to advocate the good cause. The *Correspondance* of the Association Nationale Républicaine, started in 1896, would be issued daily instead of weekly and distributed to the provincial press by telegraph rather than mail for increased effectiveness. Sympathetic candidates for the Chamber would be supported financially in their campaigns for election. In the départements groups of like-minded persons would be encouraged to form and act. For all this, he said, very considerable resources would be needed. Waldeck-Rousseau concluded his speech by appealing to the 'bonne volonté' of his listeners who 'with no ulterior motives, had no other ambition than to serve their country well'.[12]

Next, Audiffred described the work of the Association Nationale Républicaine which had increased its activity to the extent that its resources had been augmented during the past two years. He explained what needed to be done in the months ahead and appealed for funds to make it possible. Political organizations such as his, he stated, welcomed the supervision of representatives of business to assure themselves of the sound use of the funds they contributed.

Then Charles Expert-Besançon, chairman of the meeting, thanked the speakers and listeners for having attended and appealed for funds for the important electoral project which lay ahead. As to the amount expected from each person, Expert-Besançon said he did not wish to be too absolute. Not all contributions could be expected to be equal. 'One person giving 1,000 francs', he explained, 'might be less generous than another giving 100 francs.' Thus when it came to saying how much a member of the bourgeoisie should pay to a fund for the defense of his class, Expert-Besançon called for the very progressivity of contribution which he so vehemently opposed in taxation for the support of the government.[13]

Waldeck-Rousseau's final organizing effort for the 1898 general elections was to establish the Grand Cercle Républicain in cooperation with Marcel Fournier, director of the *Revue Politique et Parlementaire*. Its aim was to unite all 'bonnes volontés' (men of good will) and coordinate the efforts of the Moderate groups already in existence — including the Association Nationale Républicaine, the Comité de l'Union

11. Ibid., pp. 6, 7.
12. Ibid., pp. 9–12, 17.
13. Ibid., pp. 21–22.

Libérale, the Association des Gambettistes, the Comité de Defense et de Progrès Sociale and the Association Nationale Républicaine de Commerce et de l'Industrie. According to plans, it would have an English-style club in Paris with a reading room, dining room and library, and would serve as a gathering place for members from Paris and the provinces. The annual membership fee would be 200 francs for residents of Paris and 150 francs for those who lived outside the capital.[14]

As Waldeck-Rousseau explained it, the aim of the Grand Cercle Républicain would be to establish lines of communication between the Paris-based Moderate political organizations and the provincial bourgeoisie; therefore young emissaries would be sent out to seek members in the provinces. Waldeck was careful to indicate that the new Grand Cercle would fortify, not diminish, other bourgeois political organizations. He thus reassured his friend Audiffred who had at first been reluctant to support the Grand Cercle, apparently out of fear that it would undercut his own importance.[15]

The Coming of the Dreyfusian Revolution – The Elections of 1898

With Méline's homogeneous right coalition managing to stay in office by the narrowest of margins, the general elections of May 1898 were of great importance to the haute bourgeoisie. The loss of only a few seats by his supporters would cause Méline to lose his majority and the way would then be open to a majority of the left.

The lines of political division for the general elections were the same as they had been since 1893: left versus right, the policies of Léon Bourgeois against those of Jules Méline. *Le Temps* claimed to welcome the left-right division, holding that it would give the Republic the aspect of a true parliamentary regime. This, it stated, could be achieved because the Republic was no longer faced with the need to defend itself from the attacks of adversaries which might destroy it. Because the Republic was no longer in danger, wrote *Le Temps*, the illusion behind 'republican defense' was dead.[16]

In the 1898 election campaign Léon Bourgeois, Godefroy Cavaignac and Gustave Mesureur were the chief spokesmen for the non-socialist left. Bourgeois, as chief of the Radicals, stated in January that the main

14. Fournier, 'L'organisation du parti progressiste', pp. 240–242; Waldeck-Rousseau, papers, Bibliotheque de l'Institut de France, MS 4575 (12).
15. Pierre Sorlin, *Waldeck-Rousseau* (Paris: A. Colin, 1966), p. 384; Fournier, 'L'organisation du parti progressiste', p. 245.
16. Salles, 'Les députés sortants (1893–1898)', p. 34; *Le Temps.*, Feb. 1, Feb 15, April 28 and May 4, 1898; Charles Seignobos, *L'évolution de la Troisième République*, p. 193.

demands of his party were the impôt sur le revenu and a limited revision of the constitution to curtail the power of the Senate and prevent it from vetoing the decisions of the Chamber. Radicals also advocated opposition to 'clericalism'.[17]

Moderates opposed the Radical program, with Méline, Barthou, Waldeck-Rousseau, Poincaré and Deschanel as their chief spokesmen. The basic question of the election, they claimed, was whether the country wished to continue the policies of the Méline government or repeat the adventure of a second Bourgeois ministry. *Le Temps* saw the choice as being between the policies of Poincaré and Bourgeois, between the political groups behind Méline and those backing Bourgeois, and between the Radicals and the Moderates. On 9 May 1898, the eve of the general elections, the newspaper spelled out the alternatives before the voters: they would have to choose between the progressive and liberal program of the republican (Moderate) party which would guarantee the Republic a long future of peace, practical reforms and prosperity, and the Radical policy which, 'moving from adventure to adventure, could lead to the final catastrophe where history has shown more than one democracy had foundered'. In a similar vein the *Revue Politique et Parlementaire* stressed that the elections would orient the Republic towards 'reasoned progress or the unknown and violence'.[18]

Unlike the general elections of 1893, voter turnout was high in 1898. The results of the election were not good for the Moderates. The supporters of Méline lost ground, and the balance of power in the Chamber shifted to the left. Henceforth a majority coalition on the Méline pattern would not be possible; recognizing this, Méline left office soon after the elections.[19]

Immediately after the elections Moderate leaders such as Marcel Fournier, director of the *Revue Politique et Parlementaire* and co-organizer with Waldeck-Rousseau of the Grand Cercle Républicain, tried to put on a brave face and claimed that the makeup of the new Chamber was not significantly different from that of the old one.[20] Some historians

17. Félix Roussel, 'Chronique politique intérieure,' *RPP*, XIV (Nov. 1897), p. 466; Ibid., XV (May 10, 1898), p. 681; Ibid., XVI (May 1898), p. 467.
18. Salles, 'Les députés sortants (1893–1898)', p. 72; *Le Temps*, May 9, 1898; Marcel Fournier, 'Premiers résultats des elections',*RPP*, XVI (May 10, 1898), pp. 245, 246; Ibid., (April 1898), p. 232.
19. Marcel Fournier, 'Après les elections,' *RPP*, XXIV (June 1898), pp. 491, 498. The American *Literary Digest*, XVI (June 11, 1899), p. 713, reported: 'The Democrats, if we may classify as such the parties of the Left – Radicals, Socialist-Radicals and Socialists – have won a majority of 10 in the Chamber.' See also *The Nation*, LXV (June 16, 1898), pp. 457, 458.
20. *RPP*, XVI (June 1898), p. 704; *La Revue Diplomatique*, May 29, 1898, p. 2; Pierre Sorlin, *Waldeck-Rousseau*, p. 388.

have mistakenly accepted this claim at face value.[21] But Fournier himself acknowledged that the election results were not as good as the 'parti républicain' (by which he meant Moderates) had hoped for and indicated that the demise of the Méline coalition was imminent. Later, in 1900, Fournier wrote explicitly that the 'parti progressiste' (Moderates) had been defeated in 1898.[22]

Thus in May 1898, after the election defeat of the Méline coalition, the danger of a homogeneous left cabinet seeking the impôt sur le revenu again confronted the haute bourgeoisie. For the moment, the Chamber could avoid the question of the impôt because the Dreyfus question had, since October 1897, developed into a full-blown Affair absorbing the attention of the French political world. (It remains an open question whether, as Jacques Chastenet suggested, this was intended and perhaps engineered.) In any case, for the first year of the new Chamber, the Dreyfus Affair absorbed the attention of the French political world and provided the bourgeoisie with a respite from the threat of a ministry whose primary goal would be an impôt sur le revenu.

Period of Transition – Reorientation of the Chamber to a Concentration Pattern

After the general elections, with Méline's 'homogeneous' right coalition no longer possible, Marcel Fournier suggested that it was time for a new concentration majority in the Chamber. To form one, he wrote, the *parti progressiste* should rally, little by little, all the Radicals who were unwilling to become 'socialists'. Fournier advised that while *progressistes* (Moderates) should pursue 'concentration', it would not be good to use that term when dealing with the Radicals. He explained that the question should not be one of rallying around a flag which would soon be abandoned. This, he feared, would be the result if concentration meant

21. Pierre Sorlin made this key error in his book *Waldeck-Rousseau*. He stated (p. 388), 'Quant aux résultats [of the general elections] . . . a quelques details près, la Chambre de 1898 recopie celle de 1893.' As a result of this crucial error, Sorlin failed to understand why Méline's coalition, for which Waldeck had campaigned in 1898, was no longer viable and why the coalition which emerged from the 'dreyfusian revolution' which Waldeck engineered in 1899 was the necessary solution to the threat of the impôt sur le revenu pursued by a unified 'left.'

Sorlin's error is typical of historians writing about the results of the election of 1898. For example Herman Lebovics in *The Alliance of Iron and Wheat in the Third Republic, 1860–1914 – Origins of the New Conservatism* (Baton Rouge: Louisiana State University Press, 1988, p. 185) writes: 'the results of the elections [of 1898] were gratifying to the Opportunists [Moderates].'

22. Marcel Fournier, 'Notre oeuvre de cinq années (1894–1899)', *RPP*, XXIV (April 10, 1900), p. 37.

only a negative program, a mere surrendering of differences.[23]

Félix Roussel, who wrote the political chronicle for the *Revue Politique et Parlementaire*, made the same point. He observed that some persons believed that the political situation seemed to call for a coalition of republican groups around a program of 'limited understanding'. It would be, he wrote, under the seductive name of 'union of republicans' or 'politics of conciliation' that this return to the old practice of concentration would be advocated. Roussel stated that he could understand this way of thinking, for it responded to the natural desire of weak characters to please everyone and furnished the cunning with an easy means to fool everyone. But, he continued, though the time was right for concentration, the circumstances were not. He explained that concentration as 'republican defense' had been necessary in 1877 after the *seize mai*, in 1885 when the reactionaries attempted to exploit the criminal attitude of certain republicans against Gambetta and Jules Ferry, and in 1889 when Boulangism resulted from radical intrigues. Each time the Republic was menaced, Roussel wrote, all politics were reduced to defending it. In his view, though the situation in June 1898 was far from the same (because the Republic was not then in jeopardy), the actual division of parties within the Chamber seemed to call for a new concentration-pattern majority.[24]

The course of French politics after the general elections of 1898 to June 1899, when Waldeck-Rousseau inaugurated the longest-lived ministry of the Third Republic, reflected a reorientation of the Chamber of Deputies to a government by concentration coalition with a preponderance of Radicals – the essence of the dreyfusian revolution. During this period the Dreyfus Affair was a focus of attention.

Following the 1898 general elections, Godefroy Cavaignac's influence in the Chamber was so great that no cabinet could be formed without his support. Cavaignac's popularity had continued to grow during the Méline ministry and election campaign of 1898, so that with the fall of Méline he was clearly the most influential deputy in the chamber.[25] After Méline left office it would have been reasonable of President Faure to call Cavaignac to head a cabinet. But Faure declined to do so, probably remembering Léon Bourgeois's Radical cabinet of 1895–96 and the tension surrounding it, tension for which Cavaignac had been largely responsible as the chief advocate of the impôt.

23. Marcel Fournier, 'Après les élections générales; Situation des partis et direction politique', *RPP*, XVI (June 10, 1898), pp. 489, 499, 500, 506.
24. Félix Roussel, 'Chronique politique intérieure', *RPP*, XVII (July 10, 1898), p. 219.
25. Bredin, *The Affair*, pp. 306, 307.

Although Faure refused to call Cavaignac to head a government, Cavaignac was sufficiently influential so that no cabinet which did not have his support could survive. After Cavaignac had vetoed attempts by Ribot, Peytral and Sarrien to form cabinets, he finally consented to be Minister of War in a government led by the elderly and considered-to-be harmless Radical Henri Brisson.

In June 1898, with the Dreyfus Affair at a fever pitch, two issues concerned Cavaignac. One was to end the agitation against the Army for its role in the Dreyfus case. The other was to enact an impôt sur le revenu. To Cavaignac, the galling thing about the agitation around the Dreyfus Affair was not simply that the conviction of the traitor Dreyfus was challenged, but that the integrity of the Army itself was being attacked.

Cavaignac began his tenure with the understanding that the first item of business must be to end the storm of agitation around the Dreyfus Affair. With absolute faith in the Army that he loved, Cavaignac set about ending the Affair. Whereas the Méline government had blocked the way to *révision* (retrial) by simply refusing to discuss a judicial question which had been judged, Cavaignac was willing and even anxious to reveal the evidence on which Dreyfus had been convicted. First, he would show once and for all the basis of Dreyfus's conviction; then he would prosecute the leading Dreyfusards who had stirred up the campaign against the Army.

On 7 July 1898, as he said he would several days before, Cavaignac rose in the Chamber to present the Army's proofs against Dreyfus. He bore, in the tradition of his family, a great reputation for rectitude, honesty and incorruptibility. In 1893, at the time of the Panama Scandal, he had impressed all France by forcefully calling for a full revelation of the truth no matter who might be hurt. Now he would settle the Dreyfus Affair for good by presenting publicly on the floor of the Chamber the three strongest proofs of Dreyfus's guilt – documents which each named Dreyfus explicitly – culled from the Army's now huge dossier against Dreyfus.

Cavaignac began his speech in the Chamber by acknowledging that some of the defenders of Dreyfus were men of good faith: 'A misunderstanding threatens to arise between them and that Army whose sacred mission it is to defend the patrimony of France, not only her material patrimony, but her intellectual and moral patrimony.' It was for their benefit, Cavaignac stated, that he would expose the basis of the proof against Dreyfus. He pledged his absolute certainty in Dreyfus's guilt. Raison d'etat would never be a factor in his conclusions, he stated: 'Never could any consideration of public welfare, whatever it might be, impel me to keep an innocent man in jail . . .'[26]

He then presented the proofs of Dreyfus's guilt. One was a letter of September 1896 from Allessandro Panizzardi, the Italian military attaché in Paris, to Maximilien von Schwarzkoppen, his German counterpart. The second was the 'scoundrel D' letter which had been part of the Army's secret file in the original 1894 trial. The third was a letter which spelled out Dreyfus's name as a spy in the employ of the Germans. Regarding the latter Cavaignac affirmed 'I have assessed the material and moral authenticity of this document' and, as Jean-Denis Bredin has written, Cavaignac proceeded to demonstrate them both with considerable talent. He concluded with a ringing tribute to the Army: 'May all Frenchmen be able to come together tomorrow to proclaim that the Army which is their pride and their hope is not only mighty with its own strength . . . is not only strong with the nation's trust, but strong as well in the justice of the acts that it has accomplished.'

As Cavaignac descended from the rostrum, the entire Chamber rose in acclamation. Prime Minister Brisson insisted on noting that Cavaignac had spoken 'in the name of the government'. Unanimously, the Chamber took the exceptional action of voting to post Cavaignac's speech in each of France's thirty-six thousand communes. Only fifteen Socialists and the former Prime Minister Méline abstained. 'We had our hopes in Cavaignac,' the Socialist Dreyfusard Léon Blum would later write. 'We knew him to be upright, hardworking and methodical. And there he was declaring Dreyfus's guilt . . . And the entire Chamber had acclaimed him.'

To the overwhelming majority of Frenchmen, except for a small group of leading Dreyfusards, Cavaignac had settled the Dreyfus Affair once and for all. Only with hindsight would it become clear that he himself had opened the way to revision. Once the Minister of War made public the proofs against Dreyfus, Colonel Picquart, who had been barred from speaking because he was sworn to military secrecy, could now say what he knew about the 'evidence' against Dreyfus. On 9 July Picquart informed Prime Minister Brisson that he could prove that the two documents dated 1894 were forgeries and that the document dated 1896 had every appearance of being a forgery.

But it was Cavaignac himself who would destroy the Army's case against Dreyfus. On the evening of 13 August Captain Louis Cuignet of the War Minister's staff was meticulously reexamining the documents in the Dreyfus file. He held up to a lamp the 1896 document which named

Dreyfus explicitly and which Cavaignac had cited in his speech to the Chamber. To his horror, Cuignet saw that it was a forgery composed of two pieces of paper pasted together. The next day he showed the forgery to General Roget, head of the War Minister's *cabinet*, and both of them then took it to Cavaignac. As Jean-Denis Bredin has written: 'It was to the credit of those three men, all committed to the struggle against retrial, to have not for a moment thought of quashing their discovery.' Cavaignac was not dismayed. He kept secret the discovery of the forgery a few days, and in the meantime he continued to denounce the partisans of revision. In one speech he called them 'disloyal citizens', and in another he proclaimed: 'In the presence of the impious attempts which have been made to discredit those working for the greatness of our country, patriots must affirm, more forcefully than ever before, their love, their admiration for the Army.'[27]

On 30 August Cavaignac interrogated Colonel Henry, the source of the 1896 forgery. After tough questioning Henry admitted that he had indeed forged the document. Cavaignac immediately released the following communique to the press: 'Today in the office of the minister of war, Lieutenant-Colonel Henry was acknowledged and acknowledged himself to be the author of the letter dated October 1896 in which Dreyfus is named. The Minister of War immediately ordered the arrest of Lieutenant-Colonel Henry, who has been taken to the Fortress of Mont-Valérien.'

The revelation of the Henry forgery destroyed confidence in the evidence against Dreyfus of practically every minister in Brisson's cabinet except Cavaignac. Now Brisson decided enough was enough; retrial for Dreyfus was imperative. Léon Bourgeois acknowledged the obvious and agreed. But Cavaignac refused to budge. 'My credit has not been diminished by the discovery of the Henry forgery,' Cavaignac stated. 'On the contrary, it was I who proved that the document was counterfeit.' Brisson pleaded with Cavaignac; he wanted to step aside and have Cavaignac made prime minister and let Cavaignac himself direct the retrial. Cavaignac absolutely refused: 'More than ever,' he said, 'I remain convinced of Dreyfus's guilt.' If the cabinet insisted on retrial, Cavaignac stated, he would resign. Retrial it would be and, true to his word, Cavaignac resigned. But now, when reasonable men realized that retrial was the only sensible course of action, Cavaignac had lost the power to bring down the cabinet by his disapproval.

Now Brisson sought a new Minister of War. This turned out to be not an easy matter. Each new appointment who had expressed willingness to undertake *révision* before his appointment behaved as if he had seen

27. Bredin, *The Affair*, p. 325.

an apparition after taking office. General Zurlinden was the first. He himself had urged révision; within two days of taking office he told Brisson that there should be no retrial and that he would resign if one were decided on. The cabinet decided on retrial and Zurlinden resigned. Next General Chanoine, who was believed to favor révision, took office but within days, during a dramatic meeting of the Chamber, Chanoine also resigned. Next the Brisson cabinet itself received a vote of no confidence and left office.

The next cabinet, headed by Charles Dupuy and organized on a 'concentration' pattern with roughly equal Radical and Moderate participation, took office on 1 November 1898. It would last until 12 June 1899. Dupuy's ministry was a stop-gap measure, lacking a solid majority or a unifying issue. In the terms of Marcel Fournier, it was a coalition of negation.

Waldeck-Rousseau Forms His Concentration 'Ministry of Republican Defense'

On 3 June 1899, the United Appeals Court, having received expert opinion that the *bordereau* which had led to the conviction of Dreyfus had in fact been written by Esterhazy, ruled that Dreyfus should be retried before a military court in Rennes. The Dreyfusards had gotten their révision. Anti-Dreyfusards were furious. The ruling in favor of retrial came during a period of agitation in Paris in early June 1899; on 1 June the poet and deputy Paul Déroulède had been acquitted of the minor charge of 'provocation against the security of the State' arising from his February 'coup' attempt at the funeral of Félix Faure. On his release, Déroulède's supporters carried their hero on their shoulders through the streets, leading Clemenceau to write of 'civil war' and Jaurès to see 'reaction triumphant'. The next day, 2 June, Major Marchand, the recently returned hero of the French expedition to Fashoda on the Upper Nile, accepted the reception offered him by nationalists and expressed an opinion critical of the government. Three days later at the Auteuil race track, President Loubet's top hat was dented when the young baron de Christiani swung at him with a cane and a fracas between police and elegant young men at the races resulted in about one hundred temporary arrests.[28]

Early June's effervescence, which Paris was so adept at producing, set the stage for the resounding defeat of the Dupuy cabinet on 12 June. The Radicals who had supported Dupuy to this point now deserted him; the majority that defeated Dupuy was composed of a preponderance of

28. Sorlin, *Waldeck-Rousseau*, pp. 395–399; Guy Chapman, *The Dreyfus Case, A Reassessment* (London: Hart-Davis, 1955), pp. 257, 265, 266.

Radicals along with a few Moderates and Socialists. The Radicals thus took the opportunity to prepare the way for a concentration ministry headed by Waldeck-Rousseau in which they would form the preponderant part of the majority. Waldeck would lead a government of 'republican defense', and here was the 'threat to the Republic' to justify it.

Before inviting Waldeck-Rousseau to form a government, President Loubet offered the opportunity to Poincaré, the Moderate leader and Léon Bourgeois, leader of the Radicals. Poincaré declined; Bourgeois returned from the Hague Peace Conference to which he was a delegate and also declined, saying that it was important for him to return to the Hague 'where important developments were in the offing'. By this performance, Bourgeois demonstrated his support of the ministry Waldeck-Rousseau would organize. Throughout the tenure of that ministry, whenever Radical support threatened to waiver, Bourgeois would rally it in 'defense of the Republic'. Finally President Loubet called on Waldeck-Rousseau who proceeded to form his long-lived concentration ministry of 'republican defense', thus satisfying the need for 'concentration' under a positive banner which the *Revue Politique et Parlementaire* had indicated after the general elections a year earlier.

As Pierre Sorlin has shown, Waldeck had been moving toward the creation of a concentration ministry since January 1899, before the existence of any of the supposed 'threats to the Republic' which presumably justified it. To do this, he had the close cooperation of Raymond Poincaré and Alexandre Millerand. Poincaré, a brilliant young lawyer, had been one of several impressive young men recruited in 1889 by haut bourgeois leaders to represent their position in the Chamber. Sponsored by the powerful politician of the Meuse, Jules Develle, Poincaré had made a name for himself by playing an important part in planning the demise of Bourgeois's Radical Ministry at the 'dinner historique' of 4 April 1896 at the Durand restaurant. Since then he had dropped out of active participation in politics to concentrate on developing his lucrative practice as a lawyer for haut bourgeois clients.[29]

Millerand, a talented lawyer, was a long-time friend of Poincaré. Between 1893 and 1898 he had been an important independent Socialist deputy, and around 1898 he took on the responsibilities of a wife and child. In the months after the creation of Waldeck's ministry of republican defense, Millerand would inherit a large part of Waldeck-Rousseau's hugely profitable law practice.

29. Sorlin, *Waldeck-Rousseau*, pp. 395, 398; Emmanuel Beau de Loménie, *Les responsabilités des dynasties bourgeoises*, vol. II, *Sous la Troisième République de Mac-Mahon à Poincaré* (Paris: Les Editions Denoel, 1947), pp. 209, 251, 252; Jacques Chastenet, *Raymond Poincaré* (Paris: René Julliard, 1948), pp. 38, 43; Fernand Payan, *Raymond Poincaré* (Paris: Bernard Grasset, 1936), pp. 48, 170, 173–176.

Already in February 1899, Waldeck was preparing his justification for a ministry of 'republican defense'. After two months of intermittent street agitation related to the Dreyfus Affair, Waldeck and his friends claimed to recognize a threat to the Republic which others did not perceive. His address to the Senate on 28 February indicated the ethereal nature of the supposed threat:

> I would wish to be optimistic, but I can not be. The feeling of an increasing insecurity is spreading. Some feel all-powerful. Others feel menaced. Governmental functions are divided. Leagues form. It is the dawn of anarchy . . . The material plot is nowhere to be found but moral conspiracy is all about.[30]

On 18 June 1899 President Loubet called on the Senator from the Loire to form a cabinet. After ten days, while appropriate suspense developed, the elegant, dignified and glacial Waldeck-Rousseau produced on his second attempt his government of 'republican defense'. The coalition that supported Waldeck included a preponderance of Radicals and some Socialists and Moderates. When it was formed the government had what was most likely a deliberately slim majority of about twenty-five, provided by the support of Edouard Aynard, the liberal Catholic banker from Lyon, and about twenty of his friends. The reason Waldeck-Rousseau preferred a narrow majority to the huge one which would have been the result if all 'republicans' had supported his government was that, as the results of the 1893 general elections had shown, a huge 'republican' majority would tend to divide within itself, leading to the same left-right division of the Chamber which had produced Bourgeois's Radical ministry with its proposal for an impôt sur le revenu.

Historians have sometimes held that the deputies who opposed Waldeck-Rousseau's ministry were opposed to the Republic (for example, Alfred Cobban in his *A History of Modern France*). Nothing could be further from the truth. The majority of deputies who voted against Waldeck's ministry were Moderates who had supported the Méline ministry of 1896–98 and for whom Waldeck-Rousseau himself had strenuously campaigned before the general elections of May 1898. A minority were Catholic ralliés who had also supported the Méline ministry. Moderates and ralliés can only be described as republicans.

Waldeck's majority included about 173 Radicals, 21 Socialists and 61 Moderates. In establishing his coalition, Waldeck-Rousseau split the parliamentary Jacobins who had been united between 1893 and 1898 along their natural lines of cleavage; he divided provincial Jacobins

---

30. Sorlin, *Waldeck-Rousseau*, pp. 397, 398.

(Radicals) from the Parisian Jacobins (nationalists, typified by Henri Rochefort and his newspaper the *Intransigeant* who opposed the cabinet's presumed antagonism toward the Army). The groups which had been united in the Tivoli Vaux-Hall protest meeting after the fall of the Bourgeois ministry in April 1896 and had gone to demonstrate before the newspapers which represented their respective positions in its aftermath (see above, chapter 5), were divided by Waldeck-Rousseau in his construction of his ministry of republican defense.

Understanding that Waldeck-Rousseau designed his coalition to solve the problem posed by a Chamber in which Socialists, Socialist Radicals and Radicals comprised a majority helps explain the well-known shift of Paris's deputies from Radical to Nationalist between the 1890s and the 1900s. Philip Nord (*Paris Shopkeepers and the Politics of Resentment*) has described this transformation as taking place 'in the 1890s'. We can be more precise. This 'volte face' (Nord's words) occurred in 1899 when Waldeck-Rousseau formed his concentration coalition of republican defense.

The efforts of historians to understand the shift of Paris from Radical to Nationalist has been hampered by their use of the conventional but confusing left-to-right categories of political description. Employing these, Nord sought to explain the shift of Parisian deputies from left to right (from Figure 1 to Figure 2) while the content of their political beliefs remained constant.

Left-Right Mapping of Political Positions

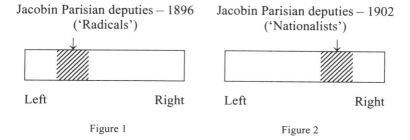

Jacobin Parisian deputies – 1896 ('Radicals')

Jacobin Parisian deputies – 1902 ('Nationalists')

Left   Right   Left   Right

Figure 1   Figure 2

An alternative mapping of political positions may be useful. With the total membership of the Chamber represented by a circle, the deputies included in the majority coalition could be represented by an inner circle and those not included by the donut-shaped outer ring.

An Alternative Mapping of Political Positions

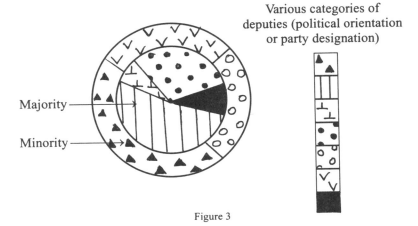

Various categories of
deputies (political orientation
or party designation)

Majority

Minority

Figure 3

With this mapping the change from the Méline to the Waldeck-Rousseau coalitions would be represented as:

■ Moderates

▦ Provincial Jacobins
(Radicals and Socialist Radicals)

• Catholic ralliés

ᐯ Socialists

≡ Catholic conservatives

▲ Parisian Jacobins
(Radicals and Nationalists)

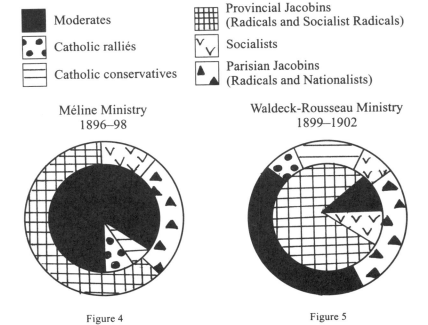

Méline Ministry
1896–98

Waldeck-Rousseau Ministry
1899–1902

Figure 4

Figure 5

Nord understood that the content of Parisian political convictions changed little if at all while Parisians were undergoing their putative transition from left to right. Before the dreyfusian revolution Parisian deputies were allied with provincial Radical deputies. Afterwards, they were outside the majority coalition in which provincial Radicals predominated. They were in opposition because Waldeck-Rousseau's dreyfusian revolution required that Parisian Jacobins be divided from provincial Jacobins to allow for a Moderate 'veto minority' within the majority coalition.

By supporting Waldeck-Rousseau's ministry, provincial Radicals exchanged pursuit of the impôt sur le revenu and social progress for the plums of patronage they had asked for but not received from Léon Bourgeois's Radical ministry of 1895–96. After 1900, provincial Radicals easily accepted the cheap but effective political glue of anti-clericalism to which Waldeck-Rousseau turned to hold together his coalition. With the Jacobin left divided and Moderates an integral part of the majority coalition, the impôt sur le revenu was no longer a threat and the problem of democracy was solved.

Though the Republic was not menaced when Waldeck-Rousseau took office, many Frenchmen (particularly Radical politicians) were content to accept the idea that it was. The reason is that without a threat to the Republic, no sense can be made of Waldeck-Rousseau's government in the terms in which it was presented, as a ministry of republican defense. The 'threat to the Republic' which Waldeck-Rousseau and his friends conjured up was just what the *Revue Politique et Parlementaire* had recommended about a year earlier in order to give lasting power to a concentration coalition. It transformed what would otherwise have been a drab coalition of compromise into a glorious one of republican defense.

Contrary to the common impression, the Republic's existence was never even remotely threatened during the Dreyfus Affair. The only supposed threat that historians have discerned occurred in early and mid-1899, toward the end of the Affair. These events of February and early June 1899 — Déroulède's farcical attempted coup, his acquittal on the charges which stemmed from it, Major Marchand's criticism of the government and the fracas at Auteuil — are the only evidence offered to show that the Republic was threatened during the Affair. Yet despite such flimsy support, the idea that the Republic was indeed menaced has been commonly accepted.[31]

31. Among the countless examples which could be cited see Douglas Johnson, *France and the Dreyfus Affair* (New York, 1966), p. 183; Leslie Derfler, *Alexandre Millerand — The Socialist Years* (The Hague, 1977), pp. 139, 146; Susanna Barrows, *Distorting Mirrors — Visions of the Crowd in the Late Nineteenth Century* (New Haven, 1984), p. 184; Phyllis

The myth that the Dreyfus Affair brought France to the verge of civil war and that anti-Dreyfusards threatened the existence of the Republic owes much of its present strength to the fact that historians have repeated it so often. Typical of what historians have written, Alfred Cobban wrote that in early 1899 'the country seemed on the verge of civil war', and provided as evidence Déroulède's 'attempt at a coup' which 'was a farcical failure'. Cobban continued: 'In the summer of 1899 it seemed that the Republican regime was breaking down. A trivial incident in June proved the turning point. In the course of a visit to the races at Auteuil by the new President of Republic, Loubet, a royalist baron knocked his hat off with a stick. This was going too far.' Cobban had the Republican regime on the verge of collapse, but cited only the incident at Autueil to support his claim.[32]

Supporters of Waldeck-Rousseau's ministry had reason to maintain the fiction that during the Dreyfus Affair the survival of the Republic was threatened. For the Radical and Socialist deputies who supported Waldeck-Rousseau, the supposed threat to the Republic was a handy rationalization for not pursuing the democratic reforms they had advocated in their election campaigns. In forming an anti-clerical coalition they were simply pursuing their long-held and loudly stated claim, false though it was, that the Catholic supporters of the Méline ministry were 'enemies of the Republic' and in some way endangered it. For Moderate politicians who supported Waldeck-Rousseau, nothing was lost in accepting the idea which justified the concentration coalition that diverted attention from the 'revolutionary' impôt sur le revenu. Only the Catholic Church would suffer when Waldeck-Rousseau's ministry turned against it claiming that it was involved in a plot which never existed.

Moderates who were not part of Waldeck's coalition ridiculed the idea that the Republic was somehow in danger in June 1899. Frances Charmes's political chronicle in the *Revue des Deux Mondes* expressed this view. On 14 June, after the fall of the Dupuy but before the formation of Waldeck-Rousseau's cabinet, Charmes mocked the idea that the Republic was threatened by the elegant rowdies, 'the chevaliers of the white carnation,' at the Auteuil races and attributed baron Christiani's assault on President Loubet to his having consumed too much champagne that day at lunch. The 30 June 'Chronique' of *Revue des Deux Mondes*, written shortly after Waldeck-Rousseau took office, sharply attacked the idea that the Republic was in danger. 'The peril which has been so much

---

Albert Cohen, review of Robert Hoffman's *More Than A Trial — The Struggle Over Captain Dreyfus* in *American Historical Review*, vol. 86, Oct. 1981, p. 861.

32. Alfred Cobban, *A History of Modern France*, vol. III (Baltimore: Penguin Books, 1965), pp. 55–56.

spoken about', wrote Francis Charmes, 'is imaginary.'[33]

The liberal Catholic *Le Correspondant* also ridiculed the idea that the Republic was somehow endangered in June 1899. It described as an 'invented plot' the supposed threat presented by the 'white carnations' at Auteuil and claimed that the counter-demonstration at the races at Longchamps had been produced as a public spectacle to confirm the transition to the politics of concentration. *Le Correspondant*, reporting that Waldeck-Rousseau invoked 'republican defense' in his ministerial declaration, approvingly quoted Méline that 'republican defense is only a lie, only an immense mystification' in which Waldeck himself did not believe.[34]

Soon after he took office, however, Waldeck-Rousseau began conjuring up threats to the Republic. After having 37 nationalists arrested in late June 1899, he had a falsely dated accusatory report fabricated in order to justify his action.[35]

Waldeck-Rousseau has long been held in high regard by the French. François Goguel, one of the foremost historians of the Third Republic, suggested that this reputation is not justified, for in fact Waldeck-Rousseau accomplished very little as premier.[36] This evaluation overlooks Waldeck's chief accomplishment, for it was he who solved the problem of democracy; how to organize a coalition majority which would be safe for the haute bourgeoisie in a Chamber of Deputies having a majority of Radicals, Socialist Radicals and Socialists.[37]

33. Francis Charmes, 'Chronique de la quinzaine', *RDM*, CLIII (June 1899), pp. 947, 955; 'Chronique,' *RDM*, CLIV (July 1, 1899), pp. 231, 232, 238.
34. Louis Joubert, 'Chronique politique', *Le Correspondant*, CXCV (June 25, 1899), pp. 1234, 1235; Ibid., CXCVI (July 10, 1899), p. 197.
35. Sorlin, *Waldeck-Rousseau*, pp. 415–416.
36. Author's conversation with François Goguel, May 11, 1971.
37. It is ironic that Pierre Sorlin in his biography of Waldeck-Rousseau evaluates the political accomplishments of his subject so differently than I do. About Waldeck-Rousseau, Sorlin wrote: 'His enduring accomplishments were of little importance . . . The only important act of his political life was the creation, in June 1899, of a ministry charged with liquidating the Affair and putting an end to the nationalist agitation . . . today these acts of courage would appear to be insufficient to place him among the great figures of the nineteenth century' (Sorlin, *Waldeck-Rousseau*, pp. 488–9). I credit Waldeck-Rousseau with a considerably greater accomplishment than his biographer. As engineer of the 'Radical republic', he deserves greater respect for his role in resolving the fin-de-siècle crisis of democracy in France.
I have called Waldeck-Rousseau the 'engineer' of the dreyfusian revolution. Perhaps 'magician' or 'conjurer' would be better terms to describe his role. After all, Waldeck-Rousseau did conjure a threat to the republic whose credibility has withstood the test of time. As for his being a magician, Waldeck-Rousseau's biographer himself appears to have not understood what his subject was doing by creating his 'ministry of republican defense'. For this Waldeck-Rousseau should be credited with a brilliant performance as well as an important accomplishment.

In one sense Waldeck-Rousseau *may* be understood to have defended the Republic with his ministry of 'republican defense' if one takes seriously what bourgeois leaders of the period frequently said – that if the Jacobin 'left' created an impôt sur le revenu against the will of the Senate, this in itself would be revolution and some sort of 'counter-revolutionary' coup against the Republic would surely follow. Thus in 1893 the *Nouvelle Revue* warned that dictatorship would follow a victory of the left when Senator Marcère, author of its political chronicle, wrote that if Jacobin socialism triumphed, it would spell its own doom.[38] In December 1894 Marcère wrote that fiscal demagoguery could bring Caesarism; and to its foes the impôt was the supreme piece of fiscal demagoguery.[39] In 1896 Ferdinand Faure wrote that the only way dictatorship would come to France would be from a crisis of 'legal socialism' resulting from 'vexatious taxes'. To its opponents, no tax could be more 'vexatious' than the impôt sur le revenu.[40]

It was during the 'Month of Crisis' between March and April 1896 that a coup was threatened by foes of the Radical ministry. The *Revue Diplomatique* described the danger clearly: 'To maintain the Bourgeois ministry in power would be to accomplish a "parliamentary coup d'etat" and open the doors to other violations.' Charles Dupuy, the former and future prime minister, warned that the Radical cabinet was letting itself get cornered into a 'revolutionary situation'.

In November 1897, no less a personage than Prime Minister Jules Méline stated that he had opposed the Bourgeois Radical ministry when its alliance with the Socialists threatened to lead to a crisis which would have been followed by an 'inevitable reaction'. Again in April 1898, just before the general elections, Méline repeated the idea: 'The first, the most important service that I believe I have rendered the Republic is to have prevented it from drifting imperceptibly into revolution which would lead to inevitable reaction . . .'[41]

Thus in the 1890s, if the Republic had been the object of a coup and parliamentary government had been replaced by autocratic rule, it would not have been the work of the socialist 'left' or the reactionary 'far right'. Rather, the coup would have been engineered by the haute bourgeoisie represented in the Chamber by the Moderates in accordance with Thiers' dictum that, 'Either the Republic will be conservative or it will not *be*.'

It was Jean Jaurès, the great Socialist orator, who did the most to secure

38. *The Encyclopaedia Britannica*, 11th edn., vol. X, p. 833.
39. Marcère, 'Chronique politique', *Nouvelle Revue*, LXXXI (March 15, 1893), p. 426; Ibid., XCI (Dec. 15, 1894), pp. 852–854.
40. Ferdinand Dreyfus, *Etudes et discourses* (Paris: Calman Lévy, 1896), p. v.
41. Simond, *Historie de la Troisième République de 1897–1899*, p. 127; Félix Roussel, 'Chronique politique intérieure', *RPP*, XIV (Nov. 10, 1897), pp. 465–466.

Socialist support for Waldeck-Rousseau's ministry. For several months before its arrival, Jaurès had written frequently about what he claimed was a threat to the Republic posed by anti-Dreyfusards. If, as I have argued, there was no significant threat to the Republic by anti-Dreyfusards, what was it that led Jaurès to claim that there was and prefer Waldeck-Rousseau's concentration ministry to the unified 'left' coalition of Radicals, Socialist Radicals and Socialists which had existed between 1893 and 1898 and had sought the impôt sur le revenu?

When the Bourgeois Radical ministry left office in April 1896, Jaurès told the packed protest meeting at the Tivoli Vaux-Hall that there should be no return to concentration (see above, chapter 5). But by 1899 he had changed his mind. Why? Could it be that he had come to take seriously the threats of those leaders of the haute bourgeoisie who warned that the triumph of 'Jacobin socialism' would spell the end of the Republic, and that given the choice between a conservative parliamentary 'Republic' and no Republic at all, Jaurès chose the former?

A paradox presented by the Dreyfus Affair may now be understood: not only did the Affair never threaten the existence of the Republic, but the Dreyfus Affair itself may have helped to save the 'Republic' (which, it should be understood, was not a republic in the classic sense, but rather a parliamentary republic) by contributing to the resolution of the true crisis of the 1890s – the crisis of democracy – which stemmed from the upper bourgeoisie's nightmare that the democratic masses threatened to overwhelm and destroy it by gaining political hegemony and confiscating its wealth by taxation. By providing the justification for a long-lived concentration ministry of republican defense which precluded the possibility of a Radical and Socialist majority coalition, Waldeck-Rousseau may well have helped prevent the 'inevitable reaction' which Moderate leaders warned would destroy the Republic if the 'revolutionary' impôt were enacted.

—9—

Conclusion

The coalition which supported Waldeck-Rousseau's concentration ministry included a majority of Radicals and minorities of Socialists and Moderates. One cost of returning to a concentration pattern in order to avoid a homogeneous coalition of the left was that henceforth Radicals would have first claim on governmental administrative patronage. As Daniel Halévy wrote, it was from the time of the Waldeck-Rousseau ministry that Radicals availed themselves of a kind of 'right' to State employment.[1]

Although it could be argued that by trading the pursuit of democratic tax reform for the pursuit of administrative patronage, Radicals had sacrificed true Jacobin ideals for 'a mess of pottage', it could also be argued that by seeking to control government administration, Radicals were simply expressing classic Jacobin values. For was not the fundamental interest of Jacobins (as Edward Fox has shown in his *History in Geographic Perspective*) the functioning of the national administration, be it called 'royal', 'Napoleonic' or 'republican'? Historians have generally emphasized the legislative side of government activity more that the administrative. (One obvious reason for this is that government's legislative activities are more in the public view than its administrative activities.) However, the idea that Jacobin politicians would be particularly interested in controlling governments's administrative activities should not be surprising.

For the haute bourgeoisie, allowing Radicals access to government patronage was a modest price for avoiding the nightmare of a homogeneous coalition of the left seeking the 'revolutionary' impôt sur le revenu. Another cost of Waldeck-Rousseau's concentration ministry was that from the election of 1902 onward haut bourgeois money helped finance the electoral campaigns of some Radical deputies. Thus in 1902 about three million francs of such funds were distributed to useful candidates through the Comité Républicain du Commerce de l'Industrie et de l'Agriculture, informally known as the 'comité Mascaraud' after

1. Daniel Halévy, *La République des comités* (Paris: B. Grasset, 1934), p. 50.

the name of its administrator, a Parisian jewelry manufacturer.[2]

With the possibility of an income tax blocked by the veto of the Moderate faction of Waldeck-Rousseau's coalition and the possibility of social welfare barred by both lack of funds and lack of interest by the coalition's majority, it was perhaps inevitable that a campaign against 'clericalism' would become the chief rallying cry of the Radicals. The beauty of anti-clericalism as a political issue was that it cost government coffers little and it was meaningful in provincial towns, where anti-clericals gathered typically at a 'café du progrès' opposite the local Catholic church and anti-clerical lawyers and school teachers competed with the local gentry and curé in the battle for the allegiance of ordinary citizens.

With the menace of a government of the left seeking 'revolutionary' 'socialistic' taxation resolved by the elegant expediency of restructuring the Chamber's majority coalition, the need that had motivated many of the bourgeoisie's proposals for social defense in the mid-1890s faded. As a result, interest in and activity to promote these proposals also faded. Thus proposals to reduce the power of the Chamber of Deputies by increasing the power of the President of the Republic and the Conseil d'Etat were laid aside.[3]

And the movement for administrative decentralization, which had flourished between 1895 and 1898, lost its raison d'etre and faded quickly. 'Proposals for administrative decentralization surge from all sides' *Le Matin* had reported in 1895. In January 1897 *Le Temps* reported that the work of the League for Decentralization was already well advanced. In early 1898, before the general elections, the *Nouvelle Revue* wrote 'people are beginning to no longer smile at plans for decentralization', and in June 1898, after the general elections, the *Nouvelle Revue* reported that 'decentralization has rallied an immense majority of votes'. In 1898 the American political scientist James T. Young, in his article 'Administrative Centralization and Decentralization in France', predicted that the growing

2. Jacques Chastenet, *Histoire de la Troisième République*, vol. III, pp. 168, 217, 218; Félix Ponteil, *Les classes bourgeoises et l'avènement de la démocratie, 1815–1914* (Paris: Albin Michel, 1869), p. 423; Francis Delaisi, 'Les financiers et la démocratie', reprinted in *Crapouillot*, Nov. 1936, pp. 2, 21 (originally published by Editions de la Guerre Sociale, 1911).

3. Proposals to increase the power of the Senate had already been realized to an extent. Boucard and Jèze in their 1896 text on State finances wrote that in recent years the Senate had played an increased role in budget formation. By forcing Bourgeois's Radical ministry to resign, the Senate established the precedent that it could remove a ministry from office and thereby act effectively as an 'emergency brake' for a Chamber of Deputies 'out of control'. Several times again during the history of the Third Republic the Senate would force a cabinet from office, thereby serving the function for which it had been designed by the authors of the Constitutional Laws of 1875.

movement for decentralization since 1890 'bids fair to bring about more important measures of this nature than any that have gone before'.[4] But the movement which had appeared to be so strong through the elections of 1898 subsided quickly after Waldeck-Rousseau formed his concentration cabinet in June 1899. The Ligue de la Décentralisation soon ceased to exist, and in September 1899 the *Nouvelle Revue* printed the last of its monthly columns on 'Decentralization' and 'The Provinces'.[5]

One reaction of the haute bourgeoisie to the Chamber's threat of 'fiscal socialism' was to increase its paternalistic activities in order to calm social unrest and enhance its legitimacy as a classe dirigeante. After Waldeck-Rousseau's restructuring of politics defused the menace of democracy a slackening of bourgeois paternalistic efforts might be expected, but whether this occurred has yet to be determined. In *The Third Republic Defended – Bourgeois Reform in France, 1880–1914* Sandford Elwitt studied bourgeois paternalism but did not gauge the level of interest in it at different times in the period he covered.

It could not be said that the chief advocates of the impôt learned nothing from their brush with the haute bourgeoisie's fury. Paul Doumer was soon enticed by an offer from his erstwhile Moderate opponents. In December 1896 Prime Minister Méline, on the suggestion of his Finance Minister Georges Cochery, appointed Doumer Governor General of the French colony in Indo-China in order to cut short his campaign in favor of the impôt. After Doumer returned to France and regained a seat in parliament in 1902, he was made administrator of the Comité des forges (Iron and Steel Council) and president of the Compagnie Générale d'Electricité. It may be assumed that by then he had paid off his debt to his former sponsor, the publisher of the anti-military *Piou-Piou de l'Yonne*. Eventually Doumer was elected to the Senate and went on, in 1931, to become President of the Republic.[6]

It was reported that Léon Bourgeois was immensely happy when the pressures of office were removed from his shoulders and he could return to his philosophy and poetry.[7] Once again he could frequent the

---

4. 'La décentralisation,' *Le Matin*, March 6, 1895, p. 2; *Le Temps*, Jan. 30, 1897, p. 1; 'Décentralisation,' *La Nouvelle Revue*, CXII (May 1, 1898), p. 154; XII (June 1, 1898), p. 540; James T. Young, 'Administrative Centralization and Decentralization in France', *Annals of the American Academy of Political and Social Sciences* (Jan.–June 1898), p. 40.

5. Robert K. Gooch, *Regionalism in France* (New York: The Century Co., 1931), p. 102.

6. Emanuel Beau de Loménie, *Les responsibilités des dynasties bourgeoises*, vol. II (Paris: Denoel, 1947), pp. 412–413; Saint Simon, *Propos de Félix Faure*, 3rd edn. (Paris: Paul Ollendorff, 1902), p. 194–195.

7. Adolphe Brisson, *Les Prophètes* (Paris: Ernest Flammarion, n.d.), p. 272.

Conclusion

Montmartre night spots where, during his term as prime minister, bourgeois patrons had made him feel less than welcome. Bourgeois, always an amiable man, a conciliator who sought to bring people together and who evidently had not enjoyed the bitter conflict which had engaged his ministry, remained a deputy but turned away from involvement in the Chamber. Twice, before and after Waldeck-Rousseau's ministry of June 1899 to June 1902, he declined the President of the Republic's invitation to attempt to form a cabinet. Bourgeois supported Waldeck-Rousseau's coalition, and when its existence was endangered by a defection of some on its 'right', Bourgeois rallied Radical support with the cry 'the Republic in danger!' Unable to achieve social reform in France, Bourgeois then turned his talents toward promoting world peace through international arbitration at the Hague Conference. Within France he continued to play the role of sage arbitrator and patriarch of the Republic for which he gained the sobriquets 'Bourgeois the just', 'the universal pacificator' and 'the angel of arbitration'.[8]

Léon Bourgeois's reaction to his experience of heading a purely Radical ministry in 1895–96 was not surprising. He had never really liked the idea of a homogeneous left ministry supported by Radicals, Socialist Radicals and Socialists, and had agreed to head such a coalition in 1895 only as a last resort at the urging of the influential Godefroy Cavaignac, as a means to enact an impôt sur le revenu. Cavaignac had urged the impôt on Bourgeois and Doumer at meetings in his home on rue Verneuil in late 1894 and early 1895. At first Bourgeois had sought to form a concentration ministry that would include Radicals and Moderates and would seek an impôt sur le revenu (see above, chapter 3); only after failing to achieve that political impossibility did Bourgeois agree to head an homogeneous Radical ministry to seek the impôt which Cavaignac believed was so urgent.

The lesson Léon Bourgeois took from his taste of the fury of the haute bourgeoisie was that class conflict is not the way to achieve social progress. If social progress was to come, he believed, it would be through changing men's minds, through education. 'Solidarité' was the name he gave to his philosophy and movement.

After Bourgeois left office, he reanimated his interest in education as the greatest force for the reform of men. In 1897, Edouard Cornély published *The Education of French Democracy*, a collection of Bourgeois's speeches concerning public education made on occasions such as prize distributions, funerals and meetings of leagues of education. Bourgeois involved himself with the Ecole des Hautes Etudes Sociales which presented courses in Paris and published books expressing the idea

8. Daniel Halévy, *La République des comités* (Paris: B. Grasset, 1934), p. 48.

that social progress would come through education. At the Ecole des Hautes Etudes Sociales he could preach his doctrine of *solidarité*, which he had proposed in an article of the same name in the *Nouvelle Revue* before he took office in 1895. In that article Bourgeois had attempted to offer the bourgeoisie a philosophic rationale as to why they should pay a fair share of taxes.

Over the years Bourgeois expanded the successive editions of *Solidarité* which achieved wide distribution as an important statement of Radical philosophy.[9] Near the turn of the century the ever-optimistic Bourgeois told a reporter from the *Vienna Neue Presse* about the 'magnificent movement' manifesting itself in support of his ideas. Conceptions of social justice and solidarity, he said, 'were coming to infuse morals and penetrate the younger generations . . . The groundwork for future progress is being laid now.'[10]

After Waldeck-Rousseau became prime minister with the support of provincial Radicals, Godefroy Cavaignac turned away in disgust from parliamentary politics and became a leader of the Comité Pour La Patrie Français. The Comité's main purpose was to oppose the government of Waldeck-Rousseau. Though it enlisted some of the brightest literary and cultural lights of the period, it failed as a political force. Cavaignac's political career never did recover in the few years he had remaining, and in 1905 he died.

The End of the Fin-de-Siècle

The Dreyfus Affair coincided with the end of the fin-de-siècle mood of lethargy and pessimism. It also coincided with the end of the 1893–96 recession and the beginning of the economic expansion which followed. The Affair came at the time when a new vigor and action animated the French spirit.

In 1893 the novelist Henry Berenger had described the fin-de-siècle

9. A recent study (Judith Stone, *The Search for Social Peace – Reform Legislation in France, 1890–1914*, Albany, State University of New York Press, 1985) has presented 'solidarity' as a philosophy whose purpose was to prevent revolution. I suggest rather that for Léon Bourgeois and the Radicals, 'solidarity' was an outcome of their decision to give up the political battle to legislate social reform with the impôt sur le revenu; henceforth they would seek reform with sweet philosophic reason rather than hard political power. While it is true that Bourgeois first published 'Solidarity' as an article in the *Nouvelle Revue* in 1895 before he headed his Radical ministry in 1895–96, it was only in the years following his ministry, years during which he declined to attempt to lead an homogeneous ministry of the left – the only type which could have achieved significant social legislation in that period – that Bourgeois expanded his 'Solidarity' article into a book and made its philosophy the basis of a 'school'.

10. Adolphe Brisson, *Les Prophètes*, p. 283.

mood in the preface to his novel *L'Effort*. He wrote of the 'morbid intellectualism — an agent of death, characteristic of our epoch, which reduces us to seeking the spectacle of life rather than the life itself and the idea of feelings rather than feelings themselves', and went on to describe the 'intellectual' of his generation as a complex and tormented being who has tried all the alternatives of modern thought but is satisfied with none and whose dry lucidity gradually crystallizes his soul.[11]

By 1899 Berenger observed, 'A literature of action is being born in France', and cited the recent works of Ricard, Barrès, Margueritte, Clemenceau, Daudet, Descaves, Emile Zola, Anatole France, J.H. Rosny and Léon Daudet to illustrate his point. 'The old divorce between thought and action, between art and life, which was dogma of previous generations,' he declared, 'is beginning to reach its end.'[12]

Bourgeois youth recovered from its fin-de-siècle malaise at the time of the Dreyfus Affair. From late 1897 the 'problem of the youth' faded quickly as educated young men threw themselves into the Affair and proved that they lacked neither energy nor will. Anatole Leroy-Beaulieu ended the anti-socialist campaign among university youth which he had led since 1894, and English-style athletics and secondary education, so much discussed in the mid 1890s, made little progress in France in the years following 1898.

The Dreyfus Affair provided bourgeois Frenchmen with a perfect end to the fin-de-siècle. If the Affair can properly be said to have 'divided French society into two camps' (these are the words which are commonly used), the society which it divided was that of upper-class Paris salons — 'society' in the narrow upper crust sense of the word — not the mass of the French population. The main division was between the two most famous 'political' salons, Mme de Loyne's which starred Jules Lemaître, and Mme Arman de Cailevet's where Anatole France reigned. For upper-class society, the Dreyfus Affair was a marvelous opportunity. After four years barren of any 'political' issue worthy of debate (because virtually all of the bourgeoisie opposed the impôt), the Affair was a perfect topic of controversy because it could engage strong passions yet divide people within, not between, class lines. The historian Douglas Johnson has pointed out that anti-Dreyfusards 'rejoiced at the fact that the opposition to Dreyfus crossed over class barriers, and brought together workers, aristocrats and others'. The same could be said for the Dreyfusards. In the Affair, members of the bourgeoisie on both sides of the issue found themselves at public meetings next to workers and students who shared their opinions. In this non-threatening proximity with society's lower

11. Henry Berenger, *L'effort*, 2nd edn. (Paris: Armand Colin, 1905), p. xv.
12. Henry Berenger, *La France intellectuelle* (Paris: Armand Colin, 1899), p. 118.

Forgotten Crisis

classes, a bourgeois could feel secure.[13]

For educated Frenchmen, the passion they could invest in the Dreyfus Affair was a welcome change from the fin-de-siècle mood which had, by that time, grown stale. Thus Romain Roland's entry in his diary of the time: 'I would rather have this life of combat than the mortal calm and mournful stupor of these last years. God give me struggle, enemies, howling crowds, all the combat of which I am capable.'[14]

The Affair was especially welcome to members of the younger generation of educated Frenchmen for it presented them with an opportunity they would otherwise have missed. Joseph Paul-Boncour, a politician active in the early years of the twentieth century, described the dearth of political battles to arouse the interest of students of the 1890s. The Dreyfus Affair came at a time when the Latin Quarter was bored.[15] To some it gave the chance to defend the Army and *La Patrie* against their enemies. To others it gave the opportunity to fight for great principles and 'defend the Republic' against its enemies; that the Republic was not the least in danger was of little psychological importance. The experience of the Affair would long remain with the leaders of France who lived through it, fertilizing their work for years to come.

France's political experience of 1893 to late 1897 – the division of the deputies in the Chamber between left and right, the Bourgeois Radical ministry seeking the impôt sur le revenu, the 'Month of Crisis' – has been suppressed or repressed in the French historical memory. Pierre Sorlin has written that this period has been a blank space in French history.[16] This helps explain the silence of history books regarding Godefroy Cavaignac's role as a political leader between 1894 and 1898, although it should be noted that contributing to this silence was Cavaignac's own preference for a role 'above parties' and the fact that he never was the nominal head of a cabinet.[17]

In his biography of Waldeck-Rousseau, Pierre Sorlin omits any discussion of the Radical ministry and the impôt sur le revenu which so

13. Douglas W. Johnson, *France and the Dreyfus Affair* (London: Blandford, 1966), p. 220.
14. Quoted from Barbara Tuchman, *The Proud Tower* (New York: Bantam Books, 1966), p. 237.
15. Joseph Paul-Boncour, *Recollections of the Third Republic*, vol. I (New York: Robert Speller & Sons, 1957), pp. 72–73; Johnson, *France and the Dreyfus Affair*, p. 1.
16. Pierre Sorlin, *Waldeck-Rousseau*. Page 364 contains his only mention (a one line footnote) of the Bourgeois Radical ministry.
17. *A Biographical Dictionary of Political Leaders Since 1870*, edited by David Bell, Douglas Johnson and Peter Morris (New York, 1990) does not include Godefroy Cavaignac, nor does the *Historical Dictionary of the French Third Republic*, (Westport, Conn., Greenwood Press, 1986), edited by Patrick Hutton.

agitated the subject of his study. Therefore Waldeck's turn from 'right' to 'left' at the time of the Dreyfus Affair has appeared to be something of a mystery. Once it is understood, however, that Waldeck-Rousseau re-entered politics in 1894 in order to oppose 'Jacobin socialism' and the impôt, his political actions make sense: either he could defeat the Radicals at the polls, or he could de-fang them by joining with some of them in a concentration coalition that would compromise their dangerous proclivity toward 'socialistic' taxation.

François Goguel, in his *Geography of French Elections under the Third and Fourth Republic*, did not include Radicals in the category of 'extreme left' for 1893–98, although he had classified them as such for the years before 1893. This is misleading for it obscures the fact that between 1893 and 1898 Radicals voted with Socialist Radicals and Socialists against Moderate ministries and in support of Léon Bourgeois's cabinet. Without realizing that between 1893 and 1898 the left was unified and in pursuit of the most 'socialist' legislation imaginable at the time – the impôt sur le revenu – the history of the period cannot be understood. It was the unified left and its program of the impôt which terrified the haute bourgeoisie. Only with Waldeck-Rousseau's concentration coalition of 'republican defense' was the Jacobin 'left' effectively split between its Parisian and provincial elements and the center coalition pattern for the remaining decades of the Republic established.[18]

Maurice Duverger has observed, that France 'has known only three years of Left government since 1789 – the Jacobins 1793–94, the Republicans 1848, and the Popular Front 1936–37 . . .'[19] Not a word of the Radicals 1895–96!

Why was the conflict over the impôt sur le revenu of the 1890s virtually forgotten and the Dreyfus Affair so well remembered? My suggestion is that for contemporary bourgeois the trauma of the conflict over the impôt and the nightmare of democracy which it reflected was too unpleasant to face and was therefore displaced by the psychologically more manageable and aesthetically more satisfying drama of the Dreyfus Affair. For historians it is because they have not stepped back from the powerful and oft-told story of the Dreyfus Affair and read the basic sources of the 1890s – newspapers, periodicals, books and parliamentary papers – with fresh eyes.

At least two different evaluations of the 1893–98 period in French history are possible. One would see it as a time in which positive social

---

18. François Goguel, *Géographie des élections françaises sous la Troisième et La Quatrième République* (Paris: A. Colin, 1970), pp. 66–67.
19. D. S. Bell and Byron Griddle, *The French Socialist Party – Resurgence and Victory* (Oxford: Oxford University Press, 1984), p. 1.

and political tendencies were derailed. From this point of view the center coalition to which France returned in 1899 had the undesirable result of producing continued ministerial instability and governmental *immobilism* which continued through the first half of the twentieth century. Instead of developing as a modern, progressive society concerned with the social welfare of her people, this interpretation would hold, France remained tied to the past by a coalition of the haute bourgeoisie and backward agricultural proprietors.[20] Further, because the development of a unified left was thwarted, French proletarians were excluded from effective political participation and therefore turned toward class struggle and revolutionary communism. It is this interpretation of the 1893–98 period which seems to prevail among historians who tend to show little sympathy with or understanding of the concerns of the capitalistic haute bourgeoisie.

A second interpretation of the 1893–98 period would see it as a time of crisis in which members of the haute bourgeoisie felt themselves and their society (we must remember that they were the leaders of French society and civilization) challenged by the rise of the democratic masses. According to this view, 1893–98 were years of vigorous experimentation by a ruling class which sought to maintain society on an even keel. In this view, Waldeck-Rousseau's concentration coalition – which has been called the 'Radical Republic,' the 'Republic of committees,' and the 'Republic of pals' – was a creative adjustment by the haute bourgeoisie to what they understood to be the danger of democracy.

The concentration pattern of coalition formed by Waldeck-Rousseau remained, with brief exceptions, *the* design of ministerial coalitions until the end of the Third Republic. This was the French solution to the problem of democracy, the problem of how, in a representative regime of universal suffrage, the wealthy few could preserve their wealth and power from confiscation by the many.

Alexis de Tocqueville had considered the problem of democracy in the 1830s and it had remained the primary concern of French political thinkers down through the 1880s. What would Tocqueville have thought of Waldeck-Rousseau's solution? I think Tocqueville would have thought well of it for what it gave France, in fact if not in ideology, was liberal, limited government protective of private property. Tocqueville would have understood that the Radicals in Waldeck-Rousseau's coalition held Jacobin values, believing that government was a legitimate tool for solving France's social problems; Radical deputies were not ideological

---

20. It has been suggested by some that a 'modern' tax system would somehow imply a modern economy and an advanced system of social welfare. This is questionable. Though rural and urban Radicals and Socialists might agree on how tax money should be raised, they might not agree on the social programs on which it should be spent.

liberals who held that the less government does the better it is. But (and this is often overlooked) provincial Radicals in Waldeck-Rousseau's concentration coalition could find as much (or more) satisfaction from controlling the lower levels of the State bureaucracy as from dealing with social problems with innovative legislation. Tocqueville also would have understood that the Moderates in Waldeck-Rousseau's coalition who were ideological liberals (and presumably not particularly interested in plums of administrative patronage) held a veto able to block the government from taking actions opposed by the haute bourgeoisie.

Tocqueville, I think, would have understood what Waldeck-Rousseau was doing in forming his concentration ministry of 'republican defense', but I doubt that he would have publicly expressed that understanding. That a concentration ministry could provide France with a barrier against the 'excesses' of democracy — which had been achieved in the United States by the federal system, the separation of powers and the national government's lack of an effective central administration — would be better left unsaid. Tocqueville, himself an advocate of limited government, would have understood that if you liked Waldeck-Rousseau's solution you would not describe it publicly for to do so would be to undermine it.

Michael Curtis has observed that in France between 1885 and 1914 there were no political thinkers of stature who wrote in defense of the Republic as Charles Renouvrier and Emile Littré had done in earlier decades. (Renouvrier, it should be remembered, had favored a 'parliamentary republic' controlled by the wealthy few, not a democratic republic of one chamber which could be expected to be dominated by the non-wealthy many.) This is understandable. From the 1890s on, the best public theoretical defense of the liberal 'parliamentary republic' was silence; to describe the Third Republic as it really was, as a government secure against challenges to the vital interests of the wealthy few by means of concentration coalitions, could only serve to undermine that control.

Because any political theorist who favored the parliamentary republic would not have wanted to describe it publicly, whatever political 'thinkers of stature' there were between 1890 and 1914 were necessarily of the far right and far left. Thinkers of both these groups responded to consequences which flowed from the nature of Waldeck-Rousseau's center coalition. On the left, thinkers responded to the fact that the Waldeckian coalition excluded the industrial proletariat from influence on government; representatives of the industrial proletariat could participate neither as members of a majority coalition nor as a 'loyal minority' formed in alliance with the Jacobin left. The result was the well-known alienation of proletarians from parliamentary politics. What is generally overlooked in discussions of this alienation is that it was not inevitable; in fact the Socialist representatives of the industrial proletariat had cooperated effectively with Radicals in support of Léon Bourgeois's ministry of 1895–96. It was the exclusion of the industrial proletariat from political influence which led to its loss of confidence in the political mechanisms of the Third Republic and its attraction to 'revolutionary syndicalism'.

The nature of the Waldeckian coalition contributed to the alienation between proletarians and Radicals. It was characteristic of the Jacobin mentality, with its hierarchic, bureaucratic conception of social order, to view labor unrest as upsetting the smooth functioning of society. Because provincial Radicals and proletarian workers were not allied after 1899, tensions and antagonisms between the two would not be tempered by efforts at mutual understanding and compromise which political allies characteristically make. That Radical ministries brutally suppressed strikes in the 1900s was therefore not surprising.

It was an irony of the Third Republic that after 1899 deputies representing the interests and ideology of the haute bourgeoisie would have more influence as members of the veto minority in concentration coalitions than as members of homogeneous coalitions of the right. Concentration ministries were bound to promote cynicism and distrust of government because their words were contradicted by their actions. Radical supporters of concentration ministries who held Jacobin values could speak in favor of government intervention to solve society's social problems. But the Moderate 'veto minority' (as well as the Radicals' own inclination to keep taxes low and the fact that their own peasant constituents were largely satisfied with things as they were) would insure that government would do little (see Judith Stone's *The Search for Social Peace – Reform Legislation in France, 1890–1914*). The dissonance between the rhetoric of politicians and action of government could not but appear as hypocritical.

Even members of the haute bourgeoisie who got the liberal government they wanted from Waldeck-Rousseau's concentration coalition could not be entirely happy with it. For one thing, it meant that provincial Radicals, 'new men' inferior to the members of the haute bourgeoisie in manners, education and culture, would act as if control of government was their birthright. This contributed to the anti-republican attitudes of people like Daniel Halévy, who was happy enough with the Third Republic when it was dominated by the 'notables' in the 1870s but was disgusted by the speechifying and sordid pursuit of influence and favors by inferior provincials in the 'république des comités'. Greatness and heroism, George Sorel recognized, had no place in the 'république des camarades'.

Prior to the 1890s the eminent political thinkers in France belonged to the establishment, were defenders of the 'parliamentary republic' and worried about the threat of democratic masses to the bourgeoisie and their civilization. After the 1890s the French political thinkers of renown – Barrès, Maurras, Sorel, Daniel Halévy – were anti-establishment voices and antagonists of democracy and the Third Republic. After 1899 the defects of the Third Republic were the defects of the Radical Republic. Universal suffrage had resulted in the election of Radical deputies who were easy targets for the scorn of highly educated and cultured critics such as Barrès, Maurras, Sorel and Halévy. These writers attacked the Republic for having a weak executive, for being incapable of vigorous coherent action (precisely what the liberal bourgeoisie wanted), for being inglorious and unheroic (provincial Radical deputies jockeying for position and favors were no one's idea of heroes) and for producing a political leadership not of the most intelligent and most able but of the most capable of flattering the masses.

With hindsight it may be understood that the French haute bourgeoisie might better have devoted some of the energy it spent opposing the impôt to other concerns such as building their country's economic wealth, a job which they claimed as their own. In their arguments against the impôt sur le revenu members of the bourgeoisie held that such a tax would cause capital to flow out of France. Yet even without it, they were happy to export their money for investments which added little to the economic strength of their country. Similarly hauts bourgeois applauded laissez-faire liberal economists like Léon Say, while they hid behind the tariff barriers constructed between 1879 and 1892 which permitted French industry the expensive luxury of lethargy while at the same time providing its owners with what would now be considered fabulously high percentage levels of profit.

It might be concluded that the French haute bourgeoisie in the 1890s was transfixed with the threat of the many beyond any reasonable measure. In itself this concern need not have been harmful. If, however, it diverted the members of France's elite from the tasks they should have pursued for the good of their society, the bourgeoisie can properly be criticized for a failure of leadership.

Among the hauts bourgeois of the 1890s there were those who understood the serious deficiencies of France's economic and financial structure. Anatole Leroy-Beaulieu understood the bad results of absorbing so much savings into non-productive State rentes. Raphael-Georges Lévy, financier and professor at the Ecole Libre des Sciences Politiques, wrote in the *Revue des Deux Mondes* about the grave deficiencies of the French banking system which prevented the nation's savings from stimulating the country's industry and trade. Knowledgeable Frenchmen in the 1890s realized that their country's economy was backward and stagnant compared with those of Germany and the United States. Paul Leroy-Beaulieu went so far as to recommend a 'United States of Europe' to face the American challenge.[21] But the leaders of French bourgeois opinion did not sufficiently promote these criticisms among their own class.

Only in the early years of the twentieth century (after the Radical ministry led by Emile Combes had been forced from office, in part by financial pressure on State rentes after he had seriously attempted to seek an impôt sur le revenu) do French writers appear to have begun to a thorough critique of their country's financial and economic system. But by then the major critics were men of the left such as Francis Delaisi and Le Tailleur ('Lysis'), and not the members of the haute bourgeoisie themselves who should have been able to do the job better.

In producing the dreyfusian revolution, the architects of the French solution to the problem of democracy had done well, serving collectively as Plato's philosopher-king, to set the conditions for sound government for the decades ahead. For the French haute bourgeoisie of the late nineteenth century, sound government meant government in which the wealthy few would not be overwhelmed by the many of democracy. In the very process of implementing their plan for the political structure of the Republic, the architects (Poincaré, Reinach, Millerand, Aynard, Waldeck-Rousseau, etc.) erased the lines of the drawing which had been their guide. The vast majority of French, members of both the few and the many, never understood just what had happened in the creation of the Radical Republic; the story of how the Third Republic was made safe for the haute bourgeoisie has never entered the pages of the history books.

Robert Mitchell wrote in his obituary for Léon Say in April 1896, that the 'magician' who had done so much to create the Third Republic had died at the very moment of the collapse of the conservative Republic. If Mitchell's obituary for the conservative Republic was a bit premature (Méline's ministry would extend it to 1898), it was not far off the mark. With the dreyfusian revolution and the coming of government dominated by representatives of the many, the conservative Republic had come to an end. But would Léon Say have been entirely dismayed by this development? As his own story of the monster and the magician indicated, Say gravely shook his head from side to side at the demise of the conservative Republic. But to himself (if he had any sense of humor at all) I think he would have smiled, justly satisfied that he had designed

---

21. *Economiste Français*, Sept. 3, 1898; Raphael-Georges Lévy, 'Les marches financiers de l'Allemagne', *RDM* (Nov. 15, 1897), pp. 430ff, and 'L'industrie Allemand', *RDM* (Feb. 15, 1898), pp. 806ff.

his 'republic' well.

I have stressed that the 1890s crisis of democracy in France was the most acute in the history of the Third Republic precisely because the conflict over the impôt sur le revenu between 1893 and 1898 pitted all the few on one side against all the many on the other side of the political divide. The design of the philosopher-kings of France made sure that henceforth majority coalitions would include a veto minority of representatives of the few together with the majority of representatives of the many. They also made sure that the vast majority of the French – few and many alike – would not understand that the structure of French politics was purposely designed to be the way it was.

Appendix:
For the Sake of the Mission – The
Military Dimension of the Dreyfus Affair

Explaining Army Motivation – The Problem

The explanations offered by contemporaries and historians as to why French Army leaders insisted on maintaining the conviction of Captain Alfred Dreyfus for espionage despite their knowledge that he was innocent have usually attributed their actions to irrational motivations. Almost never has it been suggested that they acted reasonably, according to the dictates of ordinary common sense. Rather, their motivations are variously said to have been anti-semitism, stubbornness, the inability to admit a mistake or a perverse sense of military honor. But such explanations are hardly satisfactory, for when the actions of those who made Army policy regarding Dreyfus are examined, no pattern of irrationally-motivated behavior can be found. General Mercier, the Minister of War who made sure Dreyfus would be tried and convicted and who led the Army's opposition to *révision* (retrial) throughout the Affair, was not an anti-semite.[1] Nor, in matters unrelated to the Dreyfus case, was he particularly stubborn or incapable of changing his mind.[2]

Explaining Mercier's decision to prosecute and convict Dreyfus has always been difficult for students of the Dreyfus Affair. Why – against the advice of Foreign Minister Gabriel Hanotaux, Prime Minister Charles Dupuy, President of the Republic Jean Casimir-Périer and the wartime head of the French Army General Saussier[3] – did General Mercier insist on prosecuting and convicting Dreyfus? Why did Mercier persist to the point of fabricating evidence, illegally giving a secret file of evidence to the judges in the military trial and engaging others in conspiracy even though it was clear within a few weeks of Dreyfus's arrest that the case against him was collapsing?

---

1. Guy Chapman, *The Dreyfus Case – A Reassessment* (New York: Reynal & Company, 1955), p. 64.
2. See Chapman, *The Dreyfus Case*, p. 71 for an informed evaluation of Mercier's character.
3. Ibid., pp. 66, 67.

Appendix: The Dreyfus Affair

Marcel Thomas, in *L'Affaire sans Dreyfus*, offered an assortment of reasons to explain Mercier's actions including personal ambition (based on the idea that not to have pursued Dreyfus would have cost Mercier his portfolio as Minister of War), spite (based on Mercier's animosity towards General Saussier), fear of being judged negatively by officers of the General Staff, a sincere feeling of patriotic vigilance and a desire to uphold his reputation of 'never going back on a decision.'[4] After offering these suggestions Thomas concluded: 'Doubtless, all of these contributed somewhat to Mercier's decision.'[5]

By offering such a broad range of explanations – none of which is supported with corroborating evidence – Thomas implicitly admitted that none of these explanations was based on anything more than theory. He could just as well have written: 'We do not know why Mercier pursued with such vigor the conviction of Dreyfus, though several possible but unsupported explanations have been suggested . . .'

If the explanations offered for Mercier's actions are weak, still weaker are those for the actions of other top Army leaders. Can the roles of the Chief and Assistant Chief of the General Staff in maintaining Dreyfus's conviction be reasonably ascribed, without any corroborating evidence, to their blind support of Mercier's personal ambition to be War Minister or his supposed refusal ever to change a decision?

Jean-Denis Bredin's *The Affair – The Case of Alfred Dreyfus* illustrates this problem. After describing the frenzied efforts of the Chiefs of the General Staff and officers of the Army Intelligence Service to assure the acquittal of Commandant Esterhazy (who had written the bordereau which had led to Dreyfus's arrest) when he was tried for spying for Germany in the period after Dreyfus's conviction, Bredin speculated on what motivated them:

What were they defending, [these] officers who would not recoil before any ploy? Commandant Esterhazy? The reputation of General Mercier, whose illegality they continued to cover up? The honor of the Army, whose trustees they claimed to be? Were they bound by an oath they had taken [not to divulge the irregularities in the original trial of Dreyfus], locked into discipline, captives of a complicity consolidated every day by the actions they perpetrated together? Was it hatred of Jews, a fear of the syndicate, the power of hierarchy, a love of their class, or simply the instinct of self-preservation which moved them?[6]

4. Marcel Thomas, *L'Affaire sans Dreyfus* (Paris: Arthème Fayard, 1971), p. 125.
5. Ibid.
6. Jean-Denis Bredin, *The Affair – The Case of Alfred Dreyfus* (New York: George Braziller Inc., 1986), pp. 236–237.

What is to be understood from the broad assortment of possible explanations offered by Bredin? The implication is that among them lie the key(s) to understanding what motivated Army leaders. But Bredin offers no arguments or evidence in support of any possible explanation. If the actions of lower level officers such as Colonel Henry of the Army's Intelligence Service can be adequately explained as the result of their following orders given by higher level officers, the actions of Army leaders at the highest level – the Chiefs of the General Staff and the ministers of war – require some explanation.

Logically, the alternative to explanation by irrational motivation is that Army leaders insisted on Dreyfus's conviction and opposed retrial for rational reasons which were not comprehensible to outsiders because they lacked information possessed by those Army leaders. I shall suggest that although Army leaders could not say so, there was a good reason based on the needs of national defense to convict Dreyfus and an excellent reason to maintain that conviction. To have declared Dreyfus innocent (which he surely was) would have endangered military secrets of the highest order concerning the development of France's rapid-fire field artillery.

France's 75mm rapid-fire field cannon was a superb weapon, developed by the French Army under conditions of deepest secrecy between 1894 and 1896. I believe it was the desire of the leaders of the French Army to mislead the Germans as to France's progress in developing field artillery which led them to convict Captain Dreyfus of espionage, and to refuse to review that conviction. It was this miscarriage of justice which led to the Dreyfus Affair.

This suggestion in no way changes our understanding of the public aspects of the Affair. It does not deny or minimize the anti-semitic attitudes which were expressed during the Affair and it says nothing about the campaign by Dreyfusards to obtain a new trial and, ultimately, freedom for Dreyfus. Nor is it concerned with the process which resulted in Captain Dreyfus being accused of spying for Germany by investigators in the French Intelligence Service. It does not change our understanding of the actions of any but a tiny number of individuals – the Army leaders who directed the activities aimed at misleading Germany.

Revolution in Artillery

During the 1880s the ground had been prepared for monumental innovations in weaponry. The bases of these innovations were the invention of smokeless gunpowder, which was three times more powerful than the gunpowder then in use; progress in the production of steel which resulted in an approximately 70 per cent decline in its price between 1870 and 1890; and great advances in the science of metallurgy and the development of alloy steels.

Smokeless gunpowder was first employed in small arms; the French Lebel rifle of 1886 which used it was considerably more powerful and faster firing than the Gras rifle which preceded it. But it was on artillery that the impact of smokeless powder was most profound. Because a relatively small amount of the powerful new gunpowder was needed for each shot, the modern artillery shell which combines propellant and explosive charge in one metal casing could be introduced to replace the separate powder and projectile previously used as ammunition for cannon. This artillery shell could be fired from a breach-loading cannon, which meant that weapons far more powerful and faster firing than had previously existed could be developed. A field cannon of 1870 could fire about one shot per minute; the rapid-fire French 75mm developed in 1895 and 1896 could fire over 25 much more powerful shots per minute.

From the late 1880s every modern army made the development of rapid-fire artillery a top priority. The result was a revolution in land warfare. Before this revolution the superior range and accuracy of rifle fire had largely overturned the dominant position artillery had held in the era of Napoleon I. Now with powerful rapid-fire field cannon effective at ranges far greater than rifle fire, artillery could again rule the battlefield. In 1901 Gabriel Roquerol expressed a contemporary appreciation of the significance of modern field cannon in *The Tactical Employment of Quick-Firing Artillery*:

> The adoption of the quick-firing gun has produced a feeling similar to that aroused by the introduction of smokeless gunpowder, though of yet greater intensity . . . this novel engine, which revolutionizes the methods of warfare . . .[7]

The key to developing rapid-fire field artillery was the need for some means to prevent the force of a cannon's recoil from throwing it out of aim; without this, cannon would have to be re-aimed after each firing and, although it could be loaded and fired quickly, effective rapid fire would be impossible. Rapid-fire artillery was employed first on the seas, where the problem of recoil was easier to solve on ships which could carry virtually unlimited weight;[8] one result was the well-known naval

---

7. Gabriel Roquerol, *The Tactical Employment of Quick-Firing Artillery* (London: Hugh Rees Ltd., 1903 [trans. from the French, Paris 1901]), p. v. See *Encyclopedia Britannica*, 11th edn., articles on 'Ordnance' and 'Artillery', for a good background on this subject; J. B. A. Bailey, *Field Artillery and Fire Power* (Oxford: The Military Press, 1989), pp. 5, 17.

8. 'Par un Artilleur,' *Une Merveille du génie français, Notre 75* (Paris, 1915), p. 20.

competition between England and Germany. On land, however, the need for field artillery to be of relatively light weight (that is, able to be pulled to the scene of battle by a team of six horses)[9] produced an engineering problem of formidable difficulty. The need for rapid-fire field artillery produced an intense competition between France and Germany which, because of the secrecy surrounding it and the fact that the weapons which emerged from it were modest-sized field cannon not gargantuan battle ships, is little known.

The French achieved a brilliant double success in the 1890s. They not only produced the splendid rapid-fire 75mm cannon, but they also managed to mislead the Germans into believing that they had adopted a much less powerful weapon which could fire only about six shots per minute.[10] As a result, the Germans were satisfied in 1896 to equip their own forces with a relatively primitive 'accelerated fire' (not a true rapid-fire) field cannon, roughly equivalent to the six-shot-per-minute weapon which the French had misled them into thinking they would adopt.

At the time French 75mm was ten years ahead of the field artillery of all the other Powers. In the 1890s it was the only true rapid-fire field cannon in use. Only in 1904 would Germany begin to equip its troops with its own rapid-fire field cannon. During World War I the French 75mm was still the finest field cannon in existence, and arguably saved France from defeat by Germany.

The Dreyfus Affair

To understand how Captain Dreyfus became an innocent victim of the French scheme to mislead the Germans, it will be useful to briefly review the narrative of the Dreyfus Affair.[11]

On 26 September 1894 the French Army Intelligence Service received a bordereau (list) which had been taken by one of its operatives, the charwoman Mme Bastian, from a wastepaper basket in the residence of Scwarzkoppen, the German military attaché in Paris. The bordereau referred to documents which evidently had been delivered to Schwarzkoppen, and indicated that a French officer of considerable rank was spying for the Germans. The full text of the bordereau was as follows:

9. *Encyclopedia Britannica*, 11th edn., vol. II, p. 688 ff.

10. Thomas, *L'Affaire sans Dreyfus*, p. 489; Colonel Alvin and Commandant André, *Les canons de la victoire*, 7th edn. (Paris: Charles Lavauzelle & Cie, 1923), p. 39.

11. For the narrative of the Dreyfus Affair I have relied primarily on Jean-Denis Bredin, *The Affair*, pp. 47, 53, 59–65, 81, 96, 140–143, 150, 161, 167–168, 175, 303, 316.

Having no indication that you wish to see me, I am nevertheless forwarding to you, sir, several interesting pieces of information.

1. A note on the hydraulic brake of the 120 and the manner in which that part has performed;
2. A note on covering troops (several modifications will be effected by the new plan);
3. A note on a modification of Artillery formations;
4. A note pertaining to Madagascar;
5. The Sketch for a Firing Manual for the field artillery (March 14, 1894).

This last document is extremely difficult to procure and I am able to have it at my disposal for only a few days. The Minister of War has distributed a fixed number of copies to the regiments, and the regiments are responsible for them. Every officer holding a copy is to return it after maneuvers. If you would then take from it what interests you and keep it at my disposal thereafter, I will take it. Unless you want me to have it copied in extenso and send you the copy. I am off to maneuvers.

The nature of the information referred to in the bordereau led Army investigators to think that its author was an artillery officer on the General Staff. Soon after it arrived at the Intelligence Service the bordereau was shown to General August Mercier, Minister of War. His 'emotion on reading the text', wrote Joseph Reinach in his *History of the Dreyfus Affair*, 'was quite strong as was his irritation'. Mercier's instructions to Generals Raoul de Boisdeffre and Charles Gonse, Chief and Assistant Chief of the General Staff who had the Intelligence Service under their command were simple and clear: 'The circle of inquiry is small, limited to the General Staff. Search. Find.' But the search did not find.

By the beginning of October 1894 all leads as to the author of the bordereau had been exhausted and the identity of the traitor remained as much a mystery as ever. Then on 6 October Lieutenant Colonel Albert d'Aboville, a recently appointed officer on the General Staff who had just returned from vacation, had a bright idea. He reasoned from the various types of information mentioned in the bordereau that the traitor must have had contact with the First, Second, Third and Fourth sections of the General Staff. It happened that each newly appointed officer to the General Staff spent several months as a stagiaire working in each of its departments before receiving his permanent assignment. Aboville concluded that such a stagiaire could have been the author of the bordereau. The investigators then compared handwritings and found an unmistakable similarity between the handwriting of one recent stagiaire and the bordereau. Intelligence Service investigators had found their traitor: he was Captain Alfred Dreyfus, aged 35, a Jew of Alsacian origin.[12]

On 15 October 1894 Dreyfus was placed under arrest. Army investigators then had several handwriting experts reexamine the bordereau to determine if it had been written by Dreyfus. The experts were divided in their opinions; by the end of October of the six who had examined the bordereau, three, including the two most respected, had concluded that it had not been written by Dreyfus. The case against Dreyfus appeared to be collapsing.[13]

Regardless, Mercier decided to press forward and prosecute Dreyfus. We know that Mercier did not believe that the evidence of the bordereau would be sufficient to convict because by November he was instructing the Intelligence Service to build a file of 'evidence' against Dreyfus which included forgeries fabricated by that office. On 28 November Mercier broke his public silence about the espionage case and declared to the press his absolute certainty that Dreyfus was guilty.

Dreyfus's trial before the military court began on 19 December 1894. Reflecting his belief in the insufficiency of the evidence, Mercier arranged that the file containing the forged evidence be submitted to the judges without the knowledge of Dreyfus or his attorney (or, for that matter, any other government official outside the Intelligence Service). Thus from the outset, to build the case against Dreyfus Mercier entered into profoundly illegal activities – the fabrication of evidence and use of conspiracy – to subvert justice. This set the pattern for Army behavior throughout the Affair.[14]

Between December 19 and 22 Dreyfus was tried and convicted. In February 1895 he was transported to Devil's Island to be incarcerated for the rest of his life under the most brutal conditions.

Most of France soon forgot about Alfred Dreyfus. But his family did not. Mathieu Dreyfus, with absolute faith in the innocence of his brother, put all his effort into clearing his name. In the months after the conviction, Mathieu Dreyfus gradually succeeded in discovering the weakness of the Army's case and the illegal actions it had taken to convict his brother and maintain that conviction.

In July 1895 Commandant Georges Picquart, a brilliant young officer, was appointed head of the Intelligence Service. Eight months later, in March 1896, a *petit bleu* – a blue colored pneumatic letter-telegram (in those days a pneumatic mail system served parts of Paris) – was recovered from the Paris residence of the German military attaché by Mme Bastian and passed on to the Intelligence Service. The petit bleu, torn up and

12. Bredin, *The Affair*, pp. 63–64.
13. Ibid., pp. 68, 74–76, 87.
14. Ibid., pp. 87–89.

obviously never sent, was from Schwarzkoppen to Commandant Walzin-Esterhazy of the French Army. From its content it was clear that it designated a traitor: Commandant Esterhazy, a man of questionable character and dubious finances.

Three months after the arrival of the petit bleu at the offices of the Intelligence Service in late August 1896, Picquart was examining a sample of Esterhazy's handwriting which he had obtained in his investigation into the new case of espionage. He happened to compare it with the writing of the bordereau which had led to the conviction of Dreyfus. The two were identical. The evidence struck Picquart like lightning. The bordereau had not been written by Dreyfus: It was the work of Esterhazy. The traitor was still free. The wrong man had been convicted and was languishing on Devil's Island.[15]

When Picquart went to Generals Boisdeffre and Gonse to inform them of what he had discovered, they told him in no uncertain terms to forget the matter: Dreyfus would remain in prison and Esterhazy would not be accused of the crime for which Dreyfus had been convicted. But Picquart (who happened to have been an anti-semite) could not accept such a monstrous miscarriage of justice and did not cease his efforts to rectify what had happened. As an army officer, Picquart was sworn to secrecy and could not communicate to the public or the Dreyfus family what he knew about Esterhazy's activities but, unable to abide the terrible injustice which he knew had been done, he continued to try to rectify it within the constraints of his position.

On 10 November 1896 the newspaper *Le Matin* published a facsimile of the bordereau which it obtained from the handwriting expert Tysonniere, who had kept it when he had originally examined it at the time of Dreyfus's arrest. The handwriting of the bordereau was soon recognized and it became publicly known that it had been written by Esterhazy. In mid-November 1896, Picquart's superiors, believing that it was he who had leaked the bordereau to *Le Matin* and wanting to stop his investigation into the Dreyfus and Esterhazy cases, sent him on an 'urgent' extended mission to reorganize the Intelligence Services affiliated with the various armed corps stationed on France's eastern and southwestern borders. While Picquart was away the Minister of the Army, General Billot, decided to be rid of him entirely and on 24 December ordered him transferred to Tunisia, to depart from Marseilles on 29 December.[16]

This effort to suppress the investigation failed in its ultimate purpose. From late 1896 to mid-1897 the campaign to reopen the Dreyfus case

15. Ibid., p. 162.
16. Ibid., p. 171.

gathered steam as the Dreyfus family's and Picquart's efforts expanded the circle of those who were aware of the injustice which had been done. From mid-1897 to early 1898 public controversy over the Dreyfus question reached a peak. The press was full of the Affair; petitions for revision were circulated and public demonstrations were held. Counter-petitions and counter-demonstrations followed.

Throughout the Affair, the Army accepted General Mercier's adamant insistence that Dreyfus was guilty, that the case should not be opened to a retrial and that Esterhazy, the true author of the bordereau, should not be put on trial and, if put on trial, should be acquitted. At each point that the case against Dreyfus appeared to be in jeopardy, the Army did whatever was necessary to make sure the conviction would stand including continuing to add to the file of forgeries which were presented at the original trial, and discredit Picquart who challenged it. When it became public knowledge that the handwriting of the bordereau was Esterhazy's, the Chief of the General Staff provided Esterhazy with a 'liberating document' that would assure his acquittal when he was put on trial for passing other information to the Germans.

Innovation and Deception

Artillery engineers of the 1890s understood that ideally an hydraulic brake would be the best means of ensuring that a field cannon would return to its original position after it was fired. Such a brake would essentially consist of a piston attached to the barrel of the cannon and a cylinder containing liquid fixed to its carriage; the energy of the recoil would be absorbed as the piston traveled backward through the liquid contained in the cylinder. The barrel would then be returned to its original firing position by a spring or by air compressed by the recoil movement. Less desirable would be a brakeless system; with such a system the entire cannon would roll backward, the energy of the recoil being absorbed by a spring attached to the cannon's carriage and to the ground. The cannon would then roll forward to its original position as the spring returned to its original shape.

Designing an hydraulic recoil brake for a field cannon presented great technical difficulties. If it could be perfected it would make the cannon very expensive to construct. A cannon with a spring recoil-absorbing system would be much easier to design and, because it would involve refitting existing weapons rather than building entirely new ones, would cost considerably less.

From the late 1880s French efforts to increase the rate of fire of their field artillery followed three separate paths. One line of development resulted in the '120mm short' cannon with hydraulic brake, produced in

1890. The second, directed by Commandant Ducros from 1887, sought to accelerate the fire of the field cannon then in service by adding a spring recoil system of relatively primitive design. The third line of development, led first by Commandant Deport and, after his resignation in November 1894, by Captains Rimailho and Saint-Claire Deville sought a cannon with hydraulic brake based on a 'long recoil' technology of radically new design.[17]

The brake on the 120mm short proved to be unsuitable for a field cannon.[18] When it was fired its piston lost hydraulic fluid, thereby preventing consistency of operation. The recoil of the 120 short also varied depending on the type of terrain in which the weapon was operated.[19] Try as they could, French Army engineers could not correct the brake's deficiencies.[20]

The Ducros accelerated-fire weapon worked reliably but was only able to fire about six shots per minute.[21] Each time it was fired, with its crew standing to the side, the entire cannon would roll backward and then roll forward to its original position as the spring which had absorbed its recoil returned to its original position.

The 75mm long recoil rapid-fire cannon developed by Rimailho and Sainte-Claire Deville brilliantly solved the problem of creating a field weapon with hydraulic brake.[22] It was capable of extremely accurate, rapid and powerful fire (its muzzle energy was 334 foot-tons compared with the World War I German field cannon's muzzle energy of 242 foot-tons).[23] When the weapon was fired, its crew sat on its motionless carriage behind a steel protective shield while the cannon's barrel moved backward, absorbed the recoil and returned forward to its original position. Perfected in early autumn 1896, the 75mm rapid-fire was put into large-scale production in 1897,[24] about a year after Germany had begun to equip its army with a relatively primitive accelerated-fire weapon, the model C/96 which was a modified version of the field cannon then in service.[25]

Confident that a long-recoil rapid-fire cannon could be perfected,

17. François Rimailho, *Artillerie de campagne* (Paris: Gauthier-Villars & Cie, 1924), pp. 28–31.

18. Jules Challéat, *Histoire technique de l'artillerie de terre en France pendant un siècle (1816–1919)*, vol. II (Paris: Imprimerie Nationale, 1935), pp. 168–169; Alvin and André, *Les canons de la victoire*, p. 338.

19. Alvin and André, *Les canons de la victoire*, p. 338.

20. Ibid., pp. 338–9.

21. Rimailho, *Artillerie de campagne*, p. 37.

22. Ibid., p. 1.

23. *Encyclopedia Britannica*, 11th edn., vol. 20, p. 219.

24. Michel de Lombarès, *L'Affaire Dreyfus. La clef du mystère* (Paris: Robert Laffont, 1972).

25. Ibid, p. 24; Thomas, *L'Affaire sans Dreyfus*, p. 489.

General Deloye, head of the French artillery service, undertook to mislead the Germans into thinking that France would adopt the Ducros cannon with the aim of encouraging them to equip their own forces with a similar weapon.[26] From the German point of view, parity with France in the quality of field artillery would be sufficient because German quantity – wealth, productive capacity and population – was great and continually growing greater. Even if the French did not themselves succeed in perfecting a long recoil rapid-fire field cannon, the deception would be worthwhile if it dissuaded the Germans from trying to perfect their own.

Two elements of the French deception ('intoxication' in French) are known. One was to convey the impression that the French would adopt the Ducros cannon. The other was to keep secret the existence of the 75mm rapid-fire.

To convey the impression that the Ducros cannon would be adopted, General Deloye arranged that the secrecy surrounding it be lifted and trials with it held. Rimailho described this in *Artillerie de campagne*: 'great importance', he wrote, was attributed to the trials of the Ducros cannon before the French Army's artillery committee 'by the French and evidently by the Germans', who in 1896 proceeded with the production of the accelerated-fire C/96.[27] A more detailed description of this aspect of intoxication, based on a lecture by Rimailho, was given by Colonel Alvin and Commandant André in *Les cannons de la victoire*:

In 1894, the creation of the first long recoil [rapid-fire] 75mm cannon gave the Director of Artillery the idea that he would be able to keep secret the essential principles of its brake and obtain the double result of equipping France with a weapon very superior to Germany's while leading them to construct for themselves a weapon of inferior quality.

While we perfected in secret the [rapid-fire] 75 with hydropneumatic brake at Puteaux the Director of Artillery was aware of studies pursued in Germany to produce a rigid cannon without brake capable of firing at a much lower rate. At Puteaux an analogous study was being carried on [by Ducros]. Word was spread that the study was highly successful. Supposedly 'highly secret' trials were held with the [Ducros] unbraked material at proving grounds known to be frequented by German spies. Finally we learned that the Germans had adopted a cannon without brake, the C/96, at the very time that we gained confidence in the ultimate success of the rapid-fire 75.[28]

26. Alvin and André, *Les canons de la victoire*, 7th edn., p. 39; *Une merveille du génie français*, p. 10; Rimailho, *Artillerie*, p. 59.

27. Alvin and André, *Les canons*, p. 39. See also, Challéat, *Histoire technique d'artillerie*, vol. II, p. 364.

28. Ibid., p. 39.

The second aspect of the French deception was to keep secret the existence of the 75mm rapid-fire. If the Germans were to think that the French would adopt the Ducros cannon, it was be necessary that they remain unaware of the perfected 75mm long recoil cannon. At least through early 1896, knowledge of the state of progress on the 75mm was limited to the Army officers who were working on the project and a very few politicians whose leadership was needed to obtain funding for its development.[29] Appropriations for test batteries of the 75mm were hidden in the budget, under categories such as 'modifications to artillery.'[30] This cover in particular may have been used to give the impression that the funds were being used to convert the Bange field cannon then in service to the Ducros model.

The two aspects of the French deception described above are confirmed by the testimony of Rimailho and others.[31] A third aspect of the deception would also seem to be implied. In 1894, at the time the Ducros and the rapid-fire 75mm were being developed in secret, the 120mm short recoil gun was in limited use in the French Army. Developed in 1890, the 120mm short was the first field cannon with an hydraulic brake, and in the early 1890s it received considerable favorable public attention. If the Germans were to be led to believe that the French would adopt the Ducros cannon, it would also be necessary for them to learn that the brake of the 120mm short could not be perfected. Was it possible that the French used Esterhazy to feed the Germans this true but misleading information (*true* because despite their best efforts French artillery engineers had failed to perfect the brake of the 120mm short, *misleading* because the Germans, knowing nothing about the 75mm and its hydraulic brake, would be led to conclude that the French had been unable to perfect *any* hydraulic brake)?

How could French Army leaders be sure that the Germans learned of the deficiencies of the brake of the 120mm short? [This is the one point of speculation in this appendix.] They would tell them themselves. How?

29. For a sense of the profound depth of secrecy in which the rapid-fire 75mm was developed, manufactured and maintained see Henriette Dardenne, *Godefroy Cavaignac – un républicaine de progrès aux débuts de la 3e république* (Colmar: 1969), pp. 268–269; Henriette Dardenne, 'Comment fut decidée la construction du canon 75 et l'eternelle lutte du projectile et de la cuirass', *Bulletin trimestriel de l'association des amis de l'école supérieure de guerre*, no. 20 (July, 1963), p. 68; 'par un Artilleur,' *Une Merveille du génie français, Notre 75*, pp. 20, 36; Rimailho, *Artillerie de campagne*, p. 59; Leslie E. Babcock, *Elements of Field Artillery* (Princeton: Princeton University Press, 1925), pp. 58–59; Challéat, *Histoire technique de l'artillerie*, vol. II, p. 364.

30. Rimailho, *Artillerie de campagne*, p. 59; Dardenne, *Godefroy Cavaignac*, pp. 211–212; Dardenne, 'Comment fut decidée la construction du canon de 75' p. 67; Thomas, *L'Affaire sans Dreyfus*, pp. 487–490.

31. See also *Une merveille de genie français*, Notre 75, (Paris, 1945), p. 10 and Challéat, *Histoire technique de l'artillerie,* vol. II, p. 364.

Could the French Minister of War send a letter saying as much to the German military attaché? Obviously not. The French would do better. They would have a 'spy' deliver the information. Who would play the role of spy? Let it be a French officer of questionable character and serious financial difficulties – a man like Commandant Ferdinand Walzin-Esterhazy.

The French knew that the Germans knew of the existence of the 120mm short and wanted to learn more about its brake. In his earliest contact with Schwarzkoppen, Esterhazy had said that he could provide information about its construction and how it functioned. The German military attaché was interested and agreed to pay Esterhazy for his information.[32]

French Army chiefs would provide their 'spy' with some interesting and valuable secret documents, including a 'Note on the hydraulic brake of the 120mm and the manner in which it has performed'. The information given to the Germans would be true; the Germans would be sure to test carefully whatever information they received from a French spy and false information would discredit the spy. The 'Note on the 120 short' would report the simple truth that, despite all efforts, the 120mm's brake could not be made to function satisfactorily. Esterhazy would deliver the documents to Schwarzkoppen with a covering letter in his own hand – the bordereau.

Once such a scheme of 'intoxication' would be launched, it would carry within it its own imperatives. It would be important that the intoxicator not be exposed as an agent of the French Army. If the Germans learned that Esterhazy was doing the bidding of high-ranking French officers they would understand that they had been deceived and, following the reasoning behind the deception, might deduce that the French were not deploying the Ducros accelerated-fire weapon. If they reached that conclusion, the Germans might be spurred to try to develop their own true rapid-fire field cannon with hydraulic brake.

If the scenario suggested here is correct, the arrival of the bordereau at the Intelligence Service would have endangered the French plan of intoxication. This would explain why, when the bordereau was first brought to the attention of Minister of War General Mercier, 'his emotion on reading the text was quite as strong as was his irritation'. Why should Mercier have been 'irritated'? The term suggests that he felt his plans were being thwarted. Mercier was worried that, if the eager spy hunters of Intelligence discovered that Esterhazy had written the bordereau, the Army would either have to put Esterhazy on trial as a spy or ignore the case entirely. Either course of action would entail serious risk: If Esterhazy

---

32. Bredin, *The Affair*, p. 61.

was prosecuted, to save himself and avoid life imprisonment he might say that in conveying information to the Germans he was only doing what Army chiefs had told him to do. If Mercier told the sleuths in Intelligence to forget about the bordereau and not seek its author, he would be accused of insufficient diligence, protecting a spy, or even being a spy himself.

Mercier's solution to his dilemma at this juncture can be found in his instructions to Intelligence regarding the search to be made for the author of the bordereau: 'The circle of inquiry is small, limited to the General Staff. Search. Find.' Operating under such instructions, obviously Intelligence could never find the 'spy' because Esterhazy had nothing to do with the General Staff.

As Mercier would have hoped, the search found nothing . . ..until Lieutenant Colonel Aboville returned from vacation and had the bright idea to look for the culprit among recent stagiaires with the General Staff. With the focus now on a handful of suspects, and the fact that there was a real similarity between Dreyfus's handwriting and the handwriting of the bordereau, Intelligence soon believed it had found its man. Dreyfus was arrested on 15 October 1894.

However, when several handwriting experts were consulted and the opinion of the most reliable of them held that the handwriting on the bordereau was not Dreyfus's, the case against the suspected spy was at best weak. Mercier was now faced with a dilemma. Should he release Dreyfus, or should he push ahead and prosecute him? If Dreyfus were released, then the sleuths in Intelligence would start again to hunt for the writer of the bordereau. However if Dreyfus were charged and convicted, Mercier's problem of protecting his 'spy' Esterhazy would be solved; the (supposed) author of the bordereau (Dreyfus) would be convicted and the case would be closed. On 28 November 1894, Mercier told the press that he was absolutely certain that Dreyfus was guilty and that he would be tried for espionage by court-martial.

Realizing that the case against Dreyfus was weak, Mercier arranged to have a secret file of 'evidence' against Dreyfus fabricated and given to the judges of the court-martial without informing Dreyfus or his lawyers of its existence. It was at this point that Mercier began the profoundly illegal behavior which would characterize the actions of the Army chiefs throughout the Affair. After the conviction of Dreyfus, the Army did everything possible to prevent the exposure of the 'spy' Esterhazy; Mercier strenuously resisted revision at every step and by every means, for if Dreyfus were declared innocent, Esterhazy would have to be put on trial (particularly after November 1896 when it became publicly known that the handwriting of the bordereau was his). If Esterhazy were put on trial and accused of spying for Germany the intoxication would be jeopardized by the possibility of Esterhazy declaring that he had only been doing what Army leaders had told him to do. In fact, pressure to put Esterhazy on trial did develop and in January 1898 he was tried for contact with the Germans after the incident of the bordereau; true to their policy Army chiefs arranged for the dismissal of the charges against him.[33]

Drawing on heretofore classified French military archives, Professor Allan Mitchell has described the thinking of French military leaders of the early 1890s regarding France's military strength in relation to Germany:

> In 1891 Charles de Freycinet, then the minister of war, confided to General de Miribel that Germany's 'considerable augmentations' had placed France 'in a situation of inferiority too dangerous to accept with resignation.' And, he continued, 'we cannot remain faced with such an increase in forces without taking similar measures' . . . Charles de Freycinet's confidential remark to General de Miribel that the escalation of German military prowess had placed France in a 'situation of inferiority' was not exceptional within the inner sanctum of the French army. Actually, it expressed a view widely held among responsible military experts . . . they had reason to dread the outcome of an eventual conflict.[34]

Mercier's decision to sacrifice Dreyfus in order to maintain the deception aimed at convincing the Germans to be satisfied with an accelerated-fire rather than a true rapid-fire field cannon was surely a difficult and brutal one. But given the magnitude of the stakes involved and given the fact that a military leader must think in terms of the cost in casualties needed for the success of an overwhelmingly important mission, it would have been surprising indeed if the leaders of the French Army had sacrificed the advantage of a tremendous lead in field artillery

33. Ibid., pp. 232–242.
34. Allan Mitchell, 'A Situation of Inferiority: French Military Reorganization after the Defeat of 1870', *American Historical Review*, vol. 86 (Feb. 1981), pp. 54, 60. In his book *Victors and Vanquished – The German Influence on Army and Church in France after 1870* (Chapel Hill: The University of North Carolina Press, 1984), Mitchell overlooks the vigorous effort and brilliant success of the French in developing rapid-fire artillery in the mid-1890s. Thus he describes the period of the Dreyfus Affair as one in which France 'allowed [military] matters to drift' (p. 110). Mitchell writes, 'the fact remains that in three decades [1870 – 1900] following Sedan, France's performance as a nation was mediocre at best; and during that time France virtually resigned from military and scientific leadership of Europe . . . France failed to match the hectic tempo of German development.' Aggregate evaluations and comparisons of French and German military strength aside, Mitchell overlooks France's brilliant success in developing the rapid-fire field cannon, the weapon primarily responsible for transforming warfare in the First World War. The origin of Mitchell's oversight, it seems, is that although he generalizes about the period 1870 to 1900, his detailed research on French military development only went up to about 1891.

over their country's national enemy for the liberty (or even life) of one man.

When Dreyfus was retried at Rennes in 1899, the court produced a verdict that has always appeared to make no sense. Rather than conclude that he was innocent of the charges brought against him, the Court at Rennes decided that Dreyfus was 'guilty with extenuating circumstances'. What better formula could have been found for releasing Dreyfus without requiring that Esterhazy be placed on trial?

I am not the first to have suggested that Esterhazy was used by the French Army as an agent of intoxication in relation to the development of rapid-fire field artillery.[35] However, this idea has its opponents. In *L'Affaire sans Dreyfus* Marcel Thomas, commenting on Giscard d'Estaing's *D'Esterhazy à Dreyfus*, argued that Esterhazy could not have been involved in 'intoxicating' the Germans in September 1894 because it was only in early 1895 that it was possible to seriously envision the adoption of the 75mm rapid-fire field cannon. Thomas believed that because Sainte-Claire Deville and Rimailho's rapid-fire 75mm was developed in 1895 and 1896 and definitely adopted in 1896, the deception of the Germans would have taken place in 1895 and 1896, not 1894. Others, including Douglas Johnson and Jean-Denis Bredin, who have studied the Dreyfus Affair and considered the theory of Giscard d'Estaing have rejected his hypothesis that Esterhazy was an agent of intoxication with arguments similar to those used by Marcel Thomas.[36]

In fact the first French version of a rapid-fire 75 was produced by Deport in 1894 and General Mercier, then Minister of War, ordered the construction of a number of its major components. But the main flaw in Thomas's argument stems from his failure to realize that the French aim in the intoxication was to encourage the Germans to be satisfied with producing an accelerated (six-shot-per-minute) cannon. The deception would have been worthwhile if it dissuaded the Germans from trying to develop rapid-fire field cannon even if the French would not succeed in perfecting their own.

Thomas, again arguing against Giscard d'Estaing, believed that if Esterhazy had been involved in intoxicating the Germans in regard to the 75mm rapid-fire he would not have kept his role secret throughout his life. To make his point, Thomas cited a 1920 incident in which a French writer named Rigne asked Esterhazy if he had 'passed false plans of the

---

35. See H. Giscard d'Estaing, *D'Esterhazy à Dreyfus* (Paris, 1961) and Michel de Lombarès, *L'Affaire sans Dreyfus* (Paris, 1972).

36. Bredin, *The Affair*, pp. 513–514; Douglas Johnson, *France and the Dreyfus Affair* (New York: Walker & Co., 1966), pp. 203–204.

75 to Schwarzkoppen' and, evidently, received a reply to the negative. But there is no reason to think that Esterhazy knew anything at all about the 75mm cannon at the time of the Dreyfus Affair. If the hypothesis proposed here is correct, Esterhazy's only role was to convince the Germans that the brake on the 120mm cannon could not be perfected. Thomas suggested that if Esterhazy had been involved in deceiving the Germans he would have passed false information about the 75mm rapid-fire;[37] I suggest instead that Esterhazy's role was to pass on true information about the brake of the 120mm short.

After I completed this Appendix, *Un secret bien gardé* by Jean Doise was published in Paris in January 1994. Doise's argument is similar to mine; the chief point on which we differ concerns the details of the French intoxication. Doise speculates that the Intelligence Service used Esterhazy to feed the Germans false information indicating that the French were satisfied with the brake of the 120mm short. I suggest that Esterhazy was used to feed the Germans true information about the deficiencies of the 120mm short as part of a scheme to convince the Germans that the French would adopt an accelerated-fire, not rapid-fire field cannon. One of my main sources was Rimailho's book *Artillerie de campagne (Field Artillery)*, written after the First World War, which mentions the deception directed by General Deloye.

The weakest aspect of the complex scenario proposed by Doise is that it assumes the Intelligence Service was informed about the development of field artillery and involved in the deception regarding it. This is both implausible and contrary to what is known about the French deception (see postscript, below). Doise suggests that Mercier, acting in defiance of ordinary common sense, prosecuted and drastically punished Dreyfus as a warning to others who might consider selling secrets of the 75mm rapid-fire to Germany. Doise relies on the supposed singularity of Mercier's character: 'In this horrible drama [the Dreyfus Affair] which unfolded like an ancient tragedy it was necessary that the minister of war be Mercier'.[38] According to the scenario which I have proposed, however, anyone in Mercier's position could reasonably have done what he did.

I have proposed a commonsense explanation for the actions of General Mercier and the chiefs of the General Staff in the Dreyfus Affair as an alternative to the irrational motives usually described by historians. Has this commonsense explanation been proven? Certainly the evidence

---

37. Thomas, *L'Affaire*, p. 489. Marcel Thomas maintains his opinion about the theory that Esterhazy served as an 'intoxifier' for the French in his recent book *Esterhazy ou l'envers de l'affaire Dreyfus* (Vernal: Philippe Lebaudi, 1989), pp. 391–392.
38. Jean Doise, *Un secret bien gardé* (Paris: Editions du Seuil, 1994), p. 64.

would not prove the case in a court of law; we have no 'smoking gun' or incriminating document to show that Esterhazy was working for Army leaders. However, the traditional explanations of irrational motivation are supported by no corroborating evidence at all. Anyone who doubts this can verify it for himself by reviewing the historical accounts of the Dreyfus Affair. And we do have (what has always been missing from the conventional accounts) an adequate motive for the Army's role in the Affair.

Which explanation to choose? I cannot help but think of the comparative demonstration of the Ducros brakeless cannon and the 75mm cannon with hydraulic brake presented by General Deloye, Director of French Artillery, in the spring of 1895. The demonstration took place in the Army's underground firing range at Puteaux; present were Georges Cochery (general reporter of the budget), Paul Doumer (reporter of the finance budget), and Godefroy Cavaignac (reporter of the budget for war). These parliamentary leaders were charged with deciding for which model appropriations for test batteries would be obtained from parliament. First the Ducros cannon was fired; while its crew stood to the side, the entire weapon rolled backward and then forward to its original position. Then the rapid-fire 75mm developed by Rimailho and Sainte-Claire Deville was fired with its crew seated motionless on its carriage behind a steel shield. General Deloye summarized the demonstration: 'In the first case you have a known quantity, something artless but certain . . . at 3 or 4 shots per minute. With the second there is the boldness of novelty: a more complex mechanism . . . but 25 shots.'[39]

In the traditional understanding of the actions of Mercier and the Chiefs of the General Staff, there is a well-known story with explanations worn smooth by repetition for almost 100 years—explanations so familiar that those who employ them do not even realize their improbability (turn to page 190 of Bredin's *The Affair* and find the Deputy Chief of the General Staff and the acting head of the Intelligence Service engaged in treason) or the absence of corroborating evidence in support of them. In the second case, there is a certain novelty and complexity but there is also a case which fits with what is known about the French understanding of their own military deficiencies in relation to Germany, the efforts of the French to deceive the Germans regarding their development of rapid-fire field artillery, the behavior of General Mercier (his irritation at the discovery of the bordereau, his decision to prosecute Dreyfus against the advice of the highest French officials, his decision to prosecute Dreyfus after the preponderance of expert opinion had concluded that the handwriting of the bordereau was not his, and his decision to fabricate evidence and

---

39. Dardenne, *Godefroy Cavaignac*, pp. 209–210.

present the 'secret file' to Dreyfus's court-martial thereby revealing his evident belief that the evidence against Dreyfus was insufficient to convict) and the subsequent actions by the heads of the General Staff to do whatever was necessary to protect Esterhazy and prevent a trial which would reveal his role in writing the bordereau.

The historian's problem is less difficult than that of Cochery, Doumer and Cavaignac. Those leaders of France had to choose one model of field cannon; that choice would entail spending a great deal of money and could be crucial for the destiny of their country. The historian can have both explanations and they cost him nothing. The reader can guess which I prefer. But I would be satisfied if readers were offered both explanations, that of common sense and that of irrational motivation.

Postscript

It may be of interest to consider the arguments against the scenario proposed above by the anonymous readers who considered it for publication as an article in one historical journal.

Objection: It is highly unlikely that an elaborate deception program would have been run without the knowledge of the Statistical Section [the official name of the Army's Intelligence Service]. Indeed, who would have run a deception program but the Statistical Section? Not the highest officers of the French Army, surely?
Reply: First, it should be understood that the French deception was not elaborate. The basic principles were simple: (1) keep secret the existence of one weapon (the 75mm rapid-fire field cannon), (2) hold trials, of which the Germans would be aware, with another weapon (the six-shot-per-minute Ducros cannon), and (3) convey to the Germans one piece of true information (the fact that the hydraulic brake of the 120mm short could not be perfected). Second, the assertion that the Statistical Section 'would have run a deception program' is contrary to the well-established fact that the Statistical Section had nothing whatever to do with the two parts of the deception which are known. The semi-publicized trials of the Ducros accelerated-fire cannon were planned by General Deloye, Director of French Artillery, and the secrecy around the development of the 75mm rapid-fire was maintained by the director of the Army arsenal in Puteaux, under the direction of General Deloye.

Objection: The author never asks how high a price the General Staff was willing to pay for a successful deception. Why accuse Dreyfus in the first place, when a word from Mercier could have halted the investigation of a man whom, the author believes, he knew to be innocent? It never occurs to the author that a mere word would have sufficed to halt an investigation of Dreyfus, thus protecting Esterhazy and avoiding the Dreyfus 'affair'.

Reply: This objection presumes that when Dreyfus was convicted in early 1895 that the 'General Staff' (the objector really means General Mercier) could foretell that there would be a 'Dreyfus Affair' three years later in 1897 and 1898. Further, if the scenario proposed is correct, in 1894 Mercier knew precisely the price of the deception: the unjust imprisonment and perhaps the life of one French officer. As to why Mercier could not easily halt the search for the 'spy' indicated by the bordereau, see above.

Objection: While the author considers the explanations for Mercier's behavior put forward by Thomas and Bredin unconvincing because they are unsupported by hard evidence and not 'rational', they seem more convincing to me. Not only are they based on human nature and an understanding of a military culture, they also emphasize the perverse sense of patriotic obligation which periodically surfaces in the French Army.

Reply: My point about the explanations of Thomas and Bredin (and most others writing about the Dreyfus Affair) for the actions of Mercier and the heads of the General Staff is not that they are not based on 'hard' evidence. Rather, my point is that they are supported by no evidence at all. As for the claim that I hold that Thomas's and Bredin's explanations are 'not rational', the objection misreads what I have written. I do not claim that Thomas's and Bredin's explanations are 'not rational': what I do say is that they attribute non-rational motivations to Mercier and the heads of the General Staff and, as Lewis Namier wrote: 'Although we know that man's actions are mostly conditioned by factors other than reason, in practice we have to assume their rational character until the contrary has been specifically established . . .' In the case of the irrational motivations attributed to Mercier and the chiefs of the General Staff, these have in no way been established or even supported: they have merely been asserted and repeated.

Objection: Even had they [Mercier and the chiefs of the General Staff] decided to prosecute Dreyfus in 1894, why defend the original verdict so tenaciously after 1896, when the Germans adopted the C/96, to protect Esterhazy and the deception which had run its course?

Reply: A good question, which of course does not pertain to the original conviction of Dreyfus but rather to the period after 1896, after the Germans had adopted their accelerated-fire weapon and the French had made public their adoption of a 25 shot-per-minute field cannon. The fact that they maintained the conviction of Dreyfus and continued to protect Esterhazy after 1896 simply demonstrates that French Army leaders did not want to disclose the deception they had carried out in 1894 and 1895. Why this was so remains an open (and good) question, the answer to which requires further investigation of the French deception.

Further investigation would, I suspect, yield interesting results. The scenario presented in this appendix should be considered to be only a rough sketch, not a final, detailed analysis. In the following paragraphs the possibility of a second phase of French deception is proposed.

Any study of the French effort to maintain secrecy concerning their 75mm rapid-fire field cannon in the years after 1894–95 (when they had sought to convince the Germans that they would produce an accelerated-fire, not true rapid-fire cannon) should take the following facts into account:

1. Between 1894 and 1896 the French developed three models of long recoil rapid-fire field cannon. The first, developed under the direction of Colonel Deport in 1894, was capable of rapid fire (25 shots per minute) but was not capable of sustained fire without breaking down. The second, called the 'Model I', was developed by Captains Rimailho and Sainte-Claire Deville in 1895. The third, the 'Model II', also developed by Rimailho and Sainte-Claire Deville, was perfected in the autumn of 1896 and produced in quantity in 1897 and 1898.

2. The Model II, which was very sturdy and capable of extremely powerful, accurate and enduring fire, was universally considered to be the finest field artillery piece employed in the First World War.

3. In March 1896, several months before the Model II was perfected and approximately a year before it was put into production, *Le Temps* (14 March 1896), the *Journal du Cher* (12 March 1896) and other newspapers reported that Minister of War Godefroy Cavaignac had traveled to Bourges with General Deloye and witnessed a demonstration of a new 25 shot-per-minute field cannon.

4. In 1904 a German artillery expert, J. Castner, disparaged the French rapid-fire field cannon. Castner wrote:

> The French field gun, model 1897, whose construction then [in 1897] was near completion, received the very complicated hydro-pneumatic recoil mechanism, although even then it was severely criticized by nearly every expert. It has three cylinders, two with pistons for the hydraulic brake, the third serving as air compressor for the return. This apparatus has four stuffing

boxes, one ball valve and six cylinder covers packed and screwed on, all being weak spots, easy causes for disturbance, as the vibrations in firing or on the march interfere with the packings. It is very natural that this French design has not been imitated.[40]

How can these facts be reconciled? How was it that in 1904, seven years after the French had equipped their army with what was unquestionably the finest field cannon of the era, could a German expert on artillery write that the French design was inferior and 'severely criticized by nearly every expert?' Could it be that the French had established a second phase of deception concerning their rapid-fire field cannon? Could it be that the French purposely conveyed to foreigners the misinformation that they were using the inferior Deport or Model I design when in fact they were employing the Model II? If so, this might explain why the French publicized in the press the trial of a new 25 shot-per-minute rapid-fire in March 1896, considerably before the Model II was perfected in the early autumn of 1896 or put into production in 1897, and it would explain why as late as 1904 Castner and other 'experts' had such a low opinion of the French 75mm cannon.

An article in the *Journal of United States Artillery* referred to French efforts to maintain secrecy and disseminate disinformation regarding the rapid-fire 75mm. The article stated that the gun

> was manufactured with great secrecy in the government workshops at Brouges [sic. Bourges] according to the plans and designs of Colonel Deport [sic. In fact the design was the work of Rimailho and Sainte-Claire Deville] the secret of the details of construction is not yet entirely divulged, although this material has been written about probably more than any other. *All the literature relating to the subject indicates that many of its characteristics and ballistic properties are still not known exactly. Even the data on the total weight of the piece, etc., are still variable, and it is to be noticed that French official publications contain, no doubt intentionally, false indications on this point* (italics mine).[41]

After writing the above speculation about a second phase of deception, I re-read the portion of Rimailho's *Artillerie de campagne* in which he described the French scheme to convince the Germans that they would equip their troops with the Ducros accelerated-fire weapon. There I saw what I had missed before: Rimailho's description of the second phase of deception suggested above.

Referring to the Ducros cannon, Rimailho wrote that this weapon was

40. *Journal of United States Artillery*, vol. xxi (1904), pp. 40–65, translated from *Kriegstechniche Zeitschrift*.

41. 'Present State of Field Artillery Rearmament,' *Journal of United States Artillery*, vol. xxi, no. 2, March–April, 1904.

publicized by the tests which were made before the artillery testing commission and by the field trials of 1895 and 1896. The French attributed great importance to those tests, as did the Germans who subsequently went ahead with the construction of their own accelerated-fire C/96. This was the aspect of the French deception described in the body of this appendix.

Rimailho also referred to a second phase of deception when he discussed French efforts to perfect a rapid-fire cannon in early 1896. At that time the French had just begun work on the Model II while at the same time they were trying to perfect the Model I. Rimailho wrote:

> The diverse groping efforts made during this period had several consequences. For one thing, most French officers whose functions allowed them to observe at close hand the work being done to develop rapid-fire artillery held the opinion that the various efforts would not produce a practical weapon. At this point only Deloye, Rimailho and Sainte-Claire Deville maintained confidence in their ultimate success. It was judged, at that time, that this situation should be taken advantage of by sharing with German artillery experts the skepticism about the prospects of perfecting rapid-fire artillery which were expressed in France.[42]

Here was a second aspect of deception which aimed to convince the Germans of the inadequacies of the French rapid-fire 75mm.

That the French accepted as early as March 1896 public knowledge of the approximate rate of fire of their new field cannon (which would have been impossible to hide once the weapon became standard equipment for French troops) while they misled the Germans into underestimating its operational capabilities would have allowed them to keep secret the true characteristics of their rapid-fire field cannon even after the weapon had been deployed.

Objection: In its present form the theory to explain the decision to prosecute Dreyfus is just a theory with no hard evidence at all for it.
Reply: Perhaps there is no hard evidence, but there is circumstantial evidence which is coherent with what is known about the development of rapid-fire field artillery in France and Germany and what is known about the actions of Mercier, the heads of the General Staff and General Deloye, Director of French Artillery. And the traditional explanation by irrational motivation of the actions of Mercier and the chiefs of the General Staff are 'just theories' supported by no evidence at all.

---

42. Rimailho, *Artillerie de campagne*, pp. 58–59.

A Note on Method and Sources

The thesis presented in this appendix had its origin in a question. Why in the mid-1890s did Godefroy Cavaignac, a leading member of the Chamber of Deputies, seek to have enacted a graduated income tax? What led Cavaignac, a political moderate, to advocate with all his strength a tax which in those days was considered to be radical and even revolutionary? The answer appears to lie in his awareness of the enormous cost of equipping the French armed forces with modern weapons in a period when Germany was making great efforts to increase its military strength. (The cost of equipping the French Army with the rapid-fire 75mm was 300,000,000 francs, about one-third of the country's entire annual military budget.) Rapid-fire artillery, taken for granted today, was an innovation of monumental importance in the 1890s. Surrounded by secrecy, the development of rapid-fire artillery was a prime concern of military leaders of the time.

From my reading about France's development of modern artillery there emerged a second question: Could it be that the Dreyfus Affair was in some way connected to the French development of rapid-fire artillery? After all, both did occur in the same period, between 1894 and 1897. The position of French Army leaders regarding rapid-fire artillery is easy to understand, while the Army's insistence on maintaining the unjust conviction of Captain Dreyfus has always been difficult to understand (This difficulty is reflected by the myriad of unsupported theories that have been put forward to explain it). If the two were related, then perhaps both would be comprehensible.

My approach to understanding the possible link between the two was first to learn as much as possible about how the French developed their rapid-fire artillery, maintained secrecy about it, and deceived foreigners regarding progress. My research was focused on these questions. I then tried to see to what extent these activities were congruent with the actions of Army leaders in the Dreyfus Affair. The more plausible the connection between the Dreyfus Affair and the development of rapid-fire artillery, the more reasonable would be the actions of Army leaders in the Dreyfus Affair.

Although the writings of Giscard d'Estaing, Lombarès and Doise contain conclusions similar to my own, none of them served as sources for me. It is not surprising that they and I reached similar conclusions; we all began at a similar starting point, an appreciation of how important the acquisition of rapid-fire field artillery was to French Army leaders in the 1890s – an appreciation which is conveyed by none of the standard studies of the Dreyfus Affair.

A Note on Understanding General Mercier's Motivation

Responding to *For the Sake of the Mission*, Marcel Thomas has written (in a letter to the author dated 9 October 1994) that rational motivations are adequate to explain Mercier's actions: he acted first to save his political career and then to save himself from the penalties for the misdeeds he had committed. Thomas's comments deserve an answer.

For one thing, we can see that Thomas himself was not entirely satisfied with this explanation because in his book *L'Affaire sans Dreyfus* he suggested that other motivations also drove Mercier: spite, fear of being judged negatively by General Staff officers, a sincere feeling of patriotic vigilance and a desire to uphold a reputation for never going back on a decision (see above). For another, even if Mercier's actions were motivated by political ambition, the actions of the chiefs of the General Staff and the ministers of war who came after Mercier can hardly have the same explanation. Further, the idea that Mercier's actions were politically motivated cannot withstand close examination.

The oldest and most widely-known explanation of General Mercier's decision to prosecute and convict Dreyfus was put forward in 1901 by Joseph Reinach in the first volume of his *Histoire de l'affaire Dreyfus*. According to Reinach, at the time of the discovery of the bordereau in October 1894 Mercier, who had come to be Minister of War from a career in the Army, was on the verge of losing his ministerial position due to his having alienated political leaders and his being criticized by the press.

> Thus, in September 1894, when Mercier had been Minister for less than a year, his star was fading so fast that it would soon be forgotten that it had ever shone (p.17) . . . Mercier understood that his days were numbered and that he would be sacrificed at the first opportunity (p. 20) . . . Mercier, better than anyone else, understood that his political and military position was becoming precarious. That the treason [indicated by the bordereau] was publicly known and that the traitor remained unknown, would be for him the coup de grace' (p. 39).

Given the precariousness of the War Minister's cabinet position, Reinach claimed, Mercier's actions regarding Dreyfus were intended first to secure his place in the government and then to save himself from the consequences of his misdeeds. Thus, according to Reinach, Mercier publicly proclaimed Dreyfus's guilt before his trial and proceeded to prosecute him in order to placate the press — particularly the anti-semitic press — which attacked him for not prosecuting the Jewish traitor after he was arrested. Also according to Reinach, when it became apparent that the case against Dreyfus could not be won on the evidence of the bordereau, Mercier used illegal methods and forged 'evidence' to get a conviction in order to secure his ministerial position, which would supposedly have become untenable if it turned out that an innocent French officer had been prosecuted:

> However, the acquittal of Dreyfus would destroy him [Mercier]. Everyone ... would accuse him of inefficiency, of demonstrated ineptitude, of dishonoring an innocent, of besmirching the Army. If Dreyfus were acquitted, Mercier would be removed from his ministry within an hour of the verdict (p. 235).

From then on, Army leaders continued to go from transgression to transgression in order to cover Mercier's initial transgression.

Reinach's claim that Mercier's actions were politically motivated has been repeated by historians for almost a century since the Affair. Most recently Marcel Thomas, the world's foremost authority on the documents involved in the Dreyfus case, reaffirmed Reinach's explanation in his letter to me:

> Once proceedings were instituted against Dreyfus, Mercier's political career would be ended if either the charges against Dreyfus would be dropped or if he would be put on trial and acquitted. One need only read the press of the period to understand that neither public opinion nor the prime minister would have pardoned him for having sullied the name of a French officer. It is here that it is necessary to seek the explanation of his breach of honor – odious and ignoble, to be sure, but also very logical because it was motivated by his personal interest.

Obviously Reinach's explanation of Mercier's actions cannot be conclusively proven or disproven. Besides repeating the claim, Reinach presents no clear evidence that Mercier was particularly hungry for political office. In fact, as it turned out, Mercier ceased being Minister of War on 11 January 1895 with the departure of the Dupuy ministry. This was a mere six weeks after he had publicly announced his certainty that Dreyfus was guilty of espionage and just two weeks after Dreyfus had been tried and convicted of treason. If Mercier's actions against Dreyfus were intended to keep him in office, their effect was to extend his tenure a few weeks at most. Mercier's departure from office and return to the Army as a field commander reflected the fact that he was not primarily a politician but a soldier – and an excellent technician who himself had made an important contribution to the technology of artillery shells.[43]

Reinach claimed that in September 1894, just before the arrest of Dreyfus, Mercier was on the verge of losing his position as a Minister in

---

43. Doise, *Un secret bien gardé*, p. 64.

the Dupuy cabinet. This is doubtful. Reinach also claimed that Mercier's position as Minister of War was threatened by the attacks on him by the anti-semitic press. This is also doubtful; it is unlikely that the ranting of an anti-establishment and marginal newspaper such as *La Libre Parole* could cause the removal of a minister in a very 'establishment' Moderate government such as was the Dupuy cabinet. In any case, to support these claims an historian would have to demonstrate that similar outcomes emerged in similar circumstances. This has never been done.

Ironically, if Mercier did have Dreyfus convicted as part of a scheme to 'intoxicate' the Germans regarding France's progress in field artillery, it would have served his purpose to have Reinach's explanations of his actions accepted. Reinach's explanations provided Mercier with a perfect cover. With them, there would be no reason to think that he was motivated by anything but political ambition.

Bibliography

Archival Material and Government Documents

France. Archives nationales françaises, C5550-22-2-45 (Archives de la Chambre des Députés, VI leg., 1893–98. Folder 'Voeux des conseiles généraux concernant le projet Doumer [Impôt sur le revenu]')

France. *Journal officiel de la République française: Débats et documents parlementaire, Chambre des Députés,* 1891–98

France, Ministère des finances. *Commission extra parlementaire de l'impôt sur les revenus instituée au ministère des finances, Procès-verbaux.* 2 vols. Paris: Imprimeirie Nationale, 1895

Barodet, Désire. *Rapport fait au nom de la commission chargé de reunir et de publier le texts authentiques des Programmes et engagements electoraux.* Paris: Imprimerie de la Chambre des Députés, Matteroz, 1890 and 1894

Delombre, Paul. *Rapport fait au nom de la commission du budget chargée d'examiner le projet de loi portant fixation du budget général des dépenses et de recettes de l'exercice 1897 (Impôt general sur le revenu),* 1896

Periodicals

Le Correspondant
The Economist, 1896
Economiste Français, 1893–98
Fortnightly Review (London), 1893–94
L'Illustration, 1893–96
La Nouvelle Revue, 1893–96
Polybiblion, 1893–98
Le Rentier – Journal Financier Politique, 1893–96
Revue Bleue, 1894–96
Revue des Deux Mondes, 1893–98
La Revue Diplomatique, 1893–98
Revue Politique et Parlementaire, 1894–98

Newspapers

L'Autorité
Le Courrier d'Allier
Correspondent Républicaine
La Democratie du Centre, 1893–1898
La Dépeche de Toulouse, October, 1895
Le Figaro
Le Gaulois
L'Indépendent de l'Allier, 1893–1898
L'Intransigeant
Journal de l'Aine, 1893–1898
Le Jour
Journal des Débats
Le Matin, 1893
Le Messager
Le Petit Moniteur Universel
La Petite République, 1895
Républicain de l'Ain, 1893–1898
Le Temps, 1893–1896

Books Used as Primary Sources

Alvin, Colonel and Commandant André, *Les canons de la victoire*, 7th edn., Paris: Charles Lavauzelle & Cie, 1923

Un Artilleur, *Une Merveille du genie français, Notre 75*, Paris, 1915

Avenel, Le Vicomte George d', *Le réforme administratif*, Paris: Berger-Levrault et Cie, 1891

Avenel, Henri, *Comment vote le France – dix-huit ans de suffrage universel, 1876–1893*, Paris: Librairies-imprimerie réunis, 1894

Almanach National, 1895, Paris: Berger-Levrault, 1895

Benoist, Charles, *De l'organisation du suffrage universel. La crise de l'Etat moderne*, Paris: Fermin-Didot, 1895

Bidoire, Pierre, *Budget de 1894*, Paris: Guillaumin & Cie, 1894

——, *Les budgets français – étude analytique et pratique, Budget de 1895 premiere partie – projet de budget*, Paris: V. Giard & E. Brière, 1895

Block, Maurice, *Dictionnaire général de la politique*, 2nd edn., Paris: Emile Perrin, 1884

Boucard, Max and Gaston Jèze, *Elements de la science des finances et de la legislation financière française*, 2nd edn., Paris: V. Giard et Brière, 1902

Bourgeois, Léon, *Solidarité*, Paris: A. Colin, 1896

Bourget, Paul, 'Décentralisation', in *Etudes et portraits*, vol. 3., Paris:

Plon Nourit, 1906

Boutmy, Emile, *Essai d'une psychologie politique du peuple anglais aux XIXe siècle*, Paris: Librairie Armand Colin, 1901

Blondel, Maurice, *L'action, essai d'une critique de la vie et d'une science pratique*, Paris: F. Alcan, 1893

Bray, Emmanuel de, *Traité de la dette publique*, Paris: Paul Dupont, 1895

Brisson, Adolphe, *Les Prophets*, Paris: Ernest Flammarion, n.d. (probably about 1902)

Brunetière, Ferdinand, *Education et instruction*, Paris: Didot, 1895

Caillaux, Joseph, *Mes memoires*, vol. I, Paris: Plon, 1942

Caillaux, Joseph, A. Touchard and G. Privat-Deschanel, *L'impôt en France*, 2 vols., Paris: E. Plon Nourrit & Cie, 1896

Cauwès, Paul, *Cours d'économie politique avec l'expose des principes l'analyse des questions publique et finançière*, 4 vols., 3rd edn., Paris: Le Larose, 1893

Cavaignac, Godefroy, *Pour l'impôt progressif*, Paris: Armand Colin & Cie, 1895

——, *La formation de la Prusse contemporaine*, 2 vols., Paris: Librairie Hachette, 1891

Charriaut, Henri, *Enquète sur la décentralisation*, Paris: Nouvelle Revue Internationale, 1895

Coumes, Commandant, *Aperçus sur la tactique de demain mise en rapport avec la puissance du nouvel armement et l'emploi de la poudre sans fumée*, Paris: Libraire Militaire de L. Boudin, 1892

Courcoural, Paul, *La décentralisation et la monarchie national*, Rochefort: C. Thèze, 1895

Daniel, André [André Lebon], *L'année politique, 1893–1896*, Paris: Librairie Charpentier, 1894–1897

Demolins, Edmond, *Comment éléver et établir nos enfants?* Paris: Firmin-Didot & Cie, 1893

——, *A quoi tient la supériorité des Anglo Saxons*, Paris: Firmin-Didot, n.d. [1898]

——, *L'éducation nouvelle – L'Ecole des Roches*

Deschanel, Paul, *La décentralisation*, Paris: Berger-Levrault, 1895

Dreyfus, Ferdinand, *Etudes et discourses*, Paris: Calmann Lévy, 1896

L'Ecole Libre des Sciences Politiques, *L'école libre des sciences politiques, 1871–1881*, Paris; Typographie Georges Chamerot, 1889

——, *Année scolaire, 1893–1894*

Ferrand, J., *Un avant-projet de décentralisation administrative*, Paris: Librairie Pichon, 1895

Garnier, Joseph, *Traité de finances*, 4th edn., Paris: Garnier Frères, 1883

Gide, Charles, *Principes d'économie politique*, 5th edn., Paris: L. Larose, 1896

Jugler, Clement, *La baisse du taux de l'intérêt*, Paris: imp. de Chaix, 1892

Kergall, *L'impôt démocratique sur le revenu*, Paris: A. Colin, 1896

——, *Le suicide de la République, l'impôt sur le revenu*, Paris: Fédération des contribuables, n.d.

Laffitte, Jean-Paul, *Le parti modéré; ce qu'il est, ce qu'il devrait être*, Paris: A. Colin, 1896

Lavisse, Ernest, *A propos de nos écoles*, Paris: Armand Colin, 1895

Le Bon, Gustave, *The Psychology of Socialism*, New York, 1899

Leclerc, Max, *Les professions et la société en Angleterre*, Paris: A. Colin, 1895

——, *L'éducation des classes moyennes et dirigeantes en Angleterre*, 2 vols., Paris: A. Colin, 1894

Le Play, Frederic, *La paix sociale après le desastre selon la pratique des peuples prospérés*, Tours: Alfred Mame et fils, 1874

Leroy-Beaulieu, Anatole, *Pourquoi nous ne sommes pas socialistes – séance d'ouverature du 9 janvier, 1895*, Paris: Au Siège du Comité de Defense et de Progrès Social, 1895

Leroy-Beaulieu, Paul, *L'art de placer et gérer sa fortune*, Paris: Librairie Ch. Delagrave, 1906

——, *The Modern State in Relation to Society and the Individual*, London: Ivan Sonnenschein & Co., 1891

——, *Traité de la science des finances*, 2 vols., 2nd edn., Paris: Guillaumin & Cie, 1879

——, *Traité theorique et pratique d'économie politique*, 4 vols., Paris: Guillaumin & Cie, 1896

Levasseur, G., *Anarchie et socialism – les partis et le gouvernement*, Paris: A. Charles, 1896

Levasseur, Pierre E., *La population française*, 3 vols., Paris: Arthur Rousseau, 1889, 1891, 1892

Lucoy, Comte de, *La décentralisation*, Paris: Guillaumin, 1895

Maneuvrier, Edouard, *L'éducation de la bourgeoisie sous la République*, Paris: Librairie Leopold Cerf, 1888

Marcère, E. de, *La décentralisation: projet de reforme de la loi municipale de 5 avril 1884*, Paris: Larose, 1895

Neymarck, Alfred, *Finances contemporaines*, vols. 4 and 5, *L'obsession fiscale – projets ministeriels et propositions dues a l'initiative parlementaire relatif a la reforme de l'impôt, 1872–1907*, Paris: Félix Alcan, 1907

Payot, Jules, *L'éducation de la volonté*, Paris: F. Alcan, 1894

Picavet, F., *L'éducation*, Paris: Léon Chailley, 1895

Picot, Georges, *La décentralisation et ses differents aspects*, Paris, 1896

Raffalovich, Artur, *Le marché financière*, vols. III–VII (1893–97), Paris: Guillaumin, 1894–98

Régis, Dr. Emmanuel, *La medicine et le pessimisme contemporaine*, Bordeaux: impr. de G. Gounilhou, 1898

Reinach, Joseph, *Histoire de l'affaire Dreyfus*, vols. I, IV, Paris: La Revue blanche, 1901, 1904

Renan, Ernest, *Constitutional Monarcy in France*, translated from the second French edition, Boston: Roberts Brothers, 1871

——, *La réforme intellectuelle et morale*, 5th edn., Paris: Calman-Lévy, n.d.

Reynes, Amedée, *Décentralisation*, Perpignan: impr. de l'Independent,

Ribot, Theophile, *The Diseases of the Will*, authorized translation from the 8th French edition, 4th enlarged English edition, Chicago: The Open Court Publishing Company, 1915

Rimailho, François Léon Emile, *Artillerie de campagne*, Paris: Gauthier-Villars & Cie, 1924

Rostand, Eugène, *Solutions socialistes et le fonctionnairisme*, Paris: Comité de Defense et de Progrès Social, 1896

Say, Léon and Joseph Chailley-Bert, *Nouveau dictionnaire d'économie politique*, Paris: Guillaumin & Cie, 1891, 1892

——, *Supplement au nouveau dictionnaire politique*, Paris: Guillaumin & Cie, 1897

Saint Simone, *Propos de Félix Faure*, 3rd edn., Paris: Ollendorff, 1902

Saugrain, Gaston, *La baisse du taux de l'intérêt; causes et consequences*, Paris: Larose, 1896

Stourm, René, *The Budget*, English translation from the 7th edition, New York: D. Appleton & Co. for the Institute for Government Research, 1917

——, *Cours de finance: le budget*, Paris: Guillaumin, 1896

Taine, Hippolyte Aldophe, *Notes on England*, translated with an introduction by Edward Hyams, Fair Lawn N.J.: Essential Books, 1958

Tarboureich, Ernest, *Du Conseil d'Etat comme organe legislatif*, Paris: Chevalier-Maresq, 1894

Vavasseur, A., *Qu'est ce que la bourgeoisie?* Paris: Fontemoins, 1897

Waldeck-Rousseau, René, *Action républicaine et sociale*, Paris: Charpentier, 1903

——, *Discours at the Hôtel-Continental*, Feb. 24, 1897, Paris: Association Nationale Républicaine, 1897

——, *Pour la République* (1883–1903), Paris: Charpentier, 1904

Walras, Léon, *Elements of Pure Economics or the Theory of Social Wealth*, translation of the 1926 edition by William Jaffe, London: Published for the American Economic Association by George Allan & Unwin Ltd., 1954

Worms, Emile. *Essai de legislation financière – le budget de la France dans le passe et dans le present*, Paris: V. Giard, Briere, 1894

Young, James T., 'Administrative Centralization and Decentralization in France,' *Annals of the American Academy of Political and Social Sciences*, Jan.–June, 1898

Secondary Works

Barrows, Susanna, *Distorting Mirrors – Visions of the Crowd in Late Nineteenth Century France*, New Haven: Yale University Press, 1984

Bastable, Charles F., 'Finances', in *The Encyclopaedia Britannica* (11th edn.), vol. X, pp. 347–352

Bastid, Paul, *L'avènement du suffrage universel*, Paris: Presses Universitaires de France, 1948

Beau de Loménie, Emmanuel, *Les responsibilités des dynasties bourgeoises*, vol. II, Paris: Denoel, 1947

Bergasse, Henry, *Histoire de l'Assemblée – des élections de 1789 aux élections de 1967*, Paris: Payot, 1967

Birnbaum, Pierre, *The Heights of Power – An Essay in the Power Elite in France*, Chicago: University of Chicago Press, 1982

Bodley, John Edward Courtney, *France*, 2 vols., New York: The Macmillan Co., 1898

——, 'France: History, 1870–1910', *The Encyclopaedia Britannica* (11th edn.), vol. X, pp. 873–904

Braibant, Charles, *Félix Faure a l'Elysée (Souvenirs de Louis le Gal and Notes de Jean-Pierre Busson)*, Paris: Hachette, 1963

Bredin, Jean-Denis, *The Affair – The Case of Alfred Dreyfus* (translated from the French), New York: George Braziller, 1986

Burns, Michael, *Rural Society and French Politics Boulangism and the Dreyfus Affair, 1886–1900*, Princeton: Princeton University Press, 1984

Byrnes, Robert Francis, *Antisemitism in Modern France*, vol. I., New Brunswick, New Jersey: Rutgers University Press, 1955

Colmet Daage, Félix, *La classe bourgeoise, ses origines, ses lois d'existence, son role sociale*, Paris: Nouvelles Editions Latines, 1959

Chapman, Guy, *The Republic of France, The First Phase, 1871–1894*, London: Macmillan & Co., 1962

——, *The Dreyfus Case – A Reassessment*, New York, Reynal & Co., 1955

Charle, Christophe, *Les élites de la république, 1880–1900*, Paris: Fayard, 1987

Chastenet, Jacques, *La France de M. Fallières – un époque pathetique*, Paris: Libraire Anthème Fayard, 1949

——, *Histoire de la Troisième République*, vols. I–III, Paris: Hachette, 1952–1955

——, *Raymond Poincaré*, Paris: R. Julliard, 1948

Chevallier, J.-J., *Histoire des institutions politiques de la France de 1789 a nos jours*, Paris: Librairie Dalloz, 1952

Curtis, Michael, *Three Against the Republic — Sorel, Barrès and Maurras*, Princeton: Princeton University Press, 1959

Dardenne, Henriette, *Godefroy Cavaignac — Un républicain de progrès aux débuts de la 3eme République*, Colmar, 1969

——, 'Comment fut décidé la construction du canon de 75', *Bulletin Trimestriel de l'Association des Amis de l'Ecole de Guerre*, 20, July 1963

Delaisi, Francis, 'Les Financièrs et la démocratie', *Crapouillot*, Nov. 1936 (reprint of the original published in 1911, editions de la Guerre Sociale).

Derfler, Leslie, *Alexandre Millerand — The Socialist Years*, The Hague: Mouton, 1971

Earle, Edward Mead, *Modern France: Problems of the Third and Fourth Republics*, New York: Russell and Russell, 1964

Eisenstein, Louis, *The Ideology of Taxation*, New York: Ronald Press, 1961

Elwitt, Sandford, *The Making of the Third Republic In France, 1868–1884*, Baton Rouge: Louisiana State University Press, 1975

——, *The Third Republic Defended — Bourgeois Reform in France, 1880–1914*, Baton Rouge: Louisiana State University Press, 1986

Estèbe, Jean, *Les ministères de la République, 1871–1914*, Paris: Presses de la Fondation Nationale des Sciences Politiques, 1972

Fox, Edward Whiting, *History in Geographic Perspective — The Other France*, New York: W. W. Norton, 1971

Gallaher, John G., *The Students of Paris and the Revolution of 1848*, Carbondale: Southern Illinois University Press, 1980

Giffen, Robert, 'Taxation', *The Encyclopaedia Britannica* (11th edn.), vol. XXVI, pp. 458–464

Giscard d'Estaing, Henri, *D'Esterhazy à Dreyfus*, Paris: Plon, 1960

Goblot, Edmond, *La barrière et le niveau, étude sociologique sur la bourgeoisie française moderne*, Paris: Presses Universitaire de France, 1967

Goguel, François, *Géographie des élections françaises sous la Troisième et la Quatrième République*, Paris: Armand Colin, 1970

——, *La politique des partis sous la IIIe Republique*, 2 vols., Paris: Editions du Seuil, 1946

——, *Le role financière du senat français — essai d'histoire parlementaire*, Paris: Librairie du Recueil Surez, 1937

Goldberg, Harvey, *The Life of Jean Jaures*, Madison, Wisc.: University of Wisconsin Press, 1962

Golob, Eugene O., *The Meline Tariff: French Agriculture and Nationalist*

Economy Policy, New York: Columbia University Studies in History, Economics and Public Law No. 506, 1944

Gooch, Robert K., *The French Parliamentary Committee System*, New York: Institute for Research in the Social Sciences, University of Virginia, 1935

———, *Regionalism in France*, New York: The Century Co., for the Institute for Research in the Social Sciences, University of Virginia, 1931

Gouault, Jacques, *Comment la France est devenu républicaine – les elections générales et partielles a l'assemblée nationale 1870–1875*, Paris: A. Colin, 1954

Halévy, Daniel, *The End of the Notables*, Middletown, Ct.: Weslyan University Press, 1974

———, *La République des comités*, Paris: B. Grasset, 1934

Hamburger, Maurice, *Léon Bourgeois, 1851–1925*, Paris: Librairie des sciences politiques et sociales, M. Riviere, 1932

Hamon, Augustin Frederic Adolphe et X.Y.Z., *Les maitres de la France*, Paris: Editions Sociales Internationales, 1937

Hannotaux, Gabriel, *Histoire de la nation française*

Hemmings, F. W. J. *Culture and Society in France, 1848–1898 – Dissidents and Philistines*, London: B.T. Batsford, 1971

Howarth, Jolyo and P. Cerny, (eds), *Elites in France: Origins, Reproduction, Power*, New York: St Martin's Press, 1981

Johannet, René, *Eloge du bourgeois français*, Paris: Bernard Grasset, 1924

Johnson, Douglas, *France and the Dreyfus Affair*, New York: Walker & Co., 1966

Kayser, Jacques, *Les grandes batailles du radicalism – des origines aux portes du pouvoir*, Paris: Marcel Riviere & Cie, 1962

Kropotkin, Prince Peter Alexeivitch, 'Anarchism', *The Encyclopaedia Britannica* (11th edn.), vol. I, pp. 914–919

Lachapelle, Georges, *Les Finances de la Troisième République*, Paris: Ernest Flammarion, 1937

Lebovics, Herman, *The Alliance of Iron and Wheat in the Third French Republic, 1860–1914 – Origins of the New Conservatism*, Baton Rouge: Louisiana State University Press, 1988

Lombarès, Michel de, *L'Affaire Dreyfus. La clèf du mystère*, Paris: Robert Laffont, 1972

Lorwin, Val, *The French Labor Movement*, Cambridge: Harvard University Press, 1954

Loubère, Leo, *Radicalism in Mediterranean France – Its Rise and Decline, 1848–1914*, Albany: State University of New York Press, 1974

Maitron, Jean, *Histoire du mouvement anarchiste en France (1880–1914)*, Paris: Société Universitaire d'Editions et de Librairie, 1951

Marichy, Jean-Pierre, *La deuxieme chambre dans la vie politique française depuis 1875*, Paris: P. Pinochet et R. Durand-Auzias, 1964

Marion, Marcel, *Histoire financière de la France depuis 1775*, vols. I, VII, Paris: Rousseau & Cie, 1914, 1931

Mayer, J.P., *Political Thought in France from the Revolution to the Fourth Republic*, London: Routledge & Kegan Paul, 1949

Mayeur, J.-M. and Madeleine Rebérioux, *The Third Republic From Its Origins to the Great War*, Cambridge: Cambridge University Press, 1984

Mitchell, Allan, 'A Situation of Inferiority: French Military Reorganization after the Defeat of 1870', *American Historical Review*, vol. 86, Feb. 1981

——, *Victors and Vanquished – The German Influence on Army and Church in France after 1870*, Chapel Hill: The University of North Carolina Press, 1984

Moon, Parker Thomas, *The Labor Problem and the Social Catholic Movement in France – A study in the History of Social Politics*, New York: The Macmillan Co., 1921

Morazé, Charles, *Les bourgeois conquerantes, XIXe siècle*, Paris: A. Colin, 1957

——, *La France bourgeoise – XVIII–XXe siecle*, Paris: A.Colin, 1946

Muel, Léon, *Précis historique des assemblées parlementaires et des hautes cours de justice de 1789 à 1895 d'après les documents officiels*, Paris: Guillaumin, 1896

Muret, Charlotte T., *French Royalist Doctrines Since the Revolution*, New York: Columbia University Press, 1933

Nord, Philip G., *Paris Shopkeepers and the Politics of Resentment*, Princeton: Princeton University Press, 1986

Nye, Robert, *Crime Madness and Politics in Modern France The Medical Concept of National Decline*, Princeton: Princeton University Press, 1984

Ollé-Laprune, Jacques, *La stabilité des ministres sous la Troisième République, 1879–1940*, Paris: R. Pichon et R. Durand-Auzias, 1962

Perrot, Maruerite, *Le mode de vie des familles bourgeoises, 1873–1953*, Paris: A. Colin, 1961

Ponteil, Félix, *Les classes bourgeoises et l'avènement de la démocratie, 1815–1914*, Paris: Editions Albin Michel, 1968

Rain, Pierre, *L'Ecole Libre des Sciences Politiques*, Paris: Fondation Nationale des Sciences Politiques, 1963

Ridge, George Ross, *The Hero in French Decadent Literature*, Athens, Ga.: University of Georgia Press, 1961

Sanborn, Alvan Francis, *Paris and the Social Revolution: A Study of the Revolutionary Elements of the Various Classes of Parisian Society*, Boston: Small, Maynard, 1905

Schmidt, Vivien, *Democratizing France – The Political and Administrative History of Decentralization*, Cambridge: Cambridge University Press, 1990

Scott, John A., *Republican Ideas and the Liberal Tradition in France, 1870–1914*, New York: Octagon Books, 1966

Seignobos, Charles, *L'evolution de la Troisième République, 1875–1914*, vol. VIII of *Histoire de France Contemporaine*, ed. Ernest Lavisse, 10 vols., Paris: Hachette, 1921

Seligman, Edwin R. A., *The Income Tax – A Study in the History, Theory and Practice of Income Taxation at Home and Abroad*, 2nd edn., New York: The Macmillan Co., 1914

Shapiro, David (ed.), *The Right In France, 1890–1919*, Carbondale, Ill.: Southern Illinois University Press, 1962

Shaw, Albert, *Municipal Government in Continental Europe*, New York: Century Co., 1895

Silvera, Alain, *Daniel Halévy and His Times*, Ithaca, N.Y.: Cornell University Press, 1966

Soltau, Roger, *French Political Thought in the Nineteenth Century*, London: Ernest Benn Ltd., 1931

Sonn, Richard, *Anarchism and Cultural Politics in Fin-de-Siècle France*, Lincoln, Neb.: University of Nebraska Press, 1989

Sorlin, Pierre, *Waldeck-Rousseau*, Paris: Librairie Armand Colin, 1966

Soulier, Auguste, *L'instabilité ministerielle sous la Troisieme République, 1871–1938*, Paris: Sirez, 1939

Spengler, Joseph, *France Faces Depopulation*, Durham, N.C.: Duke University Press, 1938

Stone, Judith, *The Search for Social Peace – Reform Legislation in France, 1890–1914*, Albany: State University of New York Press, 1985

Thibaudet, Albert, *La République des professeurs*, Paris: Slatkine Reprints, 1927

Thomas, Marcel, *Esterhazy ou l'envers de l'affaire Dreyfus*, Vernal: Philippe Lebaudi, 1989

———, *L'Affaire sans Dreyfus*, Paris: Arthème Fayard, 1971

Thomson, David, *Democracy in France Since 1870*, 4th edn., New York: Oxford University Press, 1964

Tocqueville, Alexis de, *Democracy in America*, vol.I, New York: Vintage Books, 1957

Trebilcock, Clive, 'British Armaments and European Industrialization, 1890–1914', *The Economic Review*, XXVI, May 1973

Warshaw, Dan, *Paul Leroy-Beaulieu and Established Liberalism in*

France, Dekalb: Northern Illinois University Press, 1991

Weber, Eugen, 'Gymnastics and Sports in Fin-de-Siècle France: Opium of the Classes?' *American Historical Review*, LXXVI, Feb. 1971, pp. 70–91

———, *France, Fin de Siècle*, Cambridge: Harvard University Press, 1986

Wright, Vincent, 'L'epuration du Conseil d'Etat (Juillet 1879)', *Revue d'Histoire Moderne et Contemporaine*, XIX, Oct.–Dec. 1972

Zeldin, Theodore, *France, 1848–1945*, vol. I, Oxford: Clarendon Press, 1973

Index

administrative decentralization, 112–7,
    159–60
anarchist violence, 91–2
anti-clericalism, 153
anti-semites, 133
arms race, 9, 174–5
Association Nationale Républicaine,
    124–5
Auteuil racetrack, 73

banquets of bourgeoisie, 16
Belleville program, 32
Benoist, Charles, 119
Berenger, Henry, 162–3
Block, Maurice, 103, 121
bourgeois youth, problems of,
    125–34
bourgeois public leaders, 15–6
Bourgeois, Léon, 41–3, 50, 53–6, 62,
    81–2, 60–2
bourgeoisie, 13–5
Boutmy, Emile, 109–11
Bredin, Jean-Denis, 173
Brunetière, Ferdinand, 128
Burdeau, August, 97

Campagnole, Edouard, 31
cannon, 75mm rapid-fire, 8, 39–40,
    175–6, 180–3
Carnot, Sadi, 50
Casimir-Périer, Jean, 26, 51–3
Cavaignac, Godefroy,
    background and education, 32–5
    his campaign for impôt sur le revenu,
        37–40, 51
    political ideals, 36–7
    role in Chamber of Deputies, 28,
        144–7
    role in promoting improved artillery,
        39–41
Chambrun, comte de, 107
Chanoine, general, 148
class lines, 120–2
Cohen, Edouard, 31
Comité National Républicain de
    Commerce et de l'Industrie, 138–9

Conseil d'état, 117
constitutional ideals of bourgeoisie,
    17–21
Curtis, Michael, 167

Delombre Report, 61–2
Deloye, general, 40, 182
Demolins, Edmond, 131–2
Deport, commandant, 181
diner historique, 72
Doise, Jean, 188
Doumer, Paul, 43, 56, 160
Dreyfus, Ferdinand, 118
Dreyfus Affair, 176–80
dreyfusian revolution, 135–6
Ducros, major, 181
Dupuy, Charles, 48–50, 148

Ecole des Roches, 131–2
Ecole Libre des Sciences Politiques,
    109–12
elections of 1893, 44–9
elections of 1898, 141–3
electoral reform, proposals for, 19–20
Elwitt, Sandford, 7, 102
Esterhazy, commandant Ferdinand
    Walzin-, 184

Faure, Félix, 53
feminist movement, 90
fin-de-siècle, end of, 163–4
Fournier, Marcel, 140, 142

Garnier, Joseph, 31
general councils, opinions regarding the
    impôt sur le revenu, 75–6
Giscard d'Estaing, Henri, 187
Goblet, René, 46
Goguel, François, 165
Grand Cercle Républicaine, 140–1
Grasserie, Raoul de la, 119
Gréard, Octave, 129
Guyot, Yves, 30

Halévy, Daniel, 2
Hariou, Maurice, 119

Index

impôt sur le revenu,
  background in France, 29–32
  Radicals promote the tax, 57–8
  income tax, 3, 9
  see also impôt sur le revenu
Intransigeant, 85
Isambert group, 54, 87

Jacobin ideals, 22–5
Jaurès, Jean, 68, 84, 151, 157
Journal des Débats, 85

L'Hopiteau, 70
labor conflict, 92–3
Lafitte, Paul, 61
Lebovics, Herman, 6
Leclerc, Max, 130
Lemaître, Jules, 128
LePlay, Frederic, 104
Leroy-Beaulieu, Anatole, 1, 74, 132–4,
  169
Leroy-Beaulieu, Paul, 2, 26–7, 30, 50,
  60, 98, 105, 122, 169
Lévy, Raphael-Georges, 133, 169
Libre Parole, 85
Ligue de la Décentralisation, 115–7

Manouvrier, Edouard, 129
Marcère, Emile de, 1, 113–6
Mascaraud, comité, 158–9
Méline, Jules, 70, 87–9
Mercier, general August, 177–8, 184–6
Millerand, Alexandre, 149
Moderates, 45
Musée Social, 107–8

national debt as lever for political
  influence, 63–7, 69–70, 77–9, 86–7
Neymarck, Alfred, 122
Nord, Philip, 151–3

parliamentary republic, 21–2
patronage, Radicals desire of
  administrative, 76–7, 153
Pelletan, Camille, 83
Petite République, 85
Peugeot, Armand, 108–9
Peytral, 28
Picot, Georges, 1
Piquart, comandant Georges
Poincaré, Raymond, 50–1, 149
problem of democracy defined, 17
Protestants, 110–1

Radical deputies, 23–4
Radicals, 46–7
Reinach, Joseph, 105, 196–7
Renan, Ernest, 19–20
Renouvrier, Charles, 20
Revue Politique et Parlementaire, 16
Ribot, Alexandre, 28–9, 54
Rimailho, captain, 181–2, 194
riots of July 1893, 93–6
Roussel, Félix, 144, 196–8

Sainte-Claire Deville, captain, 181
Say, Léon, 2, 11–2, 15, 30, 50, 68–9, 97,
  107–8
Seligman, Edwin, 3
Senate opposition to Bourgeois ministry,
  80–2
Siegfried, Jules, 107
Simon, Jules, 107, 117
Smith, Adam, 99–100
socialism, 90
Socialist Radicals, 47
Socialists, 47
Société Française des Habitations Bon
  Marché, 106
Society of Political Economy, 73–4
state socialism, 97–9
Stourm, René, 16, 104

Taine, Hyppolyte, 20
tax reform, 26–9
tax system of France, 27
Thiers, Adolphe, 5
Thomas, Marcel, 173, 187, 196–7
threats to the Republic
  by the bourgeoisie, 67, 70–1, 75,
    156–7
  by anti-Dreyfusards, 150, 154–5
Tivoli-Vauxhall protest meeting, 83–5
Tocqueville, Alexis de, 98–9, 112,
  166–7

Union Libérale Républicaine, 123–4
Unions de la Paix Sociale, 106

Vavasseur, A., 120
Villey, Edmond, 3

Waldeck-Rousseau, René, 5, 136–41,
  148–53
Worms, René, 74

Zurlinden, general, 148